Best Lake Hikes Texas

Best Lake Hikes Texas

A Guide to the State's Greatest Lake and River Hikes

Jamie Fleck

FALCONGUIDES

ESSEX, CONNECTICUT

To all my fellow Texans who appreciate and love the Lone Star State for its unique and awe-inspiring natural beauty. May this book help you continue to explore and be proud of the great state of Texas.

FALCONGUIDES®

An imprint of The Globe Pequot Publishing Group, Inc.
64 South Main Street
Essex, CT 06426
www.globepequot.com

Falcon and FalconGuides are registered trademarks and Make Adventure Your Story is a trademark of The Globe Pequot Publishing Group, Inc.

Distributed by NATIONAL BOOK NETWORK

Copyright © 2024 The Globe Pequot Publishing Group, Inc.

Photos © Jamie Fleck.
Maps by Melissa Baker and The Globe Pequot Publishing Group, Inc.

British Library Cataloguing in Publication Information available

Library of Congress Cataloging-in-Publication Data
Names: Fleck, Jamie, author.
Title: Best lake hikes Texas : a guide to the state's greatest lake and river hikes / Jamie Fleck.
Description: Essex, Connecticut: FalconGuides, 2024. | Includes index. | Summary: "Best Lake Hikes Texas is a guide to hikes with lakes across the Lone Star State. With captivating photography and up-to-date detailed directions, this visual trail guide allows readers and hikers to explore the natural grandeur that Texas has to offer"—Provided by publisher.
Identifiers: LCCN 2023046020 (print) | LCCN 2023046021 (ebook) | ISBN 9781493070817 (paperback) | ISBN 9781493070824 (epub)
Subjects: LCSH: Hiking—Texas—Guidebooks. | Trails—Texas—Guidebooks. | Lakes—Texas—Guidebooks. | Rivers—Texas—Guidebooks. | Texas—Guidebooks.
Classification: LCC GV199.42.T49 F54 2024 (print) | LCC GV199.42.T49 (ebook) | DDC 796.5109764—dc23/eng/20231108
LC record available at https://lccn.loc.gov/2023046020
LC ebook record available at https://lccn.loc.gov/2023046021

♾™ The paper used in this publication meets the minimum requirements of American National Standard for Information Sciences—Permanence of Paper for Printed Library Materials, ANSI/NISO Z39.48-1992.

Contents

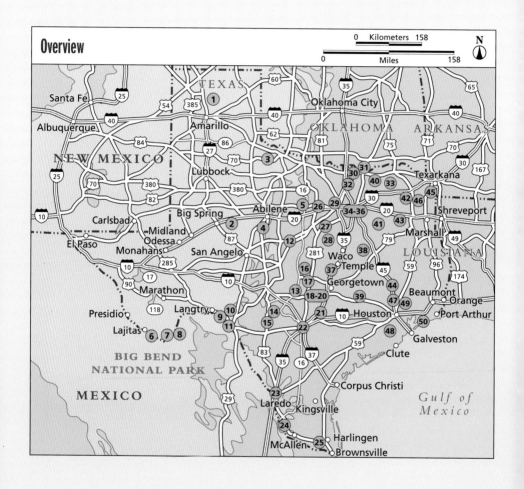

Acknowledgments

First of all, my editor at Globe Pequot, Mason Gadd. You truly are the best. Your professionalism, patience, consideration, and encouragement were all so vital in carrying this project through. Thank you for believing in me and for your complete support. There is no way I would have made this book the best that it could be without your help and valuable expertise. I am so proud to be working with you and Globe Pequot on this second publication.

Thank you to the following park and refuge superintendents, interpreters, rangers, and staff members who demonstrated kindness and took the time to provide guidance on their respective parks and refuges: Aaron Johnston, Amanda Parsons, Amanda Zumwalt, Beau Hester, Boyd Sanders, Cathryn Hoyt, Chris Bishop, Chris Campbell, Chris Caswell, Chris Chastain, Christine Donald, Connor Murnane, David Fischer, David Owens, Debbie Hicks, Deric Ivie, Doug Cochran, Eric Smith, Jamie Langham, Jamie Lee Case, Jason Hairston, Jason Schooley, Javier de León, Jeff Davis, Jessica Bullard, Joe Uribe, Kathy Whaley, Kody Waters, Lauren Hollenbeck, Leslie Mcguigan, Meredith Haley, Nate Thayer, Nikki Little, Rachel Laca, Rick Thompson, Sarah Norlin, Stephanie Croatt, Stephen Garmon, Steve Propes, Sydney Blackwell, Travis Cook, Tanya Petruney, Tom VandenBerg, and Will Speer. To all of you who helped in some way, big or small, I am thankful from the bottom of my heart.

To all of our family and friends who have expressed excitement and support for the book—I appreciate you so much. A big thank-you to my twin sister, Jennifer, and my mom, dad, and grandma for your love and unwavering support. Also, our new Texan friends that we met on one of our hiking trips for the book, Edgel and Steve Vinson. Who knew that sharing a table in a crowded breakfast place in Marfa would have given us such great friends as you two? Thank you for being people we look up to. We are so thankful for your friendship and wisdom.

Most importantly, my adventure partner for life—my husband, Koby. Wow. We thought we had a good idea of how daunting this project would be, but we were still blown away. It has been quite a whirlwind traveling around all of Texas and getting to know the state like the backs of our hands. Despite the alarm clock routinely set at 4 a.m., the hikes under the Texas sun, the never-ending warding off of mosquitos, the cancelled flights, the trails we had to redo because the GPX tracker failed, the sleepless nights at campsites and hotels, had it not been for the book, we would have not been able to travel to places we were fortunate to visit. It was worth it all, especially because you were by my side. Thank you for motivating me during the times I felt like giving up and whenever I had writer's block (so many times). You rooted for me all the way, and you will always have my whole heart.

Meet Your Guide

When her parents started taking her and her twin sister on cross-country road trips at just 5 years old, Jamie Fleck became an avid traveler. Since then, she has ventured out and experienced the outdoors in forty-five of the fifty United States and twenty-two countries worldwide. From living in Texas, Boston, Los Angeles, and Oklahoma, Jamie has experienced firsthand what Texas has to offer compared to other regions in the United States. She continues to hike, camp, and photograph the Lone Star State's state parks, national lands, and regional outdoor areas.

Jamie leans on her technical and practical skills to be accurate and detailed when traversing the trails and documenting her travels. She also taps into her creative side as a professional freelance photographer and contribution writer. She has leveraged her photography skills for more than a decade, working with numerous outdoor companies and well-recognized brands. Jamie continues to commemorate her devotion to traveling and finding underrated places outdoors to create experiences for the public through her photography.

Born in Texas and returning to live in Texas a few years ago, she currently divides her time between Texas and Oklahoma. Jamie resides with her husband and affectionate cat. She continues to hit the trails with her husband. Their cat has yet to muster the courage to go hiking with them. *Best Lake Hikes Texas* is Jamie's second publication with FalconGuides. Her first publication with FalconGuides is the successful *Hiking Oklahoma* book.

To follow along on Jamie's adventures, you can find her on Instagram: @mornings bythesea and her website: http://www.flecksoflove.com.

Sunrise at Lake Somerville (Hike 39)

Before You Hit the Trail

Best Lake Hikes Texas focuses on some of the most scenic day-hike trails to water features in Texas. While not all lake and river trails in Texas are included in this book, you will gain firsthand knowledge of popular and less-known trails that offer a rewarding view and showcase the natural beauty of Texas. There are sixty-plus hikes covered in this book that vary in difficulty to engage the novice hiker and the experienced hiker alike. Detailed information is provided for each of the trails, with chapter sections explained below.

Lake or River
This indicates what type of body of water will be featured on the hike.

Photogenic Factor
The rating is on a scale of 1 to 5, 5 being the most photogenic. The rating is subjective and is based on several factors—the condition of the lake or river, its surrounding landscape, and other notable features included on the hike. Lake and river hikes determined to have a 4 or higher photogenic factor rating made it into this guide. Please understand that if a trail got rated lower than a 5, this does not mean that it is not worthwhile. All trails that made it in this guide are scenic and had significant qualities that made them deserve to be included.

Start
This indicates the starting location for the hike.

Elevation Gain
Elevation is generally the most important factor in determining a hike's difficulty. The numbers listed indicate the total amount of elevation gained during the course of the hike.

Distance
The distance specified in each description is listed as a round-trip distance from the trailhead to the end of the route and back. Hike lengths have been estimated as closely as possible using GPS units. The final figure is the author's best estimate.

Difficulty
Assessing the difficulty of a hike is very subjective. The elevation change, trail length, trail surface, lack of shade, terrain, and physical condition of a hiker all play a role. However, even subjective ratings will give some idea of difficulty. For this guide, elevation gain and trail conditions were the most significant variable in establishing levels of difficulty.

Hiking Time

The hiking time is a rough estimate of the time within which the average hiker will be able to complete the hike. To come up with this information, an estimation was made that most people hike at 2 to 3 miles per hour. For longer hikes with more elevation changes, estimates are closer to 2 miles per hour. For short, flat hikes, 3 miles per hour can be easily attained.

Seasons/Schedule

This section specifies designated hours and days of the year that a park or trail area is open. Generally, most areas are open for day use or sunrise to sunset. Some are closed on holidays, such as national lands.

Fees and Permits

At time of publication, all of Texas's state parks charge a day-use fee. Reserving day-use passes ahead of time is highly recommended and at times, required for popular parks. Day-use passes can be purchased at park headquarters or after hours

View of Lake Texoma from the Haller's Haven Nature Trail (Hike 30)

at self-pay stations located in participating parks, online at https://texasstateparks. reserveamerica.com/, or through the TX State Parks mobile app. Annual Texas State Park Pass holders can reserve day-use passes at no cost.

Fee and permit requirements for parks owned by a local municipality vary. Some require a fee for all recreational activities, some waive the fee if you are only hiking.

Some national parks, national recreation areas, and national wildlife refuges require an entrance fee, and some do not. Consult the park or refuge website or call the headquarters prior to visiting to confirm fee and permit requirements.

Trail Contacts

The trail contacts list the name, address, website, and/or phone number of the managing agency for the lands through which the trail passes. Call or check the website for current information about the hike.

Dog-friendly

This section describes whether dogs are allowed on the trail. Verify whether a trail is dog-friendly before bringing your dog, and check for any service animal exceptions.

A quiet morning on White Rock Lake (Hike 35)

All dogs must be leashed to prevent accidents, hounding of wildlife, and/or damage to the environment. Please remember to either bury your dog's waste or pack it out with you from the trail. Some protected areas in Texas prohibit all animals, not just dogs. These areas will be specified as "no animals permitted." All buildings, facilities, and swimming areas in Texas state parks do not allow dogs.

Trail Surface
Trail surface describes the material that composes the trail. Most often it is simply a dirt path consisting of the native materials that were there when the trail was built, such as tree roots and rocks. On occasion, gravel is added or the trail may be paved. In a few instances the hike follows a dirt road or even a paved road. Be cautious when crossing vehicular roads.

Land Status
The land status simply tells which agency, usually federal or state, manages the land in which the trail lies. In this guide Texas State Parks, municipal parks and recreation departments, US Fish and Wildlife Service, USDA Forest Service, and National Park Service are the most common land managers. National park, Forest Service, and wildlife refuge areas are by far the most protected and therefore have the most rules and regulations. What might be acceptable in a state park may not be acceptable on national land.

Nearest Town

The nearest town is the closest city or town to the trailhead that has at least minimal visitor services. The listed town will usually have gas, food, and limited lodging available. Please note that in smaller towns, the hours these services are available may be limited.

Other Trail Users

This describes other users you might encounter on the hike. Mountain bikers, cyclists, paddlers, rappelers, anglers, and hunters are the most common.

Maps

The maps provided in this guide are as accurate and current as possible. When used in conjunction with the hike description and the additional maps listed for each hike, you should have little difficulty staying on track.

Most of the state parks have park and trail maps that are free to the public on the state park website, state park mobile app, and at the park offices. The National Forest Service maps do include trails, but the maps are usually broad in nature. They are still very useful for locating trailheads, campgrounds, and roads. Most of the National Park Service and National Wildlife Refuge areas have trail maps or detailed brochures available online and at the park or refuge visitor center.

United States Geological Survey (USGS) topographic quadrangles are usually the most detailed and accurate maps available when it comes to natural features. If you learn how to use them, they help you visualize many topographical features. Most of the more well-known hikes in this guide do not require a topo map; however USGS quads are particularly handy for lesser used trails and when hiking off-trail. USGS quadrangles for less-populated parts of Texas can be out-of-date and may not show newer roads and trails. USGS quadrangle maps are available at outdoor stores or online directly from USGS. To order USGS maps for a specific trail, refer to the exact map name as listed in the hike description.

GPS (Global Positioning System) units, particularly those with installed maps, can be extremely useful for finding trailheads and off-trail routes when used with paper maps. For backcountry hikers and campers, researching the area beforehand and bringing a paper map and compass with you are imperative. GPS units are not reliable in areas with no cell phone reception, and batteries for devices can fail at the least-opportune moment.

Finding the Trailhead

This section provides detailed directions to the trailhead. In general, a popular intersection or corridor in the nearest major city is used as the starting point. There are two main tiers of highways in Texas. In this guide, major state highways are used with the abbreviation "TX." The less-populated state highways, Farm-to-Market and Ranch-to-Market, are denoted with FM and RM, respectively.

View from the Summit Trail (Hike 13)

Distances were measured using Google Maps from the trailhead GPS coordinates. GPS systems on your cell phone may not be reliable or accurate, especially in remote areas with little to no cell service. Do not rely solely on online map applications.

All the hikes featured in this guide have trailheads that can be reached by a regular passenger vehicle unless otherwise noted. Check road conditions with park and refuge staff prior to venturing into remote areas or unimproved dirt roads.

Theft and vandalism can happen to vehicles parked at the trailheads. Either pack your valuables in the trunk out of sight or do not leave valuables in the car at all.

The Hike

All the hikes selected for this guide can be done easily by people in good physical condition. Some scrambling may be necessary for a few of the hikes, but none require any rock-climbing skills. A few of the hikes, as noted in their descriptions, travel across roads or are on very faint trails.

The trails are often marked with ties, blazes, plastic, or metal markings. Most of the time the trails are obvious and easy to follow, but the marks help when the paths are hard to discern. Be sure not to add your own trail markings, which could confuse other hikers. Let the official trail workers make the markings. Sometimes, especially in wooded areas, small plastic or metal markers are nailed to trees to indicate the route.

Sometimes primitive campsites are available near a trail. For national forests, there are usually few restrictions in selecting a campsite, provided that it is well away from the trail or any water source. Most state and national parks require that certain backcountry campsites be used. State parks charge a small fee; fee requirements vary for national parks.

After reading the descriptions, select the trail that appeals the most to you. Consider your physical limitations and the supplies you have on hand. Do not overextend yourself to complete any of the hikes. You are hiking because you want to enjoy nature and have a good time. You don't need to prove anything by finishing a hike!

Miles and Directions

To help you stay on course, a detailed route finder sets forth mileages between significant landmarks along the trail.

Introduction

As the second-largest state in the United States, Texas boosts over 7,000 lakes and fifteen major rivers. While most of the Lone Star State's lakes are located in its hilly central and forested eastern regions, its rivers course through all over, even in the arid regions of West Texas. Rivers in Texas are resourceful. Their impoundment created most of the lakes in Texas. Most of the lakes in Texas are man-made; this attribute does not deter them from being appreciated and loved in their own way. Both lakes and rivers in Texas serve multiple purposes—water supply, conservation, flood control, and most importantly for this book, outdoor recreation. With the abundance of lakes and rivers that the state has to offer, there is no shortage of places that Texans and out-of-state visitors can flock to in hopes of discovering refreshment and respite.

Texas is diverse in its topography and is categorized into seven regions. This guide is divided into those regions: Panhandle Plains and Big Bend Country to the west, Prairies and Lakes and Pineywoods to the east, South Texas Plains and Gulf Coast to the south, and Hill Country in the heart of the state. The Panhandle Plains is a mixture of arid prairie and canyonland, with gems like Lake Meredith and the Red River. Big Bend Country, perhaps the most unexpected region of the state, contains hauntingly beautiful deserts with escarpments carved by the Rio Grande. Prairies and Lakes is mainly that—a vivid collection of prairies and lakes. This eastern region boasts the greatest number of lakes in the state. The Pineywoods region resembles the southeastern region of Oklahoma and western Arkansas. Stately old pines congregate around photo-worthy Tyler Lake, Lake Bob Sandlin, and other lakes. The South Texas Plains region, while mostly dry, has water flowing in more fertile areas of the Rio Grande Valley. Bordered by the Gulf of Mexico, the Gulf Coast showcases marshy lakes and coastal wetlands. Hill Country, with its rolling hills and craggy topography, encases many lakes and rivers.

Inclement Weather

Texas weather can be fickle. Check the hourly weather report before embarking on any trail. Plan responsibly to make sure you complete a trail before bad weather hits or postpone the hike to a day with more favorable weather. Carrying a lightweight, waterproof jacket or poncho will help during a passing rainstorm or thunderstorm. Flash floods are infrequent but do happen. Stay on higher ground and away from water sources. Whenever you hear thunder, head to lower ground in less-exposed areas.

Most streams and creeks in Texas are seasonal and therefore filled with water only after heavy precipitation. In a scenario where you need to wade through a flowing stream, always look ahead and determine whether you feel safe going across. With swollen crossings, strong currents may exist. Rocks in the streambed can be dangerously slippery and may not be reliable ways to get across. If you feel any unsettledness, simply turn around and return the way you came.

Equipment

The right hiking shoes will probably be one of the best investments you make for your trailblazing adventures. Find a pair of hiking shoes that are durable, waterproof, have great traction, maintain ankle and sole support, have toe guards, and are comfortable. These characteristics will help make your time on the trails enjoyable as well as safer.

Wear layers of clothing to be warm during the cold mornings and evenings during the summer. Clothes made of materials that wick away perspiration but do not absorb full moisture are better to wear in summer. Hats and sunscreen will go a long way in preventing sunburn and heatstroke, no matter the season. Because wool insulates heat, clothing made of wool is better in the colder months. Bring gloves with touch-screen fingers for handling

Sunrise at Inks Lake (Hike 17)

devices and extra socks to keep you warm in the fall and winter. The types and amounts of items you bring to wear can, depending on the season, prevent you from falling victim to heat exhaustion or hypothermia.

Daypacks are useful even if you are not backpacking. They can store your water supply, meals and snacks, extra clothing, rain jacket, camera, and valuables. Bring a lightweight yet durable daypack that sits comfortably on your shoulders and back. On a long trail, the way a daypack falls on your body can make a huge difference.

Other items that would be helpful on the trail include trekking poles, a paper map, a compass, a packable first aid kit, food and water, additional clothing, insect repellent, waterproof matches, a rechargeable battery pack, and a fully charged cell phone. For longer hikes in the wilderness, a backpacking tent and blanket may be necessary.

Water

Possibly one of the most dangerous things you can do on a trail is not bring enough water. Dehydration in summer can accelerate heat exhaustion; dehydration in winter can accelerate hypothermia. Although high altitudes are not a likely scenario in Texas, it is still a good idea to drink ample amounts of water and electrolytes when hitting trails higher in elevations. Uncontaminated or safe water sources are rare along the trails, so make sure to bring an adequate amount of water in reusable water bottles. The rule of thumb is 0.5 liters of water for every hour you are on the trail—1 liter of water for every hour you are on a difficult trail or a trail with no shade in the summer. If you must resort to drinking from a natural water source, make sure to bring proper water filtration or treatment.

Should a hiker suffer from heat exhaustion, place the person in the shade and provide them with frequent drinks of electrolyte-based liquids and intermittent snacks. For a hiker suffering from hypothermia, extra dry clothes and warm fluids can help keep them warm and awake until medical care is available.

Poisonous Plants

Poison ivy, poison sumac, poison hemlock, and the Texas bullnettle are the most prevalent poisonous plants that can be found in Texas. Study visuals of these plants before hitting the trail. Nonpoisonous doppelgängers of eastern poison ivy, such as Virginia creeper and boxelder, can sometimes cause panic. Your best bet to avoid brushing up against any of these plants is just to stay on the trails. If you come into contact with any poisonous plants, quickly wash all affected areas as well as clothing with lots of warm water and soap. Reactions can take up to 72 hours to manifest, so do not assume that there was no contact. Calamine and oatmeal-based lotions, corticosteroid creams, and oral antihistamines can all help soothe minor reactions. If your reaction is abnormal or severe, make sure to receive medical assistance from a doctor as soon as possible.

Insects

Disease-bearing mosquitoes and ticks are ubiquitous during Texas summers, when the humid climate is especially welcoming. Insect repellent, long-sleeved shirts, and long pants are your friends and saviors while on the trail. If you stick to the path, you will avoid walking into unmaintained brush or grassy areas, favorite dwelling places for ticks. If you do happen to be on a trail that is a playground for ticks, make sure to remove any ticks with tweezers as soon as possible. Ticks can be very tiny and difficult to notice, so look carefully. Then wash yourself off thoroughly with soap and water. Occasionally, bees, wasps, and hornets will follow along with you. Do not swat at them. If you do, they will likely sting you as part of their defense mechanism.

Snakes

While fear of snakes is often understandable, learning about them may help you realize their importance to the ecosystem and how to avoid getting bitten. In general, snakes avoid people. It is when they are provoked or feel unsafe that they attack. Snakes do not have eardrums and therefore "hear" vibrations in the ground.

Most of the time, they know to stay back from a designated trail for their own safety, especially when they hear the pounding of hiking boots approaching. If you stay on the designated path, this will help lower your chances of encountering and getting bitten by a snake. If you find a snake in your path, do not panic. Do not try to touch or handle it either. This will give the snake a reason to attack. Turn around on the trail and return the way you came.

The most common venomous snakes in Texas are the varietal rattlesnake, cottonmouth, and copperhead. If you do get bitten by a snake, whether venomous or not, seek immediate medical help. Try to cleanse the area around the bite as best as you can; then cover it lightly

Cardinal sighting on the Paluxy River Trail (Hike 27)

with sterile wrappings. Keep the area with the bite still and below your heart until medical attention arrives.

Hunting

Hunting is considered both a recreational sport and a necessary form of wildlife management in the state of Texas. The open season for hunting in Texas usually occurs from September through February of the following year, with some hunts allowed in the spring and summer depending on the type of game being hunted. Hunting seasons vary by region, so it is imperative to check with the Texas Parks and Wildlife Department (TPWD) for the current annual hunting season calendar. Try to avoid areas that are open to hunters during the hunting season. If you end up on a trail with hunters, make sure to wear bright clothing. Most hunters wear fluorescent orange as a precaution, so that could be a good color to wear as well. For official hunting season dates, regulations, and areas that allow hunting, refer to the TPWD's website at https://tpwd.texas.gov/regulations/outdoor-annual/hunting/. Each individual park and land management's official website and social media may also include updates on hunting, especially controlled hunts.

Leave No Trace

Below are guidelines that we, as stewards of the outdoors, should adhere to so that we and future generations can continue to enjoy the trails we hike on and prolong the life of this extraordinary world we live in.

- Keep group sizes small whether hiking or camping. Try to avoid peak times to lessen the impact crowds make.
- Bring equipment that is small, lightweight, and blends in with the natural landscape.
- Be sufficiently prepared for your hike so that additional people and resources do not have to be used to rescue you.
- Whatever you bring with you, you must bring back out.
- For more on Leave No Trace principles, visit www.LNT.org.

Camping at Big Bend National Park (Hikes 6, 7, 8, and Honorable Mention Hike C)

Staying on Designated Trails

Venturing off the official trail, taking undesignated trails, and making shortcuts on switchbacks can cause many years of irreversible damage to the ecosystem and geology surrounding the trail. Trail routes are created to protect the extraordinary area that encompasses them. The specified route is to keep people away from fragile wildlife, fauna, or formations. If the route was not made to lead somewhere, do not try to create a new route to get there.

Respecting Others

Day hiking trails are some of the friendliest spots to meet people and learn new things. If the out-and-back trail you are on is narrow, make sure to leave room for people headed your way. For multiuse trails, other trail users may include cyclists, mountain bikers, and equestrians. While those on a bike should yield to hikers—and usually make some indication that they are coming near you—do not assume that they will yield; be courteous. Stay off to the side of the trail when nearing equestrians so that horses have sufficient room to pass. Respect others and nature, make new friends, and have a blast on the trails!

Map Legend

Municipal

≡⟨45⟩≡ Freeway/Interstate Highway

⟨175⟩ US Highway

⟨36⟩ State Road

⟨24⟩ County/Paved/Improved Road

├──┼──┤ Railroad Text

───── Leader Line

Trails

------ Featured Trail

- - - - - Trail or Fire Road

▌▌▌▌▌ Steps/boardwalk

•─•─•─ Utility Line/ Pipe Line

Water Features

Body of Water

River/Creek

Waterfall

Spring

Land Management

National Park/Forest

State/County Park

Reservation Area

National Wildlife Refuge/
Wilderness Area

Symbols

Boat Ramp

⌣ Bridge

■ Building/Point of Interest

⚲ Campground

† Cemetery

▲ Campsite

∩ Cave

•—• Gate

→ Hike Arrow

▲ Mountain/Peak

◇ Mileage Marker

🅿 Parking

⊞ Picnic Area

🚻 Restroom

Scenic View/Overlook

→ To Text

⑰ Trailhead

o Town (Hike Map)

Ⅱ Tower

❷ Visitor/Information Center

Panhandle Plains

An autumn scene at Lake Marvin Recreation Area (Honorable Mention Hike B)

1 Fritch Fortress Trail, Lake Meredith National Recreation Area

Majestic all year round, Lake Meredith sits among Alibates dolomite crowned mesas in the Canadian River Valley. With a geological history over 300 million years old, the surrounding Permian "red bed" landscape of Lake Meredith dotted with sunflowers, cacti, and mesquite trees also add to the enchantment. Hikers taking the Fritch Fortress Trail will get front-row views of the lake and terrain as the route traverses along the shoreline for miles.

Lake or river: Lake Meredith
Photogenic factor: 5
Start: Fritch Fortress Trailhead
Elevation gain: 2,900 to 3,121 feet
Distance: 8.96 miles out and back
Difficulty: Strenuous
Hiking time: 4-5 hours
Seasons/schedule: Open year-round; headquarters hours are 9 a.m. to 4 p.m. Mon through Fri
Fees and permits: None (subject to change)
Trail contacts: Lake Meredith National Recreation Area Headquarters, 419 E Broadway, Fritch 79036; (806) 857-3151
Dog-friendly: Leashed dogs permitted

Trail surface: Dirt and gravel
Land status: National Park Service
Nearest town: Sanford (northeast), Borger (east), Fritch and Amarillo (southwest)
Other trail users: Cyclists
Maps: USGS Sanford; Lake Meredith National Recreation Area map (available online at nps .gov/lamr/planyourvisit/maps.htm)
Special considerations: There is no shade on this trail. Start your hike early and bring adequate amounts of water. Portions of this trail can get overgrown during the summer or rainy seasons. In-ground brown markers serve as guides on this trail. Venomous snakes can be encountered on this trail.

Finding the trailhead: From the intersection of N Fillmore Street and E Amarillo Boulevard/US 66 in downtown Amarillo, head east on E Amarillo Boulevard/US 66 for 2.8 miles. Turn left onto TX 136 N. Travel northeast on TX 136 for 33.2 miles. Go left onto N Fritch Drive. After traveling on N Fritch Drive for 2.3 miles, turn right onto El Paso Drive. Continue on El Paso Drive for 0.6 miles. Turn right onto Fritch Fortress Highway. Travel southwest on Fritch Fortress Highway for 0.8 miles. Fritch Fortress Campground will be to your left. Turn left toward the restrooms and the parking lot. The Fritch Fortress Trailhead will be south of the restrooms and parking lot. **GPS:** N35° 40.823' W101° 35.901'

The Hike

Situated on the northern part of one of the largest plateaus of North America, the Llano Estacado, Lake Meredith National Recreation Area is home to the magnificent Lake Meredith and thousands of acres of grassland and canyons. Lake Meredith is a vital water supply to eleven cities in the Texas Panhandle, providing water to over 750,000 residents. It is impounded on the Canadian River by the Sanford Dam. The lake, originally called Sanford Reservoir, was renamed after former Borger city manager A. A. Meredith, who

View from the beginning of the Fritch Fortress Trail

came up with the project to construct the lake. A. A. Meredith passed away a couple of years prior to the completion of the project, but his vision transformed into and continues to be an important source of water supply and recreation for many in the area.

Morning view of Lake Meredith

The Fritch Fortress Trail is a challenging route, but completely worth it. It has endless, breathtaking views of Lake Meredith, and an incredible myriad of vegetation and wildlife. It begins south of the Fritch Fortress Campground restrooms. It primarily heads south along the shoreline of the lake with a few brief deviations to the east and west throughout the route. At 0.12 miles, you will reach your first of many spectacular vistas of Lake Meredith to your right. In the summer, you have a bird's-eye view of the mighty lake situated within red escarpments populated with flourishing sunflowers. From here you will make a 60-foot descent to the 0.14-mile mark. Switchbacks offer a degree of variety, and there are several of them on this trail. You will encounter the first series of small switchbacks at 0.14 miles with a descent of 20 feet to the 0.17-mile mark. Then there will be another switchback at 0.29 miles with a 30-foot descent to the red clay surface at 0.37 miles. You will cross over a small seasonal streambed shortly after.

From 0.87 miles to 1.84 miles, there are many opportunities to experience panoramic views of the mighty lake. You will cross over another seasonal streambed at 1.55 miles, and at this point, lake views dissipate for a while. There will be a concrete ramp to cross over at 2.05 miles, and then you will continue northwest onto the dirt path. When you reach the boat ramp at 2.08 miles, look straight ahead for the brown metal marker to reconnect with the trail. You will cross over another seasonal streambed shortly after. At around the 2.22-mile mark, during the spring and summer, this area can be blooming

Fritch Fortress Trail, Lake Meredith National Recreation Area

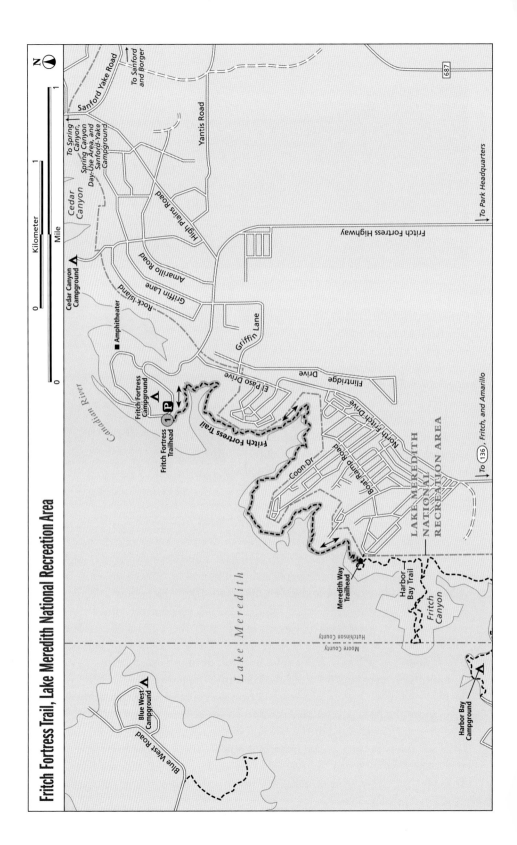

beautifully with wildflowers. A vista of Lake Meredith to your right serves as the cherry on top in this scenic area. You will then make a 20-foot ascent from 2.4 to 2.41 miles into the trail and then another wildflower area will greet you after that descent.

At 3.03 miles, bypass the offshoot to your left. There will be additional vistas to view Lake Meredith shortly after and to the 3.81-mile mark. After crossing the seasonal streambed at 3.55 miles, you will make a steep 5-foot ascent to the 3.56-mile mark. At times, after a decent rainfall, you can hear the melodic trickling of the stream to your right. Another seasonal streambed will show up at 4.2 miles, and from this point there will be significant elevation gain in the trail. It will be about a 145-foot ascent to the 4.44-mile mark through a series of switchbacks. The final lake vista on the trail will be to your right at 4.39 miles. Bear left at the fork at 4.47 miles to head toward the Meredith Way Trailhead and a composting toilet. The right side of the fork is the Harbor Bay Trail. At 4.48 miles, you will reach the parking area for the Meredith Way Trailhead. The trail commences at this point. Turn around and return the way you came.

Miles and Directions

0.0 The trail begins south of the Fritch Fortress Campground.

0.12 There will be a vista point of Lake Meredith to your right. Make a 60-foot descent to 0.14 miles.

0.14 Encounter a series of small switchbacks with a descent of 20 feet to the 0.17-mile mark.

0.29 Encounter another switchback with a 30-foot descent to the red clay surface at 0.37 miles.

0.39 Cross over a seasonal streambed.

0.87 There will be several vistas of Lake Meredith from here to the 1.84-mile mark.

1.55 Cross over a seasonal streambed.

2.05 Cross over a concrete ramp. Continue northwest onto the dirt path.

2.08 Reach a boat ramp. Look straight ahead for the brown metal marker to reconnect with the trail.

2.13 Cross over a seasonal streambed.

2.22 Reach a beautiful wildflower area and a vista to your right.

2.4 Make a 20-foot ascent to 2.41 miles.

2.66 Reach another wildflower area.

3.03 Bypass the offshoot to your left.

3.2 There will be several vistas of Lake Meredith from here to the 3.81-mile mark.

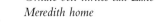
Ornate box turtles call Lake Meredith home

3.55 Cross over a seasonal streambed. Make a steep 5-foot ascent to the 3.56-mile mark.

4.2 Cross over a seasonal streambed. Make a 145-foot ascent to the 4.44-mile mark through a series of switchbacks.

4.39 Reach a lake vista to your right.

4.47 Reach a fork. Bear left to the Meredith Way Trailhead.

4.48 Return the way you came.

8.96 Arrive back at the trailhead.

2 Cactus Cut Trail, Lake Colorado City State Park

True to its name, hikers will be delighted by continuous sights of blossoming prickly pear and other cacti while on the Cactus Cut Trail. The trail also grants continuous views of Lake Colorado City. With interpretive waysides and variations in surfaces, the Cactus Cut Trail is a fun and beautiful route for anyone who enjoys hiking.

Lake or river: Lake Colorado City
Photogenic factor: 4
Start: Cactus Cut Trailhead
Elevation gain: 2,067 to 2,099 feet
Distance: 1.92 miles out and back
Difficulty: Easy
Hiking time: 30 minutes–1 hour
Seasons/schedule: Open year-round, 6 a.m. to 10 p.m.
Fees and permits: $4 per person 13 years and older (subject to change), free for Texas State Parks Pass holders
Trail contacts: Lake Colorado City State Park Headquarters, 4852 FM 2836, Colorado City 79512; (325) 728-3931

Dog-friendly: Leashed dogs permitted
Trail surface: Dirt and gravel
Land status: Texas Parks and Wildlife Department
Nearest town: Colorado City and Sweetwater (northeast), Big Spring (west), Snyder (north)
Other trail users: Mountain bikers/cyclists
Maps: USGS Lake Colorado City; Lake Colorado City State Park map (available online at www.tpwd.texas.gov/state-parks/parks-map and via the TX State Parks mobile app)
Special considerations: In-ground yellow poles serve as guides on this trail.

Finding the trailhead: From the Sayles Boulevard and I-20BL W/S 1st Street intersection in historic downtown Abilene, head west on I-20BL W/S 1st Street for 6.4 miles. Merge onto I-20 W and travel on it for 58.6 miles before taking exit 219B. Stay on I-20BL W for 2.5 miles. Turn left onto TX 163 S/Chestnut Street. Continue south on TX 163 for 6.8 miles. Turn right onto FM 2836/Ranch Road 2836. After 0.7 miles on FM 2836/Ranch Road 2836, turn right to head toward the park headquarters. Travel for half a mile, and then right toward the Mesquite Circle Camping Area and Recreation Hall. After 0.1 miles, there will be a parking area and the Cactus Cut Trailhead will be to the northeast. **GPS: N32° 19.301' W100° 55.857'**

The Hike

Originally formed on the Morgan Creek in 1949 as a water supply for nearby Colorado City and as cooling water for electricity producing condensers at the Morgan Creek Power Plant, Lake Colorado now serves as a recreational haven. It also lies within the passage of the Central Flyway Migration Corridor, allowing for visitors to spot several kinds of birds. Prickly pear cacti provide a myriad of colors throughout Lake Colorado City State Park, and the Cactus Cut Trail is no exception. With

Lake Colorado City in the summer

views of what once was the largest body of water in West Texas, and burgeoning cacti greeting hikers along the way, the Cactus Cut Trail is an enjoyable route to hike.

The Cactus Cut Trail begins northeast of the parking area, heading east. The first diversion to bypass occurs to your right about 220 feet into the trail. The trail then heads primarily north for the rest of the way. You will need to bypass another diversion to your right shortly after. There will be two more diversions to bypass, one at the 0.11-mile mark and one at the 0.14-mile mark. A dip in the path will occur in between these two points. Bear left at the fork at 0.14 miles to continue on the trail.

At 0.19 miles, there will be a "What Is Hidden in That Midden?" interpretive wayside to your right. You will come upon a vista of a cove of Lake Colorado City to your right at the 0.22-mile mark, and then cross over a wooden footbridge shortly after. When you reach Mesquite Circle Camping Area Road at 0.27 miles, watch for vehicles before crossing the road. Head straight toward the in-ground yellow pole to reconnect with the trail. Rocky ledges and sandy sloughs start to reoccur as part of the path surface from 0.33 miles to 0.36 miles. All throughout this time, make sure to follow the in-ground yellow poles, as the route can get confusing. Make sure to head north toward the yellow pole, especially at the 0.38-mile mark. Lake views will be offered to you at 0.7 and 0.72 miles to your right. Take some time to enjoy the view.

You will encounter an additional interpretive wayside, this time titled "Wildlife Detectives" to your right at 0.73 miles. There will be a mild descent of less than 5 feet down a rocky ledge shortly after. You will cross over a slab of rock at 0.84 miles, before bearing left at 0.88 miles. Once you reach the Lakeview Camping Area, there will be

Cactus Cut Trail, Lake Colorado City State Park

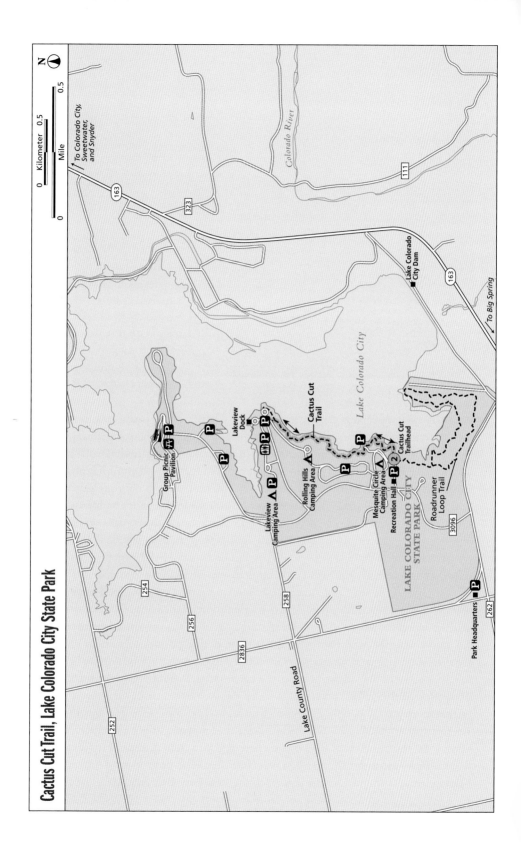

Prickly pear in full bloom   *Cacti along the Cactus Cut Trail*

more views of Lake Colorado City. At this point, you can turn around and return the way you came.

Miles and Directions

0.0 The trail begins northeast of the parking area.

0.04 and 0.05 Bypass the diversion to your right.

0.11 Bypass the diversion to your right.

0.14 Reach a fork. Bear left.

0.22 Reach a vista of a cove to your right.

0.23 Cross over a wooden footbridge.

0.27 Reach Mesquite Circle Camping Area Road. Watch for vehicles before crossing the road to reconnect with the trail straight ahead. Head toward the yellow pole.

0.33 and 0.36 Traverse over some rocky ledges. Follow the yellow pole.

0.38 Head north toward the yellow pole.

0.39 Head north toward the lake. Follow the yellow poles.

0.7 and 0.72 Views of the lake will be to your right.

0.8 Make a mild descent down a rocky ledge.

0.84 Cross over a slab of rock.

0.96 Reach the Lakeview Camping Area. Return the way you came.

1.92 Arrive back at the trailhead.

3 Juniper Ridge Nature Trail (combined with Rocky Ledges Loop), Copper Breaks State Park

The desolate, unspoiled beauty of Copper Breaks State Park continues to astound visitors. The remote location of the park makes it a surreptitious gem in the Panhandle flatlands of Texas. Within the area, the picturesque Lake Copper Breaks and limitless Pease River rest among million-year-old, craggy mesas swathed in mesquites and junipers.

Lake or river: Lake Copper Breaks and Pease River

Photogenic factor: 5

Start: Juniper Ridge Nature Trailhead

Elevation gain: 1,332 to 1,439 feet

Distance: 2.15-mile loop with an additional lollipop

Difficulty: Moderate to difficult due to uneven terrain and a steep descent

Hiking time: About 2 hours

Seasons/schedule: Open year-round, 7 a.m. to 10 p.m.

Fees and permits: $3 per person 13 years and older (subject to change), free for Texas State Parks Pass holders

Trail contacts: Copper Breaks State Park Headquarters, 777 Park Road 62, Quanah 79252; (940) 839-4331

Dog-friendly: Leashed dogs permitted

Trail surface: Dirt and gravel

Land status: Texas Parks and Wildlife Department

Nearest town: Quanah (north), Crowell (south)

Other trail users: Mountain bikers/cyclists

Maps: USGS Margaret; Copper Breaks State Park map (available online at www.tpwd.texas .gov/state-parks/parks-map and via the TX State Parks mobile app)

Special considerations: There is no shade on this trail. Start your hike early and bring adequate amounts of water. Wooden signs with arrows serve as guides for the Rocky Ledges Loop. This park has designated Dark Sky Park status.

Finding the trailhead: From downtown Amarillo, merge onto I-40 E/US 287 S. Stay on I-40 E for 8.4 miles, before taking exit 78 for US 287 S. Continue on US 287 S for 135 miles. When you reach the town of Quanah, turn right onto TX 6 S/S Main Street. After traveling south on TX 6 for 12.4 miles, turn right into Copper Breaks State Park. Stay on State Highway Park Road 62 until you reach the Kiowa Campground. Go left and in about half a mile after you have passed the Cottonwood Group Campground, the road will loop. The Juniper Ridge Nature Trailhead will be to the north of the loop and parking area. **GPS:** N34° 06.457' W99° 44.816'

The Hike

The stunning Copper Breaks State Park gets its name from the "copper" banded ancient geological formations and juniper breaks that populate the region. Two main

Lake Copper Breaks at sunset

water sources are nestled within the park—Lake Copper Breaks and the Pease River. Lake Copper Breaks can be seen from the Juniper Ridge Nature Trail, while the Pease River is visible from the Rocky Ledges Loop. This guide will take you on both trails, beginning with the Juniper Ridge Trail.

The Juniper Ridge Trail can be taken in any direction. Wooden steps will occur frequently throughout the Juniper Ridge Trail. A way to make sure you are staying on the main route and not going on a side trail is to look for wooden steps in the path. There will also be several interpretive waysides on geology along the Juniper Ridge Trail. They include details on the following topics: "Pangea," "Stratigraphy," "Clear Fork Group," "Pease River Group," "Pleistocene," "Holocene," "Missing History," "Erosion," "Copper," "Gypsum," and a designation of the Permian Sea Tide Ripples feature. At 145 feet into the trail, an overlook of Lake Copper Breaks will be to your left.

At 285 feet within the trail, another view of Lake Copper Breaks will be presented to you to your left. The trail primarily heads north until you pass the Juniper Ridge Overlook and reach the 0.39-mile mark. You will eventually go through a wildflower meadow. Bypass the side trail to your right at 0.21 miles. Be mindful of the Permian Sea Tide Ripples prior to reaching the fork at 0.29 miles. These ancient

BATTLE OF PEASE RIVER

The Pease River may be recognized for its beauty, but it is also well-known for a raid on the Comanche people by the Texas Rangers that took place in the winter of 1860. The attack came as a surprise to the Noconi Comanche people, who had made the Pease River their home. Many Comanche people were massacred, and a few captured. One of the captives during the raid was Cynthia Ann Parker (also known as Naduah). Although not born Comanche, she had been captured by the tribe, adopted, and then married to a Comanche chief. She was the mother of Quanah Parker, who would eventually become a historically prominent Comanche leader. After her recapture by the Texas Rangers, Cynthia Ann Parker was never permitted to return to the Comanche people.

sandstone ripples were formed millions of years ago. Take the right side of the fork and stay on the designated trail with the wooden steps. The trail will ultimately head west to curve around the vista point. Bypass the side trails from the left and the right. You will reach the wooden shelter with a bench at the Juniper Ridge Overlook at 0.33 miles.

After taking in the enchanting views at the vista, continue toward the fork at 0.35 miles. Both sides will converge heading northwest. Head up the rocky ledges. Another overlook of Lake Copper Breaks will be to your right at 0.39 miles. The trail then heads south. Use caution when going across the footbridge, as it may be unstable. At 0.6 miles, you will meander through an area populated with cacti, particularly the plum-crowned prickly pear. When you return to the spur portion of the lollipop route shortly after, go straight down the log steps back to the parking lot to conclude the Juniper Ridge Nature Trail.

When you reach the parking lot and loop, bear left to connect with the Rocky Ledges Loop. This portion of the trail is undefined until you reach the Rocky Ledges Loop Trailhead at the 0.84-mile mark. Curve along the loop and watch for vehicles. You will go through a gate at 0.66 miles. Continue east on the MTB Trail that connects to the Rocky Ledges Loop. Once you come upon the junction at 0.71 miles, there will be a sign indicating to bear right to reach the Rocky Ledges Loop and River Run Trail. The left side of the fork is a continuation of the MTB Trail that goes to the park headquarters. Head south until you reach another sign to your right at the 0.84-mile mark. This sign will point you to the entrance to the Rocky Ledges Loop. Bear left to start on the Rocky Ledges Loop. Use the wooden signs with arrows as guides for this trail.

The trail primarily heads in an easterly direction until the 1.3-mile mark. Heed caution of where you step around 1.05 miles. The path can get overgrown with sunken spots in the trail surface. After heading up some rocks at 1.08 miles, bypass the side trail to your right. Then bear right across the rocky ledge shortly after. You will be afforded several vista points to your right starting at 1.13 miles. Make sure to bypass the subsequent side trails by continuing east. Once you reach the small alcove to your right, go around it and then you will cross over a couple seasonal streambeds shortly after. The trail eventually heads south at the 1.3-mile mark. Up to 1.45 miles, watch for trail surface erosion as it changes to soft red clay.

Several vistas of the magnificent Pease River will begin to your left, shy of a mile and a half into the trail. At 1.55 miles, pay attention to the "Sudden Drop Off" warning sign. You will descend about 40 feet until the 1.61-mile mark. The most notable view of the Pease River will occur at 1.6 miles, as the trail heads west. The 100-mile river, named after former

Bird's-eye view of the Pease River

Texas governor Elisha M. Pease, appears to curve endlessly through the flatlands.

After heading down some rocks, you will reach the end of the Rocky Ledges Loop. Bear right onto a portion of the River Run Trail to return to the Rocky Ledges Loop Trailhead. Bypass the side trails to your left along the way back. Once you reach the Rocky Ledges Loop Trailhead at 1.92 miles, continue straight to return to the junction originally from the 0.71-mile mark that connects with the MTB Trail. The mileage clocks at 2.04 miles when you reach the junction. Bear left. Watch for vehicles before walking along the sides of the loop and returning to the Juniper Ridge Nature Trailhead and parking area. If you have free time and happen to be in Copper Breaks State Park on a Friday or Saturday, they do a fun in-person feeding with their small herd of Texas longhorns at 2 p.m. Check with the park headquarters to confirm the feeding is taking place prior to visiting.

Juniper Ridge Nature Trail (combined with Rocky Ledges Loop), Copper Breaks State Park

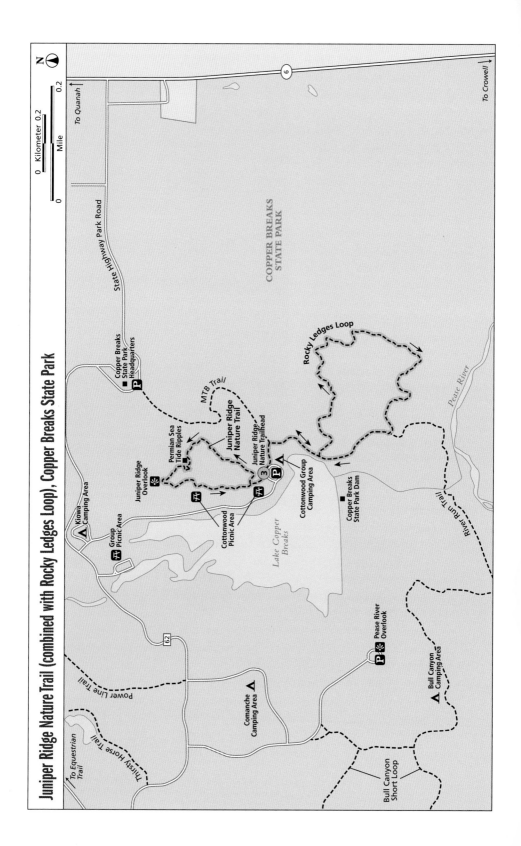

N

0 Kilometer 0.2

0 Mile 0.2

To Quanah

6

To Crowell

State Highway Park Road

Copper Breaks State Park Headquarters

COPPER BREAKS STATE PARK

MTB Trail

Permian Sea Tide Ripples

Juniper Ridge Nature Trail

Juniper Ridge Nature Trailhead

Juniper Ridge Overlook

Kiowa Camping Area

Group Picnic Area

Cottonwood Picnic Area

3

Rocky Ledges Loop

Cottonwood Group Camping Area

Copper Breaks State Park Dam

Lake Copper Breaks

Pease River

62

Power Line Trail

To Equestrian Trail

Thirsty Horse Trail

Comanche Camping Area

Pease River Overlook

River Run Trail

Bull Canyon Camping Area

Bull Canyon Short Loop

Miles and Directions

0.0   Start at the Juniper Ridge Nature Trailhead.

0.03 Reach a fork. Bear right. An overlook of Lake Copper Breaks will be to your left.

0.05 Additional views of Lake Copper Breaks will be to your left. Go through a wildflower meadow.

0.21 Bypass the side trail to your right.

0.29 Reach a fork. Bear right. The trail curves west around the vista point. Bypass the side trails to your left and right.

0.33 Reach a wooden shelter.

0.35 The path splits and eventually merges. Head northwest up the rocky ledges.

0.39 An overlook of Lake Copper Breaks will be to your right.

0.42 Go across the footbridge (may be unstable).

0.6   Enter a cacti area.

0.62 Reach the spur portion of the lollipop route. Go straight down the log steps back to the parking lot.

0.65 Reach the parking lot. Bear left to connect with the Rocky Ledges Loop. The trail is undefined until you reach the Rocky Ledges Loop Trailhead at the 0.84-mile mark. Curve along the loop and watch for vehicles.

0.66 Reach a gate. Continue on the MTB Trail that connects to the Rocky Ledges Loop. Bear left.

0.71 Reach a junction. Bear right to reach the Rocky Ledges Loop and River Run Trail.

0.84 Reach the entrance to the Rocky Ledges Loop. Bear left. Follow the wooden signs with arrows.

1.05 The trail surface can get overgrown with sunken spots.

1.08 Head northeast up some rocks. Bypass the side trail to your right.

1.09 Bear right across the rocky ledge.

1.13 There will be several vista points to your right starting from this point.

1.15 Bypass several side trails. Continue heading east.

1.19 Go around the small alcove to your right and then cross over a couple seasonal streambeds shortly after.

1.3   Bear right.

1.4   The path becomes eroded and then the surface changes to soft red clay up to the 1.45-mile mark.

1.48 Bear right. Vistas of the Pease River will be to your left starting from this point.

1.55 Heed the "Sudden Drop Off" warning sign. You will descend about 40 feet until the 1.61-mile mark.

1.6   The best view of the Pease River occurs at this point.

1.73 Reach a junction. Bear right to return to the Rocky Ledges Loop Trailhead.

1.9   Bypass a couple side trails to your left.

1.92 Reach the Rocky Ledges Loop Trailhead. Continue straight to head to back to the loop and parking area.

2.04 Reach the junction originally from the 0.71-mile mark that connects with the MTB Trail. Bear left. Watch for vehicles before walking along the sides of the loop.

2.15 Arrive back at the trailhead.

4 Abilene Dam Road, Abilene State Park

Originally intended as a water source for the growing city of Abilene in the early 20th century, Lake Abilene now serves as a popular recreation area. Surrounded by fiery-red clay banks and situated on the upper Elm Creek, Lake Abilene can be enjoyed by hikers on the Abilene Dam Road Trail.

Lake or river: Lake Abilene
Photogenic factor: 4+
Start: Abilene Dam Road Trailhead
Elevation gain: 1,996 to 2,079 feet
Distance: 5.3 miles out and back
Difficulty: Easy
Hiking time: 2–3 hours
Seasons/schedule: Open year round; headquarters hours are 8:15 a.m. to 4:45 p.m., lake hours are 6 a.m. to sunset (gated)
Fees and permits: $5 per person 13 years and older (subject to change), free for Texas State Parks Pass holders
Trail contacts: Abilene State Park Headquarters, 150 Park Road 32, Tuscola 79562; (325) 572-3204
Dog-friendly: Leashed dogs permitted

Trail surface: Asphalt for a portion of the trail, mixture of red clay and gravel for the remainder
Land status: Texas Parks and Wildlife Department
Nearest town: Abilene and Buffalo Gap (northeast), Tuscola (southeast)
Other trail users: Mountain bikers/cyclists, equestrians
Maps: USGS Lake Abilene; Abilene State Park map (available online at www.tpwd.texas.gov/state-parks/parks-map and via the TX State Parks mobile app)
Special considerations: There is no shade until you reach the 1.63-mile mark. Start your hike early and bring adequate amounts of water. Hunting is permitted in some areas of Abilene State Park. Try to avoid areas that are open to hunters during hunting season.

Finding the trailhead: From historic downtown Abilene, head south on Sayles Boulevard for about 2 miles until it changes into Buffalo Gap Road. Continue on Buffalo Gap Road for 10.2 miles, and then it becomes East Street. Travel on East Street for 0.4 miles. Turn left onto Appleton Street. Appleton Street becomes West Street after 0.1 miles. After traveling on West Street for 0.3 miles, take the curve heading west onto Vine Street. Vine Street becomes Litel Street after 0.2 miles. Continue on Litel Street for 0.4 miles and then turn right onto FM 89 W. Continue west on FM 89 for 5.1 miles. You will pass the main entrance to Abilene State Park headquarters to your left. Turn right on Abilene Dam Road to enter the Lake Abilene Unit of Abilene State Park. In less than 200 feet, you will see a small parking area to your right by the gate. The trailhead for Abilene Dam Road is northeast of the parking area. **GPS:** N32° 13.883' W99° 53.473'

The Hike

While the previous landscape where Lake Abilene was formed has drastically changed, it still maintains its beauty and usefulness. At sunrise and sunset, the lake is especially beautiful. Its waters are calm and its colors contrast with the saturated red clay of the

Sunrise at Lake Abilene

hills and greenery of woodlands that encompass it. Elm Creek Valley serves as a dramatic backdrop for Lake Abilene while hikers traverse Abilene Dam Road. The lake is also situated where the town of Bethel from the early 1900s used to be. The formation of Lake Abilene forced the residents of the once populated town to relocate. The Bethel Cemetery was also moved—and the gravesites can be found at the nearby Buffalo Gap Cemetery.

Abilene Dam Road starts off with an asphalt surface and heads northeast from the parking area. A private residence will be to your right shortly after you begin the trail. Keep in mind that there is no shade on the trail until you reach the 1.63-mile mark, so make sure to bring adequate amounts of water. In 600 feet, the trail heads north. You will be afforded views of Lake Abilene to your left. The trail heads northwest at 0.68 miles. About 1 mile into the trail, there will be a 15-foot descent to the 1.02-mile mark. The trail surface then changes to a mixture of red clay and gravel, corresponding to the makeup of the hills to the north. At 1.1 miles, the trail heads north and heads away from the lake. Then the trail heads primarily west until the 1.9-mile mark. Portions of the trail can get muddy after a decent rainfall from this point on. (This is also noticeable at the 1.38-, 1.51-, 2.83-, 2.9-, 3.07-, 3.14-, 3.19-mile marks, respectively.) You will start to encounter several offshoots for mountain biking paths at the 1.59-mile mark. Bypass the first mountain biking offshoot to your right. Cross over a seasonal streambed at 1.62 miles, and then you will reach the loop portion of the lollipop route quickly after. This portion of the trail has partial shade. Use the sign with the words "N Lake TR" as a guide. Bear right to take the loop in a counterclockwise direction.

At 1.85 miles, there will be a 50-foot ascent from here to the 1.9-mile mark. When you reach the fork at 1.9 miles, bear left to continue on the trail. To your right is another mountain biking offshoot. The trail primarily heads south until the 2.55-mile mark. Continue straight at the junction at the 2.22-mile mark. To your right will again

Abilene Dam Road, Abilene State Park

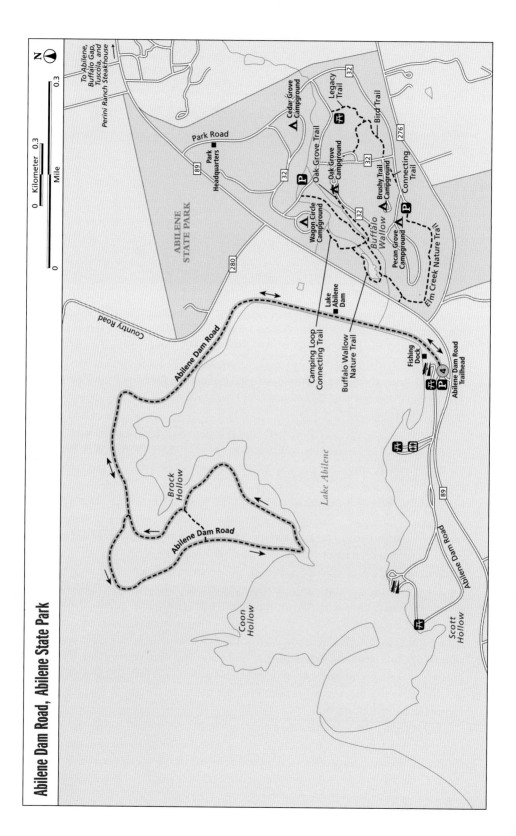

be another mountain biking offshoot, and to your left will be a shortcut connecting to the return route of the loop. Lake views will be offered to you again at 2.44 miles. There will be a 30-foot descent from the 2.5-mile mark to the 2.56-mile mark. You will come upon a vista of Lake Abilene at the end of the descent. Make sure to stop and enjoy the panoramic view of the serene lake with graceful wind turbines nestled among the grandeur of Elm Creek Valley. The trail curves northeast after this point.

After a 5-foot ascent from 2.83 miles to 2.85 miles, lake views will occur once again to your right. The trail heads north at 2.9 miles, and then curves northwest. Partial lake views will be available to your right. At the fork at 3.4 miles, continue straight. To your left will be the shortcut you encountered at the 2.25-mile mark. The trail begins to curve northeast at 3.52 miles, and then any lake views on the loop portion of the lollipop route will dissipate shortly after. At 3.67 miles, the loop portion concludes, and you will reach the spur part of the lollipop route from the original 1.63-mile mark. Bear right to return the way you came. Grab a bite to eat at the famous and award–winning Perini Ranch Steakhouse in the nearby town of Buffalo Gap to reward yourself after the hike.

Miles and Directions

0.0 Head northeast from the parking area on the asphalt surface. There will be a private residence to your right shortly after.

1.0 Make a 15-foot descent to the 1.02-mile mark. The trail surface changes to red clay and gravel.

1.24 This portion of the trail can get muddy. (Portions of the trail also can get muddy at the 1.38-, 1.51-, 2.83-, 2.9-, 3.07-, 3.14-, 3.19-mile marks.)

1.59 Bypass the mountain biking trail to your right.

1.62 Cross over a seasonal streambed.

1.63 Reach the loop portion of the lollipop route. Follow the sign with the words "N Lake TR." Bear right to take the loop in a counterclockwise direction.

1.85 Make a 50-foot ascent from here to the 1.9-mile mark.

1.9 Reach a fork. Bear left.

2.22 Reach a junction. Continue straight.

2.5 Make a 30-foot descent from here to the 2.56-mile mark.

2.55 Reach a vista of the lake.

2.83 Make a 5-foot ascent from here to the 2.85-mile mark.

3.19 Partial lake views will be to your right.

3.4 Reach a fork. Continue straight.

3.67 The loop portion of the lollipop concludes at this point. Bear right to return the way you came.

5.3 Arrive back at the trailhead.

Vista point from Abilene Dam Road

5 Lakeview Trail, Possum Kingdom State Park

Surrounded by imposing cliffs and valleys cloaked in oaks, junipers, mesquite, and redbuds, the nearly 20,000-acre Possum Kingdom Lake is a mighty body of water. Hikers can enjoy the view of the clear waters and beautiful landscape from the Lakeview Trail.

Lake or river: Possum Kingdom Lake
Photogenic factor: 4
Start: Lakeview Trailhead
Elevation gain: 974 to 1,083 feet
Distance: 1.55-mile lollipop
Difficulty: Easy
Hiking time: 30 minutes–1 hour
Seasons/schedule: Open year-round, no gate; headquarters hours are 8 a.m. to 5 p.m.
Fees and permits: $4 per person 13 years and older (subject to change), free for Texas State Parks Pass holders

Trail contacts: Possum Kingdom State Park Headquarters, 3901 State Park Road 33, Caddo 76429; (940) 549-1803
Dog-friendly: Leashed dogs permitted
Trail surface: Dirt and rocky path
Land status: Texas Parks and Wildlife Department
Nearest town: Graham (north), Breckenridge (southwest), Mineral Wells (east)
Other trail users: Mountain bikers/cyclists
Maps: USGS Cove Creek; Possum Kingdom State Park map (available online at www.tpwd.texas.gov/state-parks/parks-map and via the TX State Parks mobile app)

Finding the trailhead: From the US 180 and US 281 intersection in Mineral Wells, travel on US 180 W for 35.2 miles. Make a slight right to connect with TX 252 Loop W. Stay on TX 252 Loop W for 0.8 miles before turning right onto State Park Road 33. Travel on State Park Road 33 for 16.7 miles and you will enter Possum Kingdom State Park. Continue for 0.2 miles. You will pass by the park store and Spanish Oaks Camping Area. The Lakeview Trailhead will be west of the last parking area. **GPS:** N32° 52.934' W98° 33.884'

The Hike

While short and sweet, the Lakeview Trail is full of beauty and wonderment. Interchanging between wildflower prairies and wooded areas, views of Possum Kingdom Lake are also afforded along the way. The trail begins west of the parking area and heads southwest. At 0.11 miles, you will come upon a worn-out gate, a trail map exhibit, and a hiking trail sign. Bypass a couple of side trails to your right shortly after. The trail curves north at 0.16 miles. You will then reach the loop portion of the lollipop route at 0.21 miles. This guide takes the loop in clockwise direction by bearing left.

Vista of Possum Kingdom Lake

From the 0.39-mile mark to the 0.47-mile mark, you will make a 40-foot ascent as the trail heads northwest. Bear left to continue on the Lakeview Trail when you get to the fork. The right side of the fork is the Longhorn Trail. At 0.53 miles, you will make a rocky 80-foot descent to the 0.63-mile mark. In between, views of Possum Kingdom Lake will be available straight ahead. Shortly after the descent, you will come upon an overlook for Possum Kingdom Lake. The trail then heads northeast. Views of the lake will continue on your left. Be aware of any fallen tree trunks at this point and also when you cross over a rock slab at 0.96 miles.

You will make a rocky 20-foot ascent from the 1.06-mile mark to the 1.08-mile mark as the trail heads away from the lake.

Blackfoot daisies along the trail

The path surface turns to grass as you get closer to the primitive campsites. Primitive campsite number 10 will become visible at 1.15 miles. Bear right to continue on the trail. Bypass the connection to the Longhorn Trail to your right at 1.17 miles and continue straight. Primitive campsites 9 through 1 will be visible from the 1.21-mile mark to the 1.33-mile mark. At 1.35 miles, the loop portion of the lollipop route ends at the original 0.21-mile mark. Bear left, heading southeast (the route eventually curves northeast) back down the spur portion of the route to return the way you came.

Lakeview Trail, Possum Kingdom State Park

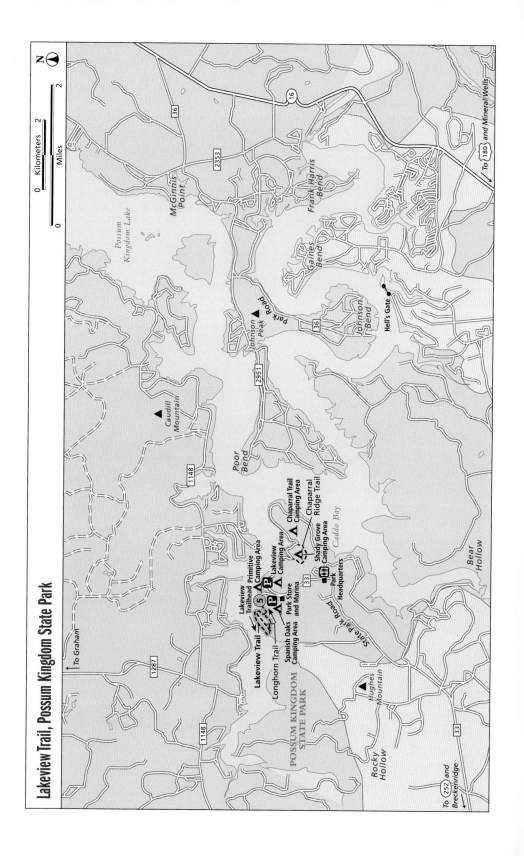

THE BOYS FROM POSSUM KINGDOM

While the topography that encompasses Possum Kingdom Lake is ideal for a possum habitat, seeing an actual possum these days is a rare feat. The name of the lake is based on a story about a possum hide peddler from the early 1900s. The peddler's name was Ike Sablosky, and he was drawn to the nearby Mineral Wells area for the health benefits of the mineral water. Once his health improved, he started a possum hide business, with most of the best resources coming from the Palo Pinto County where Possum Kingdom Lake now lies. Ike Sablosky would refer to his best hunters as "the boys from Possum Kingdom." The name stuck and became widely used for the region.

If you have the opportunity to see Hell's Gate, it is a must-see landmark. Hell's Gate is a popular highlight of Possum Kingdom Lake. With two 90-foot cliffs granting entry to one of Possum Kingdom Lake's southern coves, it is quite a marvel. While it is not accessible by foot from Possum Kingdom State Park, it is accessible by boat.

Miles and Directions

0.0 The trail begins west of the parking area.

0.11 Reach a gate, a trail map exhibit, and a hiking trail sign. Bypass a couple of side trails to your right shortly after.

0.21 Reach the loop portion of the lollipop route. Take the loop in clockwise direction by bearing left.

0.39 Make a 40-foot ascent from here to the 0.47-mile mark.

0.47 Reach a fork. Bear left to continue on the Lakeview Trail.

0.53 Make a rocky 80-foot descent from this point to the 0.63-mile mark.

0.59 Views of Possum Kingdom Lake will be available straight ahead.

0.64 Reach an overlook for Possum Kingdom Lake. Be aware of any fallen tree trunks at this point.

0.96 Cross over a rock slab. Be aware of any fallen tree trunks at this point.

1.06 Make a rocky 20-foot ascent to the 1.08-mile mark as the trail heads away from the lake.

1.13 The path surface turns to grass.

1.15 Reach primitive campsite number 10. Bear right to continue on the trail.

1.17 Bypass the connection to the Longhorn Trail to your right.

1.21 to 1.33 Primitive campsites 9 through 1 will be to your left.

1.35 The loop portion of the lollipop route ends at the original 0.21-mile mark. Bear left down the spur portion of the route to return the way you came.

1.55 Arrive back at the trailhead.

Honorable Mentions (Panhandle Plains)

A Lake Rita Blanca Loop, Lake Rita Blanca City Park

A typical morning at Lake Rita Blanca consists of flocks of birds fanning out over its glassy surface and dragonflies waltzing among the mixture of buffalo grasses and blue grama along its shoreline. It is an uplifting scene and for those looking to get a peaceful workout, the trail that encircles the lake is the perfect route.

Lake or river: Lake Rita Blanca
Photogenic factor: 4+
Start: Lake Rita Blanca Loop Trailhead #3
Elevation gain: 3,868 to 3,918 feet
Distance: 5.08-mile loop
Difficulty: Moderate
Hiking time: 2–3 hours
Seasons/schedule: Open year-round, sunrise to sunset
Fees and permits: None (subject to change)
Trail contacts: City of Dalhart Parks Department Office, 205 Rock Island Avenue, Dalhart 79022; (806) 244-5511

Dog-friendly: Leashed dogs permitted
Trail surface: Dirt and gravel
Land status: City of Dalhart Parks Department
Nearest town: Within Dalhart city limits
Other trail users: Mountain bikers/cyclists
Maps: USGS Dalhart West; no official maps available, however trail is easy to follow from Trailhead #3
Special considerations: Cattle roam freely on this trail. Maintain a respectful and safe distance from livestock.

Finding the trailhead: From the intersection of Railroad Street and Denver Avenue in Dalhart, travel on Railroad Road for half a mile. Turn right onto E 7th Street, and after 190 feet, turn left onto Tennessee Avenue. After 0.8 miles, Tennessee Avenue changes to Lake Drive. Lake

Dawn at Lake Rita Blanca

Drive changes into FM 281 after 0.3 miles. In 0.3 miles, go left after passing the Rita Blanca Community Center. A parking area and Trailhead #3 will be to your left after 0.4 miles. **GPS:** N36° 02.203' W102° 30.424'

B Lake Marvin Shore Trail, Lake Marvin Recreation Area

Dazzling in the fall, Lake Marvin is modest in size but boasts beautiful scenery and foliage. The trail that meanders along its shoreline is a peaceful one. Another advantage—if you are there in October, you can experience the fall foliage festival held annually in the nearby city of Canadian after you are done with the hike.

Lake or river: Lake Marvin
Photogenic factor: 4
Start: Lake Marvin Shore Trailhead
Elevation gain: 2,215 to 2,280 feet
Distance: 2.13 miles out and back with an optional spur
Difficulty: Easy
Hiking time: 2–3 hours
Seasons/schedule: Open year-round, sunrise to sunset
Fees and permits: None, if hiking only (subject to change)
Trail contacts: Black Kettle and McClellan Creek National Grasslands District Office,

18555 Highway 47A Suite B, Cheyenne 73628; (580) 497-2143
Dog-friendly: Leashed dogs permitted
Trail surface: Dirt
Land status: USDA Forest Service
Nearest town: Canadian (west), Pampa and Amarillo (southwest)
Other trail users: Anglers
Maps: USGS Lake Marvin; USDA Forest Service map for Lake Marvin (available online at https://www.fs.usda.gov/recarea/cibola/recarea/?recid=64092)

Finding the trailhead: From the intersection of Main Street and 2nd Street in Canadian, travel on US 60 E for 1.9 miles. Turn right onto FM 2266 E. After 10.7 miles, FM 2266 changes to CR K. CR K then changes into CR L after 0.4 miles. Continue on CR L for 0.7 miles and the trailhead will be to your left near the boat ramp. **GPS:** N35° 52.900' W100° 10.976'

Lake Marvin in the fall

Big Bend Country

The Rio Grande at sunset (Hike 7)

6 Santa Elena Canyon Trail, Big Bend National Park

The dramatic, 1,500-foot limestone walls of Santa Elena Canyon soaring over the Rio Grande are something to see. Short, yet worthwhile, the Santa Elena Canyon Trail leads hikers through the northern portion of Santa Elena Canyon with breathtaking river views along the way.

Lake or river: Terlingua Creek and Rio Grande
Photogenic factor: 5
Start: Santa Elena Canyon Trailhead
Elevation gain: 2,236 to 2,322 feet
Distance: 1.58 miles out and back
Difficulty: Moderate
Hiking time: 1–2 hours
Seasons/schedule: Open year-round; entrance fee stations and visitor centers are closed after regular business hours (Panther Junction and Chisos Basin are open year-round; Rio Grande Village, Persimmon Gap, and Castolon Visitor Centers are only open Nov through Apr)
Fees and permits: $30 per vehicle (subject to change), free for Interagency Pass holders and on designated days (check with park website for yearly designated fee-free days)
Trail contacts: Big Bend National Park Headquarters (Panther Junction), 1 Panther Junction, Big Bend National Park 79834; (432) 477-2251
Dog-friendly: No animals permitted
Trail surface: Dirt and gravel

Land status: National Park Service
Nearest town: Marathon (north), Terlingua (west)
Other trail users: None
Maps: USGS Castolon; Big Bend National Park map (available online at nps.gov/bibe/plan yourvisit/maps.htm)
Special considerations: There is minimal shade on the trail. Temperatures in Big Bend National Park can reach 110+°F in the summer. Make sure to bring 1 gallon per person per day and hike in the early morning. Venomous snakes can be encountered on this trail. This trail requires crossing Terlingua Creek. At times, the water level of Terlingua Creek can be high and flowing, making it impassible. Exercise caution when crossing and do not attempt to cross if there is any doubt. Do not use social paths to avoid getting wet from the creek. Only stay on the officially designated route and follow the sign. All other unofficial paths are dangerous and not maintained. Verify with the park headquarters on current water levels before attempting the hike.

Finding the trailhead: From the intersection of NE 1st Street and US 385 S in Marathon, head south on US 385 S for 39.8 miles. It will change into Main Park Road. Continue on Main Park Road for 27.5 miles. Turn right onto Gano Springs Road. Travel on Gano Springs Road for 12.7 miles before going left onto Ross Maxwell Scenic Drive. Ross Maxwell Scenic Drive will change into Santa Elena Canyon Road after 21.9 miles. Travel on Santa Elena Canyon Road for 9 miles until you reach the parking lot for the Santa Elena Canyon Trail. The Santa Elena Canyon Trailhead will be southwest of the restrooms. **GPS:** N29° 10.039' W103° 36.628'

Vista of the Rio Grande and Terlingua Creek   *Entrance to Santa Elena Canyon*

The Hike

Formed by the Terlingua Fault, the spectacular, 7-mile-long Santa Elena Canyon is unarguably one of the highlights of Big Bend National Park. And rightly so—with its extraordinary, vertical cliffs, its narrow passage allowing the Rio Grande to flow through, and its stark beauty that can be seen miles away during the daytime. The Santa Elena Canyon Trail offers several vistas and interpretive waysides along its path, adding to its appeal.

You will begin the Santa Elena Canyon Trail by heading west across a boardwalk. The trail heads north at 195 feet, and then at 430 feet, the boardwalk ends. The path surface then changes to dirt and gravel. You will encounter several interpretive way-sides along the route. These signs include information on the following topics: "Into the Canyon," "Partners in Protection," "Retama Flower," "Calcite Crystal," "Feathered Beauty," "Diminished River," "Fossil," "Canyon Anatomy," "Limestone Lovers," "Looking Back," "False Agave," "Leatherstem," "Strawberry Pitaya," "Lechuguilla," "Blind Prickly Pear," "Ocotillo," "Honey Mesquite," "Canyon Music," "Geology in Action," Desert Beaver," and "Go with the Flow."

Santa Elena Canyon Trail, Big Bend National Park

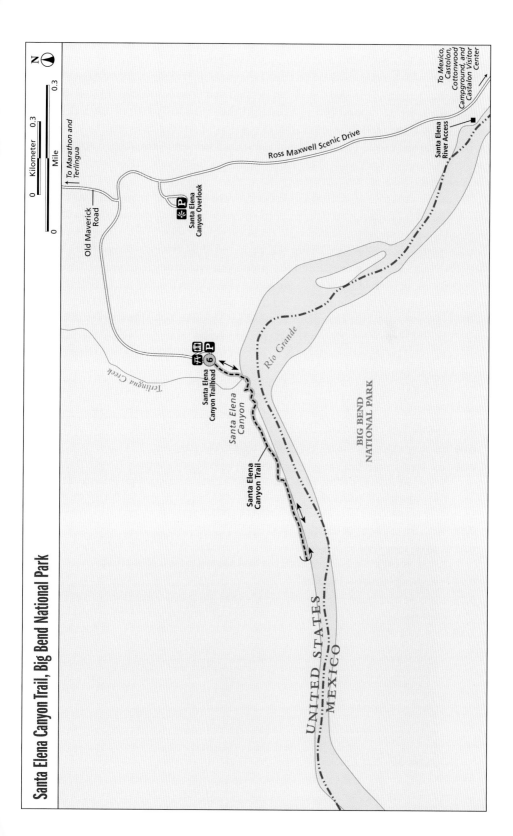

At 0.16 miles, pay extra attention. Look for brown signs with hiker symbols. These signs will direct you where to cross Terlingua Creek. After a decent rainfall or during rainy seasons, Terlingua Creek can be high and flowing, making it impassable. Please take extreme caution before crossing if the creek has water. If you feel any doubt about crossing, do not cross. Do not go on any social trails that head west to go around the creek. Those are unofficial trails. They are unmaintained and dangerous. Be sure to check with the park headquarters to confirm water levels before attempting the hike.

If you are able to cross Terlingua Creek, you will reach land at around the 0.18-mile mark. At 0.21 miles, you will begin to enter the mouth of the canyon. You will head up some stone steps, beginning a series of switchbacks. There will be several vantage points along the way facing the river and the canyon, offering bird's-eye views of photo-worthy scenes. From this point, you will make an ascent of close to 90 feet to the 0.47-mile mark and then descend to the 0.55-mile mark, where the path levels out back to a dirt surface. You will pass through some tall boulders shy of three-quarters of a mile into the trail, and then the path ends shortly after at 0.79 miles. You will know you have reached the end when you come upon the front-facing side of a cliff and where the Rio Grande cuts off. After enjoying the river, turn around and return the way you came.

Miles and Directions

0.0 Start the Santa Elena Canyon Trail by heading west across a boardwalk.

0.08 The boardwalk ends, and the path surface turns to dirt and gravel.

0.16 Look for the brown sign with hiker symbols that indicate where to cross Terlingua Creek. Please take extreme caution before crossing if the creek is flowing. If you feel any doubt about crossing, do not cross. Do not take any social trails to go west around the creek. Those are unofficial trails and are unmaintained and dangerous.

0.18 Reach the other side of Terlingua Creek.

0.21 Wind up some stone steps, beginning a series of switchbacks. From here, make about a 90-foot ascent to the 0.47-mile mark, and then descend to the 0.55-mile mark.

0.74 Pass through some tall boulders.

0.79 Reach the front-facing side of a cliff and where the Rio Grande cuts off. Return the way you came.

1.58 Arrive back at the trailhead.

7 Hot Springs Trail, Big Bend National Park

Touted to have healing properties, the mineral-rich waters of the Langford Hot Springs in Big Bend National Park continue to lure many visitors. While the hot springs are the highlight of the Hot Springs Trail, the trail also provides views of historical structures, Indigenous petroglyphs, and the stunning Rio Grande.

Lake or river: Rio Grande and Langford Hot Springs
Photogenic factor: 5
Start: Hot Springs Trailhead
Elevation gain: 1,821 to 1,939 feet
Distance: 1.18-mile lollipop
Difficulty: Easy
Hiking time: 1–2 hours, depending on additional time spent at the hot springs
Seasons/schedule: Open year-round; entrance fee stations and visitor centers are closed after regular business hours (Panther Junction and Chisos Basin are open year-round; Rio Grande Village, Persimmon Gap, and Castolon Visitor Centers are only open Nov through Apr)
Fees and permits: $30 per vehicle (subject to change), free for Interagency Pass holders and on designated days (check with park website for yearly designated fee-free days)
Trail contacts: Big Bend National Park Headquarters (Panther Junction), 1 Panther Junction, Big Bend National Park 79834; (432) 477-2251

Dog-friendly: No animals permitted
Trail surface: Dirt and gravel
Land status: National Park Service
Nearest town: Marathon (north), Terlingua (west)
Other trail users: None
Maps: USGS Rio Grande Village; Big Bend National Park map (available online at nps .gov/bibe/planyourvisit/maps.htm)
Special considerations: There is minimal shade on the trail. Temperatures in Big Bend National Park can reach 110+°F in the summer. Make sure to bring 1 gallon per person per day and hike in the early morning. This guide is for the Hot Springs Trail, not the lengthier and more primitive Ernst Ridge Trail. It is advised by park management that the Hot Spring Trail be used as the one to reach the hot springs. When the Rio Grande floods, the hot springs can be filled with mud and silt. The temperature of the hot springs stays at a constant 105°F. Exercise caution when bathing in the springs. Venomous snakes can be encountered on this trail.

Finding the trailhead: From the intersection of NE 1st Street and US 385 S in Marathon, head south on US 385 S for 39.8 miles. It will change into Main Park Road. Continue on Main Park Road for 27.5 miles. Turn left onto Park Route 12. Travel on Park Route 12 for 16.8 miles before turning right onto Hot Springs Road. Hot Springs Road is a narrow, gravel road. RVs and oversized vehicles are not allowed on this road. The trailhead will be east of the parking lot. **GPS:** N29° 10.650' W102° 59.959'

The Hike

With a year-round temperature close to 105°F, the Langford Hot Springs draws people to its geothermally heated, therapeutic waters. Once housed by a two-story

Langford Hot Springs

Historical post office of Hot Springs

bathhouse commissioned by Joseph O. Langford in the early 1900s, the hot springs now lie within the remains of the bathhouse foundation. The hot springs were the main reason the Hot Springs settlement was formed, and you can see remnants of the settlement along the Hot Springs Trail, including an old post office building. However, the history of the healing properties of the hot springs goes further back than the 1900s. Vestiges of the Indigenous peoples can be seen by the petroglyphs and pictographs engraved on the limestone walls paralleling the hot springs and Rio Grande.

The Hot Springs Trail commences east of the parking lot. About 145 feet from the trailhead, you will come upon a fork. Continue straight to start on the loop in a counterclockwise direction. The aforementioned historic post office building from the Hot Springs settlement and a "Hot Spring Historic District" interpretive wayside will be to your left.

"If You Build It" and "Reminders of the Past" interpretive waysides will be to your left at 435 feet and 520 feet into the trail, respectively. The trail begins to head northeast at 0.12 miles, and a vista of the majestic Rio Grande will be to your right. This view is particularly beautiful at both sunrise and sunset. There will be stairs leading to an area to view Indigenous petroglyphs on the rocks to your left at the 0.15-mile mark. At 0.28 miles, a "Healing Water" interpretive wayside will be to your right, detailing the supposed health benefits of the hot springs. You will come upon the Langford Hot Springs to your right at 0.3 miles. If you are wearing the proper swimwear and are interested, this is your chance to experience the hot springs. The hot springs stay at a steady 105°F, so keep that in mind when entering.

Hot Springs Trail, Big Bend National Park

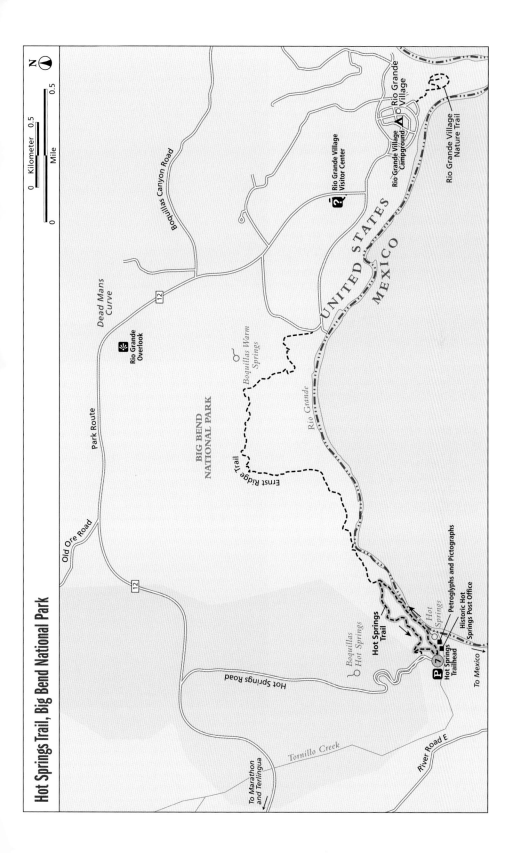

N

0   Kilometer   0.5

0   Mile   0.5

Boquillas Canyon Road

Dead Mans Curve

Rio Grande Overlook

12

Park Route

Old Ore Road

12

BIG BEND NATIONAL PARK

Boquillas Warm Springs

Ernst Ridge Trail

Rio Grande

UNITED STATES

MEXICO

Rio Grande Village Visitor Center

Rio Grande Village Campground

Rio Grande Village

Rio Grande Village Nature Trail

Boquillas Hot Springs

Hot Springs Road

Hot Springs Trail

Hot Springs

Hot Springs Trailhead

Petroglyphs and Pictographs

Historic Hot Springs Post Office

To Mexico

Tornillo Creek

River Road E

To Marathon and Terlingua

The path surface turns rocky after the hot springs area. When you reach the fork a little over half a mile into the trail, bear left to continue on the Hot Springs Trail. The right is the Ernst Ridge Trail entrance. You will make an ascent of 100 feet to the 0.68-mile mark. The trail then heads south at three-quarters of a mile into the trail, and then southwest at 0.82 miles. You will make a descent of about 50 feet from the 0.95-mile mark to the 1.15-mile mark. In between the descent, the trail heads south. You will reach the fork (spur portion of the lollipop) from the original 145-foot mark. Bear right to return to the trailhead and parking area.

Prehistoric pictographs on the canyon walls

Miles and Directions

0.0 The Hot Spring Trail begins left of the parking area.

0.03 Reach a fork. Continue straight to begin the loop. A historic post office building and "Hot Spring Historic District" interpretive wayside will be to your left.

0.12 A vista of the Rio Grande will be to your right.

0.15 There will be stairs leading to some Indigenous petroglyphs and pictographs on the rocks to your left.

0.3 Reach the Langford Hot Springs to your right.

0.39 The path surface turns rocky.

0.51 Reach the connection to the Ernst Ridge Trail. Bear left to continue on the Hot Springs Trail. Make an ascent of 100 feet to the 0.68-mile mark.

0.95 Make a descent of 50 feet to the 1.15-mile mark.

Sunset on the Hot Springs Trail

1.15 Reach the fork from the original 0.03-mile mark. Bear right back to the trailhead and parking area.

1.18 Arrive back at the trailhead.

8 Boquillas Canyon Trail, Big Bend National Park

Boquillas Canyon is one of four canyons within Big Bend National Park. Hikers on the Boquillas Canyon Trail are rewarded with stunning views of the Rio Grande carving through the canyon's limestone cliffs.

Lake or river: Rio Grande
Photogenic factor: 5
Start: Boquillas Canyon Trailhead
Elevation gain: 1,745 to 1,890 feet
Distance: 1.4 miles out and back
Difficulty: Moderate
Hiking time: 1–2 hours, depending on additional time spent on the riverbank
Seasons/schedule: Open year-round; entrance fee stations and visitor centers are closed after regular business hours (Panther Junction and Chisos Basin are open year-round; Rio Grande Village, Persimmon Gap, and Castolon Visitor Centers are only open Nov through Apr)
Fees and permits: $30 per vehicle (subject to change), free for Interagency Pass holders and on designated days (check with park website for yearly designated fee-free days)

Trail contacts: Big Bend National Park Headquarters (Panther Junction), 1 Panther Junction, Big Bend National Park 79834; (432) 477-2251
Dog-friendly: No animals permitted
Trail surface: Dirt and gravel
Land status: National Park Service
Nearest town: Marathon (north), Terlingua (west)
Other trail users: None
Maps: USGS Rio Grande Village; Big Bend National Park map (available online at nps .gov/bibe/planyourvisit/maps.htm)
Special considerations: There is minimal shade on the trail. Temperatures in Big Bend National Park can reach 110+°F in the summer. Make sure to bring 1 gallon per person per day and hike in the early morning. Venomous snakes can be encountered on this trail.

Finding the trailhead: From the intersection of NE 1st Street and US 385 S in Marathon, head south on US 385 S for 39.8 miles. It will change into Main Park Road. Continue on Main Park Road for 27.5 miles. Turn left onto Park Route 12. Travel on Park Route 12 for 19.3 miles before turning left onto Boquillas Canyon Road. After traveling on Boquillas Canyon Road for 3.6 miles (and bypassing the road to Boquillas Canyon Overlook to your right), you will reach the parking lot for Boquillas Canyon Trail. The trailhead will be to the east of the parking lot. **GPS:** N29° 12.039' W102° 55.159'

The Hike

There are several tales surrounding the naming of the region that encompasses Boquillas Canyon. The most popular version is one that supposedly occurred in January 1882. A group of surveyors led by the Texas Rangers came upon some horses belonging to the Indigenous peoples in the mouth of Boquillas Canyon. The group was unable to take the horses with them. Fearing that the Indigenous people might

Entrance to Boquillas Canyon   *The Rio Grande bordering Mexico*

retrieve the horses, the captain of the Texas Rangers ordered that all the horses be killed. Due to this incident, the mountain range north of Boquillas Canyon is known as Sierra del Caballo Muerto, or Dead Horse Mountains. With small arroyos coming through its narrow corridor, the name "Boquillas," which translates to "little mouths," for Boquillas Canyon seems fitting. The "little mouths" reference could also infer to the small holes in the limestone walls of the canyon.

The Boquillas Canyon Trail leads hikers along the Rio Grande and into the looming Boquillas Canyon. It begins east of the parking lot. After 90 feet, the trail heads north, and you will make an ascent of 30 feet until you reach 485 feet into the trail. In between all this, the trail heads southeast at 225 feet and views of the Rio Grande and the quaint village of Boquillas, Mexico, will appear to the west and the south. The scenic views of the river are exceptional at this point.

After the ascent, the trail levels out and heads south. At the 0.14-mile mark, the trail heads east and then south again. You will encounter a series of small, rocky switchbacks at 0.2 miles. The trail then heads east toward Boquillas Canyon shortly after. At 0.43 miles, the trail heads northeast into the canyon, and then its surface gets rocky as you meander along the riverbank. The trail reaches a stopping point at the 0.7-mile mark when you come upon a vista of the Rio Grande and Boquillas

Boquillas Canyon Trail, Big Bend National Park

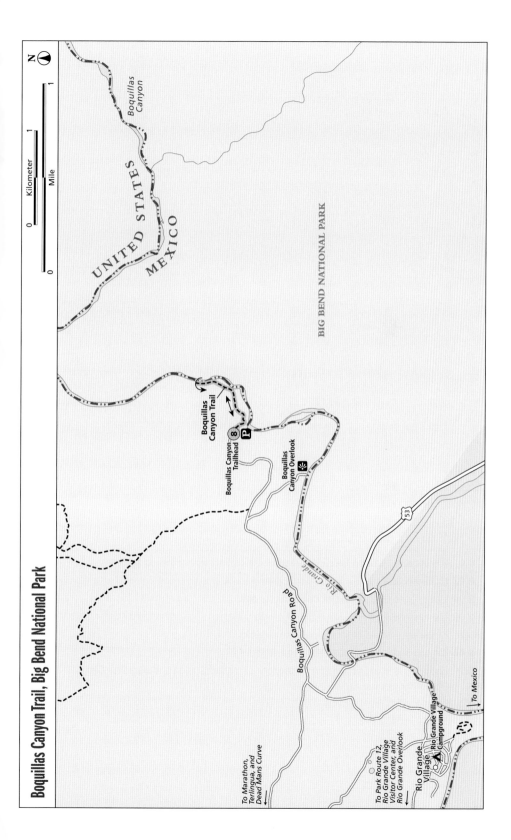

The Rio Grande bordering Mexico

Canyon. Take in the expansive view of the cliffs towering over a thousand feet above the river before turning around and heading back the way you came.

Miles and Directions

0.0 The Boquillas Canyon Trail begins east of the parking lot and heads southeast.

0.02 Make an ascent of 30 feet to the 0.09-mile mark.

0.04 Views of the Rio Grande will begin to your right.

0.09 The trail levels out.

0.2 Encounter a series of small, rocky switchbacks.

0.46 The trail surface gets rocky along the riverbank.

0.7 Reach the end of the trail and an overlook of the Rio Grande and Boquillas Canyon. Return the way you came.

1.4 Arrive back at the trailhead.

9 Rio Grande Trail (with Panther Cave Overlook), Seminole Canyon State Park and Historic Site

With its soaring limestone cliffs and the numerous prehistoric pictographs that it houses, Seminole Canyon is as distinctive as it is magnificent. The Rio Grande Trail, with some overlap of the Canyon Rim Trail, includes several astonishing overlooks of the Amistad Reservoir, Seminole Canyon, and the treasured Panther Cave.

Lake or river: Amistad Reservoir
Photogenic factor: 5
Start: Rio Grande Trailhead
Elevation gain: 1,132 to 1,384 feet
Distance: 5.65-mile lollipop
Difficulty: Moderate
Hiking time: 3–4 hours
Seasons/schedule: Open year-round, no gate; headquarters hours are 8 a.m. to 4:15 p.m.
Fees and permits: $4 per person 13 years and older (subject to change), free for Texas State Parks Pass holders
Trail contacts: Seminole Canyon State Park and Historic Site Headquarters, 434 Park Road 67, Comstock 78837; (432) 292-4464
Dog-friendly: Leashed dogs permitted
Trail surface: Dirt and gravel
Land status: Texas Parks and Wildlife Department

Nearest town: Comstock (east), Del Rio (southeast)
Other trail users: Mountain bikers/cyclists
Maps: USGS Seminole Canyon; Seminole Canyon State Park and Historic Site map (available online at www.tpwd.texas.gov/state-parks/parks-map and via the TX State Parks mobile app)
Special considerations: There is no shade on this trail. Start your hike early and bring adequate amounts of water. Venomous snakes can be encountered on this trail. There are trail mileage signs posted throughout this trail. Mileage calculations in this guide differ from the trail mileage signs, but the trail mileage signs are also useful. This guide includes portions of the Canyon Rim Trail to include the Panther Cave Overlook.

Finding the trailhead: From the intersection of E Gibbs Street and US 277/US 377/US 90/Veterans Boulevard in Del Rio, head north on Veterans Boulevard for 4.3 miles. Keep to the left to continue on US 277/US 90. Stay on US 90 for 36.5 miles. Turn left onto Park Road 67. Continue on Park Road 67 for 1.4 miles (the park headquarters will be half a mile into the road when you enter the park). The Rio Grande Trailhead is north of the metal gate and east of the Desert Vista Camping Area. Four parking spaces are available at the trailhead. Additional parking is available right before the Roadrunner Flat primitive camping area. **GPS:** N29° 41.737' W101° 19.127'

The Hike

In the spring of 1873, three courageous Black Seminole scouts from Fort Clark, protecting Lieutenant John Bullis from an onslaught by Comanche warriors, stayed the

Vista of the Amistad Reservoir

night in what is now known as Seminole Canyon. These scouts were each awarded the Medal of Honor for saving John Bullis's life, and the canyon is named in honor of them. Seminole Canyon is home to numerous archeological sites, some dating back to the Early Archaic Age Period from 7,000 BC. The canyon also offers a scenic experience as well. Situated in three major vegetation zones, the wildlife and flora are wide-ranging. With its sheer cliffs and the flow of the Amistad Reservoir coursing through, its landscape is enchanting.

The Rio Grande Trail begins east of the Desert Vista Camping Area. The trail heads primarily south for a good portion of the route. In about 240 feet, you will need to pass through a metal gate. There will be two signs at this point, one titled "Rio Grande and Canyon Rim Trail System" and the other "Adapt and Perish." Continue straight on the Rio Grande Trail when you reach the fork at 0.45 miles. The left side connects to the Canyon Rim Trail. The site for a transcontinental railroad crossing from 1883 is also at this point. Once again, continue straight on the Rio Grande Trail when you reach the fork at 0.6 miles. This time, the left side is the Middle Fork Trail.

The first of several shelter areas will become available to your left at 0.8 miles. Take advantage of these shelters by taking a break within them, especially during the summer. The trail heads southeast after the bench to your right at 1.14 miles. At 1.4 miles, the trail returns heading south. Another connection to the Middle Fork Trail appears to your left at the 1.47-mile mark. Continue straight.

Once you are two miles into the trail, you will reach a fork and a water trough. The right side is part of the Canyon Rim Trail. This guide heads this way in order to do the loop portion of the lollipop trail in a counterclockwise direction. The left side is the Rio Grande Trail. This will be the return route of the loop. A quarter of a mile later, the path surface turns rocky for a brief period. A short loop to a vista of Amistad Reservoir will be presented to you at 2.28 miles. Take the short loop, and you will be rewarded with a beautiful panoramic view of Amistad Reservoir when the mileage clocks at 2.36 miles. The loop for the vista concludes at 2.42 miles. Bear right to head toward the Panther Cave Overlook. The trail begins to narrow, and you will make a 40-foot rocky descent from here to the 2.57-mile mark. Make sure to follow the sign in the meantime to keep you on the trail.

When the trail begins to head east at 2.67 miles, expansive views of the Amistad Reservoir surrounded by cascading ravines will be straight ahead of you. You will encounter a small switchback shortly after. The path levels out back to dirt and gravel at the 2.77-mile mark and there will be several overlooks to your right shortly after. Make sure to stop and take some pictures of the awe-inspiring scene in front of you. From 2.88 miles to 2.9 miles, you will make a rocky 10-foot ascent. At the fork, bear right to traverse along the canyon rim. The left side is a shortcut. The trail begins to head north shy of 3 miles, and Panther Cave will be visible from a distance. An overlook for Panther Cave will be to your right at the 3-mile mark, and then an overlook of Seminole Canyon to your right at the 3.07-mile mark. When you reach shade shelter #4 at 3.1 miles, there will be a sign for the official Panther Cave Overlook. The shortcut from the 2.9-mile mark converges at this point from the southwest. When you take a look at Panther Cave to the east, marvel at the 100-foot-long prehistoric pictograph panel painted with all natural elements that has been preserved for thousands of years. The most popular feature of this Lower Pecos River Style art form is the 9-foot panther. Other large felines and humans adorned with feline-eared headdresses also accompany the scene. Panther Cave is not accessible by foot, but

Panther Cave

Rio Grande Trail (with Panther Cave Overlook), Seminole Canyon State Park and Historic Site

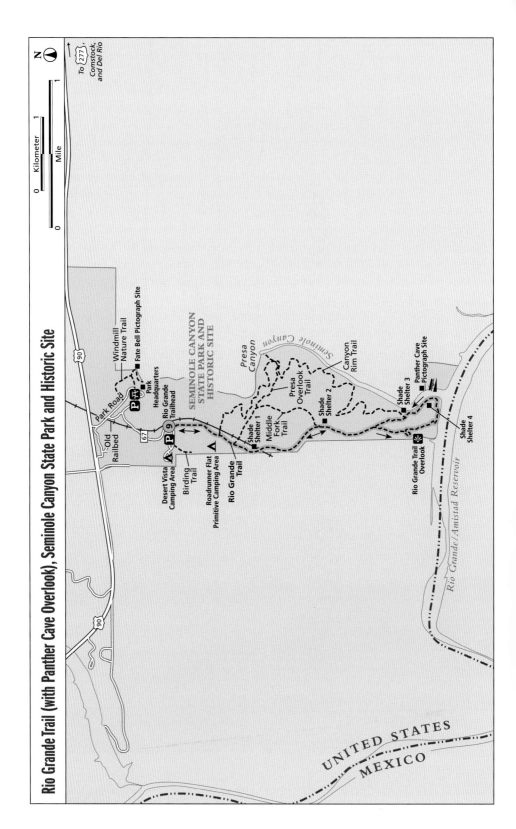

N

To 277, Comstock, and Del Rio

0 Kilometer 1

0 Mile 1

Park Road

90

Old Railbed

67

Windmill Nature Trail

Fate Bell Pictograph Site

Park Headquarters

P

Rio Grande Trailhead

9

P

Desert Vista Camping Area

Birding Trail

Roadrunner Flat Primitive Camping Area

Rio Grande Trail

SEMINOLE CANYON STATE PARK AND HISTORIC SITE

Presa Canyon

Seminole Canyon

Shade Shelter 1

Middle Fork Trail

Presa Overlook Trail

Canyon Rim Trail

Shade Shelter 2

Shade Shelter 3

Panther Cave Pictograph Site

Rio Grande Trail Overlook

Shade Shelter 4

Rio Grande/Amistad Reservoir

UNITED STATES

MEXICO

people can view it up close by taking a boat from the Pecos River boat ramp in the Amistad National Recreation Area.

After taking in the sights of Panther Cave, continue straight to shade shelter #3 at the 3.25-mile mark. Continue straight on the Rio Grande Trail when you reach the fork at 3.35 miles. To your right is a connection to the Canyon Rim Trail. You will encounter the fork from the original 2-mile mark at 3.65 miles. Head straight back to the trailhead. For more up-close views of Seminole Canyon and a vista of Presa Canyon, hike the 7-mile, more challenging but worthwhile, Canyon Rim Trail.

Miles and Directions

0.0 The trail begins east of the Desert Vista Camping Area.

0.05 Go through a metal gate.

0.45 Reach a connection to the Canyon Rim Trail to your left. Continue straight. This is also the site for a railroad bed crossing from 1883.

0.6 Reach a connection to the Middle Fork Trail to your left. Continue straight.

0.8 Shade shelter #1 will be to your left.

1.14 A bench will be to your right.

1.47 Bypass the connection to the Middle Fork Trail to your left.

2.0 Reach a fork and water trough. The right side is part of the Canyon Rim Trail. This guide heads this way to do the loop portion of the lollipop trail in a counterclockwise direction. The left side is the Rio Grande Trail. This will be the return route of the loop.

2.25 The path surface turns rocky for a brief period.

2.28 Take the short loop to your right for a vista of Amistad Reservoir.

2.36 Reach the vista of Amistad Reservoir.

2.42 The loop for the vista concludes. Bear right to head toward the Panther Cave Overlook. Make a 40-foot rocky descent from here to the 2.57-mile mark.

2.5 Follow the sign to keep you on the trail.

2.67 Views of Seminole Canyon will be straight ahead.

2.7 Encounter a small switchback.

2.77 The path levels out back to dirt and gravel. There will be several overlooks to your right shortly after.

2.88 Make a rocky 10-foot ascent to the 2.9-mile mark.

2.9 Reach a fork. Bear right to traverse along the canyon rim.

3.0 An overlook for Panther Cave will be to your right.

3.07 Reach an overlook of Seminole Canyon to your right.

3.1 Reach shade shelter #4 and a sign for the Panther Cave Overlook. The shortcut from the 2.9-mile mark converges at this point from the southwest. Continue straight.

3.25 Reach shade shelter #3.

3.35 Bypass the connection to the Canyon Rim Trail to your right.

3.65 Reach the fork from the original 2-mile mark. Return to the trailhead.

5.65 Arrive back at the trailhead.

10 Devils River Trail to Finegan Springs, Devils River State Natural Area (Del Norte Unit)

The 40-mile-plus-long Devils River is enjoyed by many for its crystal-clear waters and the unspoiled landscape it carves through. Nourished by many springs and flowing over limestone bedrock, the river provides refuge for threatened species and respite for outdoor enthusiasts. The Devils River Trail ends at the river itself and also leads hikers to the mesmerizing Finegan Springs.

Lake or river: Devils River
Photogenic factor: 5
Start: Devils River Trailhead
Elevation gain: 1,283 to 1,447 feet
Distance: 2.86 miles out and back
Difficulty: Easy
Hiking time: 2 hours
Seasons/schedule: Open year-round, Fri through Mon 8 a.m. to 5 p.m. (closed Tues, Wed, and Thurs)
Fees and permits: $5 per person 13 years and older (subject to change), free for Texas State Parks Pass holders
Trail contacts: Devils River State Natural Area Headquarters, 21715 Dolan Creek Road, Del Rio 78840; (830) 395-2133
Dog-friendly: Leashed dogs permitted
Trail surface: Dirt and gravel

Land status: Texas Parks and Wildlife Department
Nearest town: Comstock (southwest), Del Rio (southeast)
Other trail users: None
Maps: USGS Dolan Springs; Devils River State Natural Area map (available online at www.tpwd.texas.gov/state-parks/parks-map and via the TX State Parks mobile app)
Special considerations: Poison ivy grows around Finegan Springs. Make sure to stay a good distance while viewing Finegan Springs to avoid contact with poison ivy and to protect the fragile ecosystem. There is no shade on this trail. Start your hike early and bring adequate amounts of water. This park has designated Dark Sky Sanctuary status.

Finding the trailhead: From the Gibbs Street and Veterans Boulevard/US 377 intersection in Del Rio, head northwest on Veterans Boulevard/US 377 for 4.3 miles. Turn right to continue on US 377. Travel for 22.2 miles on US 377. At the next fork, continue straight onto US 277 N. After 17.9 miles, turn left onto Dolan Creek Road. Dolan Creek Road is a gravel road. Drive with extra care and at a slower speed on this road. In about 6 miles, go right and head northwest. It will be about 17.6 miles on the gravel road to reach the park headquarters, and then another extra 3.6 miles to the trailhead from the park headquarters. The Devils River Trail begins at the gate southeast of the parking area. **GPS:** N29° 54.230' W100° 59.646'

The Hike

Formerly named the San Pedro (Saint Peter) River by Spanish expeditioners, the spring-fed Devils River got its new moniker from a Texas Ranger in the 1840s after he deemed it so. In defiance to its new title, the Devils River is a beautiful sight to

Riverbanks of Devils River

behold. Its waters are clear as day. It serves as a haven for several endangered species and state listed species—the Devils River minnow, Rio Grande darter, Conchos pupfish, and Proserpine shiner, just to name a few. The Devils River Trail brings hikers to the riverbanks and also connects them to one of the river's sources, the lush Finegan Springs.

The Devils River Trail begins at the gate southeast of the parking area and heads in a southeasterly direction. When you reach the fork shy of a quarter of a mile into the trail, bear right. You will cross over some rock slabs as you make a 30-foot ascent to the 0.27-mile mark. The trail then heads back southeast. Continue heading southeast at the fork shortly after. The left will be an area closed to the public. You will make an ascent of 25 feet from the fork to the 0.42-mile mark. At the final fork of the Devils River Trail at 0.55 miles, continue straight as the trail curves southwest. A covered shelter will be to your right. From this point, you will make a 50-foot ascent to the 0.85-mile mark, where views of the Devils River will become available to you straight ahead.

At 0.9 miles, there will be a composting toilet to your left. You will make a 40-foot descent from here to the 0.94-mile mark where the Devils River Trail ends at the riverbank. After taking a break in the shade of the surrounding oak trees and enjoying the glistening waters of the Devils River, you have the option to turn around and return the way you came. If you would like to check out Finegan Springs, continue right on the Finegan Springs Trail. The trail surface will be rock slabs for a short portion of the route. At the 1.17- and 1.20-mile marks, portions of the trail through the reeds can get overgrown and flooded from river overflow. Unobscured views of Devils River will be to your left at a mile and a quarter on the route. You will pass by a large boulder shortly after.

Access to a swimming area will occur to your left at 1.35 miles. In the summer months, this area can be very popular. Exercise caution if you decide to take a dip

Devils River Trail to Finegan Springs, Devils River State Natural Area (Del Norte Unit)

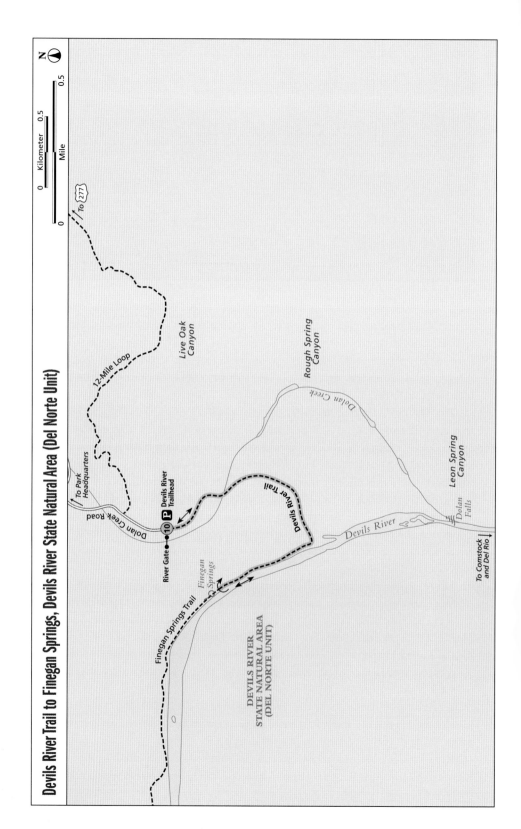

in the water, as no lifeguards are on duty. Overflow from the river can also occur on the trail after heading away from the swimming area, so you may need to walk through waterlogged areas. Watch your step as going over rocks will be very slippery. You will reach Finegan Springs to your right at 1.43 miles. The magnificent Finegan Springs can be enjoyed at a distance as poison ivy grows in abundance around it. Finegan Springs is a source for the Devils River and can produce up to 22,000 gallons of water per minute. After marveling at the charming force of nature, turn around and return the way you came.

Miles and Directions

Scenery along the Devils River Trail

0.0 The Devils River Trail begins at the gate southeast of the parking area.

0.2 Reach a fork. Bear right. Cross over some rock slabs and make a 30-foot ascent to the 0.27-mile mark.

0.35 Reach a fork. Continue straight. Make an ascent of 25 feet from this point to the 0.42-mile mark.

0.55 Reach a fork. Continue straight. A covered shelter will be to your right. From this point, make a 50-foot ascent to the 0.85-mile mark.

0.9 A composting toilet will be to your left. Make a 40-foot descent from here to the 0.94-mile mark.

0.94 The Devils River Trail ends at the riverbank. You have the option to turn around and return the way you came. This guide continues on to Finegan Springs by bearing right. The trail surface will be rock slabs for a short portion of the route.

1.17 This portion of the trail through the reeds can get overgrown and flooded. Take the right side of the path.

1.2 This portion of the trail can get overgrown and muddy.

1.35 Access to a swimming area will be to your left.

1.4 From this point, you may need to walk through water overflowing from the river. Watch your step as going over rocks will be very slippery.

1.43 Reach Finegan Springs to your right. Watch for poison ivy. Return the way you came.

2.86 Arrive back at the trailhead.

The magnificent Finegan Springs

11 Diablo East Green and Blue Trail Loops, Amistad National Recreation Area

The crystal-clear waters and mild temperature of Lake Amistad help make it a recreation paradise. The absence of soil in the reservoir and the pollutant-free tributaries that feed it contribute to its pristine nature. The terrain of the Amistad National Recreation Area is rich in biodiversity, making it a beautiful backdrop for the reservoir. Hikers taking the Green and Blue Trail Loops in the Diablo East area will be able to behold the picturesque scenery that the area has to offer.

Lake or river: Amistad Reservoir
Photogenic factor: 4+
Start: North Trailhead
Elevation gain: 1,132 to 1,190 feet
Distance: 1.35-mile loop
Difficulty: Easy
Hiking time: 30 minutes–1 hour
Seasons/schedule: Open year-round; visitor center hours are 8 a.m. to 4:30 p.m.
Fees and permits: None (subject to change)
Trail contacts: Amistad National Recreation Area Visitor Center, 10477 US 90 W, Del Rio 78840; (830) 775-7491

Dog-friendly: Leashed dogs permitted
Trail surface: Dirt and gravel
Land status: National Park Service
Nearest town: Del Rio (south)
Other trail users: None
Maps: USGS Amistad Dam; Amistad National Recreation Area map (available online at nps .gov/amis/planyourvisit/maps.htm)
Special considerations: There is no shade on this trail. Start your hike early and bring adequate amounts of water. This guide combines the Green Trail Loop and the Blue Trail Loop into one hike, starting with the Green Trail Loop.

Finding the trailhead: From the intersection of E Gibbs Street and US 277/US 377/US 90/ Veterans Boulevard in Del Rio, head north on Veterans Boulevard for 4.3 miles. Keep to the left to continue on US 277/US 90. Stay on US 277/US 90 for 7.3 miles before turning right onto Diablo East Road. After traveling on Diablo East Road for 0.7 miles, the North Trailhead will be west of the restrooms. **GPS:** N29° 28.566' W101° 00.928'

The Hike

The stunning Amistad Reservoir is a result of cooperation and goodwill demonstrated by the United States and Mexico. Thus, the body of water was granted its name, Amistad, which in Spanish means "friendship." Two bronze eagles are situated at the Amistad Dam as symbols of that friendship. The location of Amistad National Recreation Area, which includes Amistad Reservoir, is a combination of three different ecoregions, resulting in a myriad of plant species. These ecoregions are the Tamaulipan Mezquital, the Chihuahuan Desert, and the Edwards Plateau. Hiking in the Diablo East area of the Amistad National Recreation Area allows hikers to enjoy the rich diversity of the landscape.

View from the Green Loop Trail

This guide begins the hike at the North Trailhead (also one of the entrances to the Green Trail Loop), west of the restrooms. The trail initially heads northwest, and then at 215 feet, it curves south. About 400 feet into the trail, the trail heads west. From this point to the 0.2-mile mark, you will be afforded views of the Amistad Reservoir to your right. The trail curves southeast at the 0.2-mile mark, and then a sheltered bench will be available to your left a quarter of a mile into the trail. Since there is no shade on this route, make sure to take advantage of the sheltered benches offered on this trail.

Bear right when you reach the fork at 0.35 miles to start on the Blue Trail Loop. The left side is a continuation of the Green Trail Loop. This guide will not do the Green Trail Loop in its entirety in efforts to hike as much of the Blue Trail Loop as possible. Views of the Amistad Reservoir will be available to your right once again shortly after. The trail heads northwest at 0.43 miles, and you will be granted views of the Amistad Reservoir to your right once again prior to the trail curving southwest.

You will come upon the second sheltered bench to your left a little over half a mile into the route. The trail then heads southeast. At three-quarters of a mile into the trail, the last bench on the route, this time unsheltered, will be available to your left. The trail heads east shortly after. At the 0.97-mile mark, you will encounter the South Trailhead for the Blue Trail Loop. Bear left to continue on the Blue Trail Loop. When you reach the undefined barren area at 1.21 miles, head northwest across the open dirt area to hike along the western edge of the parking lot. Watch for vehicles

Diablo East Green and Blue Trail Loops, Amistad National Recreation Area

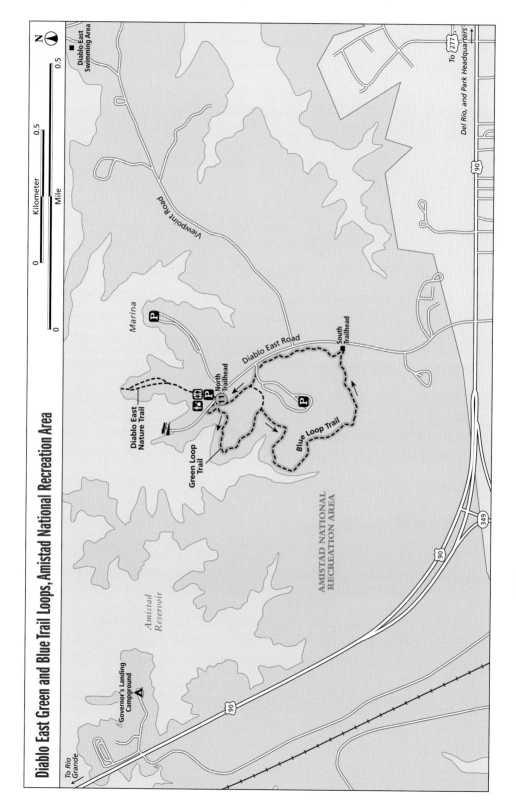

Amistad Reservoir in the summer

as you make your way across the parking lot. You will reconnect with the trailhead at 1.35 miles.

Miles and Directions

0.0 The trail begins at the North Trailhead, west of the restrooms.

0.08 From this point to the 0.2-mile mark, there will be views of the Amistad Reservoir to your right.

0.25 A sheltered bench will be to your left.

0.35 Reach a fork. Bear right to start on the Blue Trail Loop. Views of Amistad Reservoir will be available to your right again shortly after.

0.53 Views of the Amistad Reservoir will be available to your right once again.

0.55 Another sheltered bench will be to your left.

0.75 There will be a bench (not sheltered) to your left.

0.97 Reach the South Trailhead for the Blue Trail Loop. Bear left.

1.21 Reach an undefined area. Head northwest across the open dirt area to go along the western edge of the parking lot. Be alert for moving vehicles.

1.35 Arrive back at the trailhead.

Honorable Mention (Big Bend Country)

○ Rio Grande Village Nature Trail, Big Bend National Park

The picturesque Rio Grande Village Nature Trail includes enchanting aerial views of the Rio Grande. It has no shortage of wonderful surprises. With its idyllic boardwalk to its changes in elevation, the trail is informative with its interpretive waysides as it is scenic with its overlooks.

Lake or river: Rio Grande
Photogenic factor: 5
Start: Rio Grande Village Nature Trailhead
Elevation gain: 1,785 to 1,942 feet
Distance: 0.73-mile lollipop
Difficulty: Moderate
Hiking time: 1–2 hours
Seasons/schedule: Open year-round; entrance fee stations and visitor centers are closed after regular business hours (Panther Junction and Chisos Basin are open year-round; Rio Grande Village, Persimmon Gap, and Castolon Visitor Centers are only open Nov through Apr)
Fees and permits: $30 per vehicle (subject to change), free for Interagency Pass holders and on designated days (check with park website for yearly designated fee-free days)
Trail contacts: Big Bend National Park Headquarters (Panther Junction), 1 Panther Junction, Big Bend National Park 79834; (432) 477-2251
Dog-friendly: No animals permitted
Trail surface: Dirt and gravel
Land status: National Park Service
Nearest town: Marathon (north), Terlingua (west)
Other trail users: None
Maps: USGS Rio Grande Village; Big Bend National Park map (available online at nps.gov/bibe/planyourvisit/maps.htm)
Special considerations: There is minimal shade on the trail. Temperatures in Big Bend National Park can reach 110+°F on a daily basis in the summer. Please make sure to bring 1 gallon per person per day and hike in the early morning. Venomous snakes can be encountered on this trail.

Finding the trailhead: From the intersection of NE 1st Street and US 385 S in Marathon, head south on US 385 S for 39.8 miles. It will change into Main Park Road. Continue on Main Park Road for 27.5 miles. Turn left onto Park Route 12. Travel on Park Route 12 for 20.3 miles before going left onto Daniels Ranch Road. After 0.2 miles, turn right toward the Amphitheater parking lot. (Note: If you are not camping at Rio Grande Village Campground, you will need to park at the Amphitheater parking lot and connect to the Rio Grande Village Nature Trailhead from there.) The Rio Grande Village Nature Trailhead will be 0.34 miles east of the Amphitheater parking lot, south of Rio Grande Village Campground site #18. **GPS:** N29° 10.750' W102° 57.241'

Overlook of the Rio Grande

Hill Country

Bluebonnets are plentiful in the spring in Hill Country (Hike 17)

12 Texas Oak Trail, Lake Brownwood State Park

Wildflowers and prickly pears blossom plentifully along the Texas Oak Trail during the spring. Abundant oaks also flourish along its path. To top it all off, the Texas Oak Trail also extends views of Lake Brownwood, making it quite a delightful hike.

Lake or river: Lake Brownwood
Photogenic factor: 4+
Start: Texas Oak Trailhead
Elevation gain: 1,404 to 1,476 feet
Distance: 1.67-mile lollipop
Difficulty: Moderate
Hiking time: 1 hour
Seasons/schedule: Open year-round, 6 a.m. to 10 p.m.
Fees and permits: $5 per person 13 years and older (subject to change), free for Texas State Parks Pass holders
Trail contacts: Lake Brownwood State Park Headquarters, 200 State Highway Park Road 15, Brownwood 76801; (325) 784-5223

Dog-friendly: Leashed dogs permitted
Trail surface: Dirt and rocky path
Land status: Texas Parks and Wildlife Department
Nearest town: Lake Brownwood (southwest), Brownwood (south)
Other trail users: None
Maps: USGS Lake Brownwood; Lake Brownwood State Park map (available online at www.tpwd.texas.gov/state-parks/parks-map and via the TX State Parks mobile app)
Special considerations: The best time to hike this trail is in the spring, when the wildflowers and cacti are blooming.

Finding the trailhead: From historic downtown Abilene, get onto TX 36 S via 11th Street. Travel south on TX 36 for 42.5 miles. Turn right onto TX 206 S. TX 206 S changes into TX 279 S after 1.1 miles. After traveling on TX 279 S for 17.1 miles, go left onto State Highway Park Road 15. Continue on State Highway Park Road 15 for 6.2 miles (the park headquarters will be along the way). Turn left toward the Willow Point Camping Area. After 0.2 miles, go left toward the Willow Point Camping Area (opposite direction of the boat launch area). The trailhead will be south of the parking area, across from the fishing pier after 0.4 miles.
GPS: N31° 51.725' W99° 01.598'

The Hike

The Texas Oak Trail gets its name from the many Texas red oak, post oak, and live oaks that thrive along its path. The oaks are joined by flowers, cacti, and shrubs in an array of hues. The trail commences south of the parking area, across from the fishing pier. At 45 feet into the trail, bear right at the fork to continue on the Texas Oak Trail. The left is a connection to the Council Bluff Trail. Bypass the offshoot to the lake to your right at 0.3 miles, and then you will encounter another connection to the Council Bluff Trail, this time to your left. Bear right to continue on the Texas

Lake Brownwood in the summer

Oak Trail. Also from this point, you will be treated with views of Lake Brownwood to your right. This will continue intermittently to the 0.81-mile mark. You will cross over a seasonal streambed shortly after, and then the path surface turns rocky.

At 0.42 miles, you will reach the loop segment of the lollipop route. Bear right to take the loop in a counterclockwise direction. Be aware of some unearthed tree roots within the path at this point. Portions of the trail can get muddy after a decent rainfall, most noticeably at the 0.48- and 0.67-mile marks. Just shy of half a mile into the trail, you will descend about 15 feet to the 0.53-mile mark. At 0.59 miles, you will encounter your first of several rock outcrops to either go around or go through. Other rock outcrops are present at the 0.61-mile mark and the 0.69-mile mark. In between, you will make a 5-foot rocky descent from the 0.62-mile mark to the 0.63-mile mark.

Just as it can get muddy in portions of the trail during a decent rainfall, portions of the trail get overgrown. The segment of the trail where it occurs the most prominently is close to three-quarters of a mile into the trail. Spring and summer seasons can also encourage overgrowth on the trail. At 0.77 miles, you will come upon an up-close vista of Lake Brownwood to your right. Take a moment to enjoy the peaceful view. After the vista, the trail curves and heads south away from the lake. You will make a 15-foot ascent from the 0.81-mile mark to the 0.83-mile mark.

Shortly after, in the springtime, you will reach an area that is flourishing with vivid wildflowers (including American basketflower, lemon beebalm, goldeneye phlox, agarita, and Mexican buckeye). When in bloom, the colorful scenery is like something out of a fairy tale. Bypass the offshoot to your left at 0.88 miles, and then at 0.95 miles, there will be another wildflower area for you to enjoy. The path splits at this point and eventually merges. Continue heading east.

When you reach the fork at 1.2 miles, bear left to continue on the Texas Oak Trail. The right is the Office Trail. The Office Trail leads to the park headquarters if you need to go there. At 1.22 miles, the trail heads west, and you will make a 20-foot

Texas Oak Trail, Lake Brownwood State Park

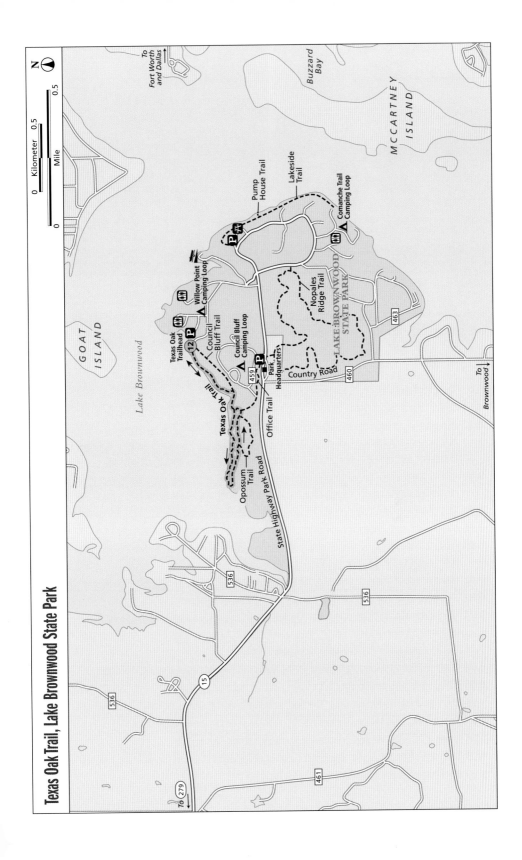

GOAT ISLAND

Lake Brownwood

To Fort Worth and Dallas

N

0   Kilometer   0.5

0   Mile   0.5

Buzzard Bay

McCARTNEY ISLAND

Pump House Trail

Lakeside Trail

Comanche Trail Camping Loop

Willow Point Camping Loop

Texas Oak Trailhead

Council Bluff Trail

Council Bluff Camping Loop

Nopales Ridge Trail

LAKE BROWNWOOD STATE PARK

Park Headquarters

Country Road

Texas Oak Trail

Office Trail

Opossum Trail

State Highway Park Road

To Brownwood

To

View of Lake Brownwood from the trail   *Wildflowers bloom among oak trees*

descent down some stone steps. The loop segment of the lollipop route concludes at a mile and a quarter into the trail. Bear right to return the way you came.

Miles and Directions

0.0 The trail heads south from the parking area.

0.01 Reach a fork. Bear right.

0.3 Bypass the offshoot to the lake to your right.

0.32 Reach a fork. Bear right. Periodically, Lake Brownwood will be visible to your right from this point to the 0.81-mile mark. Cross over a seasonal streambed shortly after.

0.42 Reach the loop segment of the lollipop route. Bear right to take the loop in a counterclockwise direction. Be aware of unearthed tree roots within the path.

0.48 This portion of the trail can get muddy after a decent rainfall.

0.49 Make a 15-foot descent from this point to the 0.53-mile mark.

0.59 There will be a few rock outcrops to either go around or go through at this point, the 0.61-, and the 0.69-mile mark.

0.62 Make a 5-foot rocky descent to the 0.63-mile mark.

0.67 This portion of the trail can get muddy after a decent rainfall.

0.74 This portion of the trail can get overgrown after a decent rainfall or during spring and summer.

0.77 Reach a vista of Lake Brownwood to your right.

0.81 Make a 15-foot ascent from here to the 0.83-mile mark. Enter a wildflower area.

0.88 Bypass the offshoot to your left.

0.95 Enter another wildflower area. The path splits and merges back at the 1.01-mile mark.

1.2 Reach fork. Bear left.

1.22 Make a 20-foot, westerly descent down some stone steps.

1.25 The loop segment of the lollipop concludes. Bear right to return the way you came.

1.67 Arrive back at the trailhead.

13 Moss Lake Trail (combined with Summit Trail and Echo Canyon Trail), Enchanted Rock State Natural Area

The Enchanted Rock State Natural Area has many sights to see, including the popular dome itself, fairy-tale-like Echo Canyon, and quaint Moss Lake. Although Moss Lake is small, it provides a rewarding perspective of Enchanted Rock and the route to it is surrounded by ever-changing scenery.

Lake or river: Moss Lake
Photogenic factor: 5
Start: Summit Trailhead
Elevation gain: 1,345 to 1,811 feet
Distance: 2.78 miles out and back, with an additional spur
Difficulty: Moderate to strenuous due to steep ascents and descents and uneven, rocky path
Hiking time: 2–3 hours
Seasons/schedule: Open year-round, 6:30 a.m. to 8 p.m.
Fees and permits: $8 per person 13 years and older (subject to change), free for Texas State Parks Pass holders
Trail contacts: Enchanted Rock State Natural Area Headquarters, 16710 Ranch Road 965, Fredericksburg 78624; (830) 685-3636

Dog-friendly: No animals permitted
Trail surface: Dirt and rock, with portions of the trail on slabs of rock
Land status: Texas Parks and Wildlife Department
Nearest town: Llano (northeast), Fredericksburg (south)
Other trail users: None
Maps: USGS Crabapple; Enchanted Rock State Park map (available online at www.tpwd.texas.gov/state-parks/parks-map and via the TX State Parks mobile app)
Special considerations: Yellow arrow markers on wooden posts serve as guides for this trail. This park has designated Dark Sky Park status.

Finding the trailhead: From the Main Street and Milam Street intersection in Fredericksburg, head northeast on Milam Street for 1.4 miles, where it then changes to Ranch Road 965. Continue for 15.5 miles on Ranch Road 965. Turn left into the Enchanted Rock State Natural Area. After passing the park headquarters, turn right at the fork to head toward the day-use parking area. The Summit Trailhead will be close to the stone step bridge to your left near the center of the day-use parking area. Try not to get it confused with the Loop Trailhead, which is at the picnic area at the end of the day-use parking lot. **GPS:** N30° 29.843' W98° 49.102'

The Hike

Enchanted Rock, shrouded by myth and folklore, continues to spellbind visitors today. Hikers make the trek to its summit, not only to be mesmerized by the grand view below, but to be fascinated by the rare vegetation and trees that affix themselves to the granite batholith. Although Enchanted Rock is by far the star of the park,

View of Turkey Peak while on Enchanted Rock

Moss Lake and Echo Canyon are worthy highlights as well. A unique panorama of Enchanted Rock can be seen from Moss Lake, and the modest lake itself makes a peaceful resting stop.

Moss Lake can be accessed by starting at the Summit Trailhead and then continuing on the Echo Canyon Trail. To include summiting Enchanted Rock as part of the experience, this guide incorporates hiking the full length of the Summit Trail. From the day-use parking lot, head north across the 25-foot stone step bridge to start on the Summit Trail. After crossing over the stone step bridge, bypass the restroom (to the east) and the picnic area (to the west) 265 feet into the rocky trail. Head toward the gazebo housing the informational plaques at the 0.11-mile mark. Then head about 30 feet down the log steps. You will cross over a large rock and reconnect with the rocky path.

When you reach a fork, continue straight onto the Summit Trail. The right side is the Frontside Trail. Shortly after, go up the rocks. Make sure to stop and turn around and enjoy the panoramic view before you.

At the 0.38-mile mark, you will come upon the entrance to the Echo Canyon Trail to your left. Continue straight up the rocks following the sign for the Summit Trail. It will be an ascent close to 400 feet until you reach the summit at 0.73 miles. The path will mostly be undefined. Follow where the path has been worn into the rock. When you reach the summit of Enchanted Rock you will be at 1,815 feet in elevation, and you will be on top of the second-tallest bedrock hill in the United States. Views of Moss Lake will be to your left, Turkey Peak to your right, and both Freshman Mountain and Buzzard's Roost to your northeast. After enjoying the astounding panoramic view, return to the Echo Canyon Trail entrance at the 0.38-mile mark, which will clock at 1.07 miles. Bear right to begin the Echo Canyon Trail.

At 1.14 miles, you will go down some rocky steps. This portion can be undefined. Look ahead for the wooden stake with a yellow arrow to your northwest. When you cross over the large slab of rock at 1.25 miles, look for the wooden stakes with the yellow arrows on the dirt path toward your left. A beautiful vista of Echo Canyon will appear before you shortly after with Little Rock to your left. Look for the rock with a mushroomlike appearance, and once you go toward it, you will see another wooden stake with a yellow arrow. Continue on the rocky base of the charming Echo Canyon through the oak trees. Some scrambling over boulders will need to be done. The path continues to be undefined, but as long as you traverse north toward the trees through Echo Canyon you are headed in the right direction.

Look for the wooden stake with the yellow arrow at 1.34 miles, and then the path levels out through the wooded area shortly after. Curve around the large rock formation to your left. Once you reach the fork at 1.41 miles, take the right side of the fork to continue onto the Echo Canyon Trail. The left side is the Connecting Trail, which is a route that also leads to Moss Lake. You will come upon another fork at 1.42 miles; this one connects to the Purple Trail and the Green Trail to the northeast. Continue straight on the Echo Canyon Trail. From this point, during the spring and summer many butterflies will congregate in this area. It is truly a delightful experience to be surrounded by them as they waltz in the breeze through Echo Canyon. Motorboat Rock can be seen to your right.

You will cross over a large slab of rock 1.5 miles into the trail before you reconnect with the dirt path ahead. This part of the trail becomes undefined once again. As always, use the wooden posts with the yellow arrows as your guide. Continue straight on the slabs of rock. To your right will be a path that is the Base Trail. It alternates between dirt paths and slabs of rock several times between the 1.58-mile mark and 1.63-mile mark. Follow the wooden posts to the northwest.

Entrances to the Moss Lake Primitive Camping Area will occur at the 1.68-mile mark and 1.73-mile mark. Bypass those entrances and continue northwest on the trail. After the second entrance, take the left side of the fork toward Moss Lake. Once you reach Moss Lake, the Connecting Trail will be to your left. The Moss Lake

View of Moss Lake

Moss Lake Trail (combined with Summit Trail and Echo Canyon Trail), Enchanted Rock State Natural Area

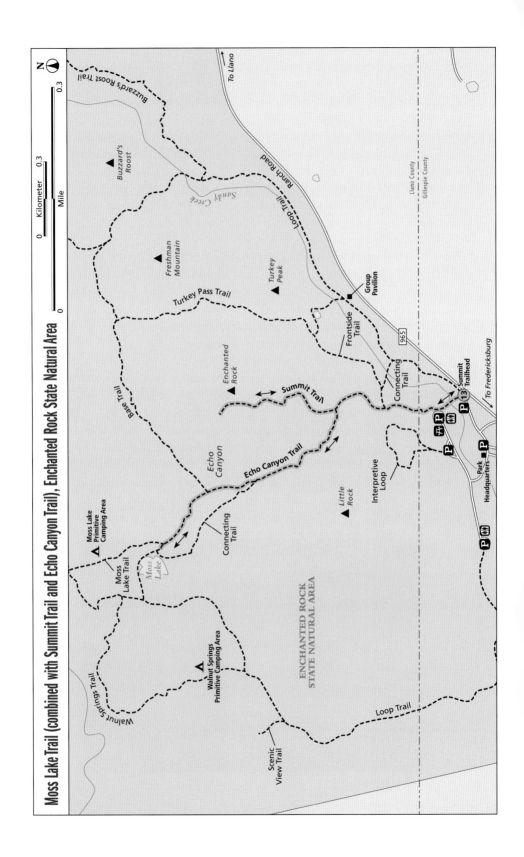

Trail continues to wind on the northwest side of the lake. After going on the spur around the quaint and peaceful lake and enjoying the view with Enchanted Rock in the background, turn around and return to the Echo Canyon Trail and Summit Trail connection. The mileage will clock close to 2.38 miles when you return to the Summit Trail entrance. Bypass the spur to Enchanted Rock and return to the trailhead and day-use parking lot.

Miles and Directions

0.0 From the day-use parking lot, head north across the 25-foot stone step bridge to start on the Summit Trail.

0.05 Bypass the restrooms to your right and the picnic area to your left. Head toward the gazebo at the 0.11-mile mark and then down the log steps.

0.2 Reach a fork. Continue straight.

0.38 Bypass the entrance to the Echo Canyon Trail to your left. Continue straight up the rocks following the sign for the Summit Trail. It will be an ascent of 400 feet until you reach the summit at 0.73 miles and the path will mostly be undefined. Follow where the path has been worn into the rock.

0.73 Reach the summit of Enchanted Rock. After enjoying the panoramic view, return to the Echo Canyon Trail entrance at the 0.38-mile mark.

1.07 Reach the Echo Canyon Trail entrance. Bear right onto the Echo Canyon Trail.

1.14 Go down some rocky steps. This portion can be undefined.

1.26 Reach a vista point of Echo Canyon.

1.3 Continue onto the rocky base of Echo Canyon. Some scrambling over boulders will need to be done. The path continues to be undefined, but as long as you traverse north toward the trees through Echo Canyon you are headed in the right direction.

1.41 Reach a fork. Bear right.

1.42 Reach a fork. Continue straight.

1.5 Continue straight on the slabs of rock. This part of the trail is undefined.

1.58 Between this point and the 1.63-mile mark, the trail surface alternates between dirt and slabs of rock.

1.68 Bypass the entrance to the Moss Lake Primitive Camping Area.

1.73 Reach a fork and the second entrance to the Moss Lake Primitive Camping Area. Bear left toward Moss Lake.

1.75 Reach a fork and Moss Lake. After going around the lake and enjoying the view, turn around and return to the Echo Canyon Trail and Summit Trail connection.

2.38 Reach the Summit Trail entrance. Bypass the spur to Enchanted Rock and return to the trailhead.

2.78 Arrive back at the trailhead.

Common Buckeye butterfly in Echo Canyon

14 East Trail (combined with Maple Trail and East-West Trail), Lost Maples State Natural Area

Each year in the fall, visitors flock to the Lost Maples State Natural Area to catch a glimpse of the dazzling display of fall colors the region showcases. The landscape seen from the East Trail is majestic. The Sabinal River winds through the valley of bigtooth maples, sycamores, and Texas madrones, and the halcyon Can Creek Pond sits against limestone escarpments painted by nature.

Lake or river: Sabinal River and Can Creek Pond

Photogenic factor: 5

Start: East Trailhead

Elevation gain: 1,772 to 2,264 feet

Distance: 4.7-mile loop; trail is undefined in the day-use area portion

Difficulty: Easy for the Maple Trail and East-West Trail, strenuous for the East Trail

Hiking time: 3–4 hours

Seasons/schedule: Open year-round; headquarters hours are 8:30 a.m. to 4:30 p.m.

Fees and permits: $6 per person 13 years and older (subject to change), free for Texas State Parks Pass holders

Trail contacts: Lost Maples State Natural Area Headquarters, 37221 FM 187, Vanderpool 78885; (830) 966-3413

Dog-friendly: Leashed dogs permitted

Trail surface: Dirt and rock

Land status: Texas Parks and Wildlife Department

Nearest town: Vanderpool (south)

Other trail users: None

Maps: USGS Sabinal Canyon; Lost Maples State Natural Area map (available online at www.tpwd.texas.gov/state-parks/parks-map and via the TX State Parks mobile app)

Special considerations: Yellow metal circles with arrows serve as guides for the Maple Trail, and green metal circles with arrows serve as guides for the East Trail. Lost Maples State Natural Area is well-known for its fall foliage. Be sure to make plans well in advance to visit the park during peak times, usually the last week of October to late November. The park offers a weekly fall foliage report each year starting in the middle of October. The fall foliage report is available online at https://tpwd.texas.gov/state-parks/lost-maples/foliage-reports. You can also check ahead of time with park staff to confirm the status of fall colors in the area.

Finding the trailhead: Get onto I-10 W/US 87 N from downtown San Antonio and stay on it for 28.3 miles. Take exit 540 for TX 46 toward New Braunfels/Bandera when you reach the town of Boerne. Turn left on TX 46 W/W Bandera Road. Continue on TX 46 W for 11.1 miles before turning right onto TX 16 N/State Highway 16 S. After reaching the town of Bandera in 11.9 miles, go right onto TX 16 N/Main Street. Continue on TX 16 N for 13.7 miles. When you reach the town of Medina, turn left onto FM 337/Ranch Road 337. Stay on FM 337/Ranch Road 337 for 26.2 miles until you reach the town of Vanderpool. Turn right onto Ranch Road 337/RM 187 (a sign will say Ranch Road 187 N). Shy of 5 miles on Ranch Road 337/RM 187, go left into the Lost Maples State Natural Area. After 0.8 miles, turn right toward the day-use area and parking lot. The East Trailhead will be at the very northern end of the day-use parking lot. **GPS:** N29° 49.000' W99° 34.246'

A place to rest on the Maple Trail

The Hike

Melodic streams, looming limestone bluffs, painterly vistas, Edwards Plateau grass-lands, and endless captivating fall foliage, the route of the East Trail combined with the Maple Trail and East-West Trail has it all. Along this star-studded course, the Sabinal River will accompany you, and Can Creek Pond and Can Creek will greet you with photo-worthy moments.

You will begin the route with the East Trail. It commences at the very end of the day-use parking lot, to the north. Shortly into the hike, there will be "Maple Haven" and "Texas Mountain Laurel" interpretive waysides to your right. Several interpretive waysides will be displayed throughout the Maple Trail and East Trail from this point to the 0.73-mile mark. These signs include information on the "Virginia Creeper," "Guadalupe Bass," "Travertine," "Frostweed," "Ball Moss," "Ashe Juniper," "American Sycamore," "Texas Persimmon," "Twistleaf Yucca," and "Texas Madrone." Bypass the side trail to your left at 250 feet and bear right onto the East Trail. When you reach the Maple Trail entrance at 520 feet, bear left up the rock steps onto the Maple Trail. You can also continue straight on the East Trail. This guide takes the Maple Trail to experi-ence the fall foliage that makes the Lost Maples State Natural Area so popular.

The scenery along the quiet Maple Trail is spectacular during the fall and well worth the diversion from the East Trail. The trees around you are ablaze in crimson, fiery hues; the forest is a collection of vivid colors unmatched throughout most of Texas. Falling leaves from bigtooth maples, sycamores, and Texas madrones float around in the stillness and embellish the dirt path. You will come upon some rock steps and a wooden footbridge shortly after. The Sabinal River will be to your right. This will be the first of a few other rock steps that will be in the path—others will occur at the 0.14-, 0.16-, and 0.21-mile marks. A few picturesque benches will be along the path before you cross over the seasonal rocky riverbed at 0.42 miles. You will also need to bypass the side trail to the Sabinal River on your right in between these points. The Maple Trail ends at 0.48 miles. Reconnect with the East Trail by heading north. Follow the sign indicating the East Trail. Cross over a seasonal river-bed at the 1.07-mile mark.

At 1.17 miles, there will be an optional spur to Monkey Rock to your left. This guide ventures on that spur. You will reach the very unique limestone formation as well as the Sabinal River at 1.21 miles. Marvel at the monkey-like appearance of the outcrop before turning around and heading back to the East Trail. The mileage clocks at a mile and a quarter when you reconnect with the East Trail. Continue on the East Trail by heading northwest.

The trail heads north at 1.29 miles. Cross over the first of several seasonal river-beds at the 1.32-mile mark, with more to cross at 1.57, 1.64, and 1.67 miles. At 1.39 miles, you will reach Primitive Campsite A. Bear left to continue on the East Trail. A composting toilet will be available to your left at 1.49 miles. There will be a lovely overlook to a grotto at 1.73 miles. The maidenhair fern–festooned grotto hovers over a luminous, trickling stream. The trail heads south shortly after.

At 1.79 miles, you will begin the first challenging portion of the East Trail. From this point to the 2.06-mile mark, there will be a steep rocky ascent of about 290 feet. An overlook will be to your left in the middle of the ascent at 1.85 miles. The trail heads west around 2.20 miles. A spur to a scenic overlook to your left will occur at 2.30 miles. This guide bypasses the spur and continues straight on the East Trail. Portions of the trail can get muddy after a decent rainfall from the 2.38-mile mark to the 2.68-mile mark. At 2.62 miles, you will be afforded a bird's-eye view of the Sabinal River winding through the valley to your left. Make sure to take photos of the panorama, or at the very least, bask in the grand view before you. Once you return onto the trail, bypass the trail to your right that leads to Primitive Campsite B at 2.89 miles. Continue straight to continue on the East Trail.

The second challenging portion of the East Trail happens at 2.93 miles. You will make a steep rocky descent of about 335 feet to the 3.25-mile mark. The trail heads south before winding east. When the descent and East Trail end at 3.25, you will see Can Creek Pond, a composting toilet, and the West Trail connection to your right. Feel free to roam around the area before continuing straight onto the East-West Trail. A picturesque vista of Can Creek Pond will be to your right at the 3.31-mile mark. You will cross over Can Creek a couple times before reaching the West Trail connection at 3.97 miles. The West Trail will be to your right. Continue southeast on the East-West Trail.

There will be one more interpretive wayside to your right at 4.1 miles, this one detailing "A Home for Hawks." Cross over Can Creek one more time at 4.25 miles, and then the East-West Trail ends shortly after. This portion of the route becomes a little less defined. You will see a parking lot to your right. Continue straight on the asphalt. Watch for passing vehicles coming through the parking lot. At 4.36 miles, you will see a sign for the Trail to Day-Use Area. Bear left onto the Trail to Day-Use Area, and then cross over a seasonal creek bed shortly after. When you reach the park road

Can Pond from the East-West Trail

Fall foliage on the Maple Trail   *Monkey Rock on the East Trail*

at 4.41 miles, watch for vehicles before continuing west along the park road. There will be a pedestrian crosswalk to reconnect with the Trail to Day-Use Area at 4.46 miles. Again, watch for vehicles, and then when it is safe to do so, go across the cross-walk. You will reach the day-use area when the mileage clocks at 4.5 miles. Continue straight through the day-use area to the East Trailhead and where you parked your car.

East Trail (combined with Maple Trail and East-West Trail), Lost Maples State Natural Area

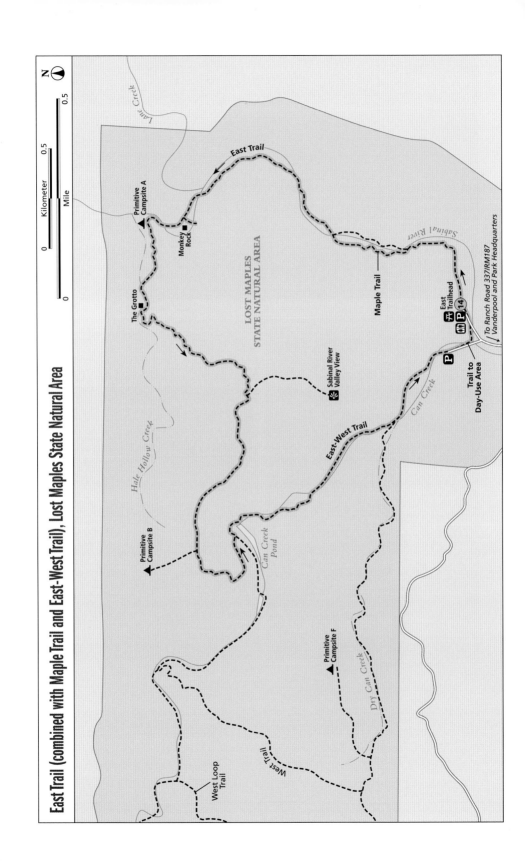

Miles and Directions

0.0   Start at the East Trailhead north of the very end of the day-use parking lot.

0.05 Bypass the side trail to your left. Bear right onto the East Trail.

0.1   Reach the Maple Trail entrance. Bear left up the rock steps onto the Maple Trail.

0.12 Reach some rock steps and a wooden footbridge.

0.14 There will be rock steps in the path at this point and the 0.16- and 0.21-mile marks.

0.35 Bypass the side trail to the Sabinal River on your right.

0.42 Cross over a rocky seasonal riverbed.

0.48 Reconnect with the East Trail and head north.

0.9   Bypass the side trail to your right.

1.07 Cross over a seasonal riverbed.

1.17 Take the optional spur to Monkey Rock to your left.

1.21 Reach Monkey Rock and the Sabinal River. Turn around and return to the East Trail.

1.25 Reconnect with the East Trail and head northwest.

1.32 Cross over a seasonal riverbed at this point, and at 1.57, 1.64, and 1.67 miles.

1.39 Reach Primitive Campsite A. Bear left.

1.49 A composting toilet will be available to your left.

1.73 Reach an overlook to a grotto.

1.79 Make a steep rocky ascent of about 290 feet to the 2.06-mile mark.

1.85 Reach an overlook to your left.

2.3   This guide bypasses the spur to your left to the scenic overlook. Continue straight.

2.62 Reach a "Birdseye View" vista of the Sabinal River to your left.

2.89 Bypass the trail to your right that leads to Primitive Campsite B. Continue straight.

2.93 Make a steep rocky descent of 335 feet to the 3.25-mile mark.

3.25 Reach Can Creek Pond, a composting toilet, and the West Trail connection to your right. Continue straight.

3.31 There will be a vista of Can Creek Pond to your right.

3.38 and 3.6 Cross over Can Creek.

3.97 Reach the West Trail entrance/exit to your right. Continue southeast onto the East-West Trail.

4.25 Cross over Can Creek.

4.27 The East-West Trail ends. Reach a parking lot to your right. Continue straight on the asphalt. Watch for passing vehicles.

4.36 Bear left onto the Trail to Day-Use Area.

4.38 Cross over a seasonal creek bed.

4.41 Reach the park road. Continue west along the park road and watch for vehicles.

4.46 Go across the pedestrian crosswalk to reconnect with the Trail to Day-Use Area.

4.5   Reach the day-use area.

4.7   Arrive back at the trailhead.

15 Blinn River Trail (entrance from Madrone Walkway), Garner State Park

The Frio River has been a life source to many over the centuries—from the Indigenous peoples to European settlers centuries ago to Texans today. Its waters are clear, and its sparkling beauty flowing over limestone can be enjoyed by hiking the Blinn River Trail. The Madrone Walkway connects to the Blinn River Trail and offers scenic views of the Frio River as well.

Lake or river: Frio River
Photogenic factor: 4+
Start: Madrone Walkway Trailhead
Elevation gain: 1,357 to 1,457 feet
Distance: 1.13-mile lollipop
Difficulty: Easy
Hiking time: About 1 hour
Seasons/schedule: Open year-round, 8 a.m. to 10 p.m.
Fees and permits: $8 per person 13 years and older (subject to change), free for Texas State Parks Pass holders
Trail contacts: Garner State Park Headquarters, 234 RR 1050, Concan 78838; (830) 232-6132
Dog-friendly: Leashed dogs permitted

Trail surface: Majority of Madrone Walkway is asphalt; Blinn River Trail is dirt and gravel
Land status: Texas Parks and Wildlife Department
Nearest town: Leakey (north), Utopia (east)
Other trail users: Mountain bikers/cyclists on the Madrone Walkway portion, anglers on the Blinn River Trail portion
Maps: USGS Magers Crossing; Garner State Park map (available online at www.tpwd.texas .gov/state-parks/parks-map and via the TX State Parks mobile app)
Special considerations: The Blinn River Trail is situated close to the banks of the Frio River. During times of heavy rainfall or flooding, this trail can be closed due to erosion. Please contact the park headquarters for trail conditions.

Finding the trailhead: From downtown San Antonio, take I-35 S for 2.6 miles until you take exit 153 for US 90 W. Merge onto US 90 W and stay on it for 59 miles until you reach the town of Sabinal. Turn right onto TX 127 N/N Center Street and continue for 21.1 miles. Turn right when you reach the town of Concan to travel onto US 83 N. Stay on US 83 N for 8.3 miles. Turn right on FM 1050 E. Continue on FM 1050 for 0.2 miles before going right into Garner State Park. After 0.9 miles, turn right onto New Park Road 29 (opposite the Live Oak and Rio Frio camping areas). Go left onto State Park 29 Road after 0.6 miles (opposite the River Crossing camping area). After another 0.6 miles, you will see the Pavilion Gift Shop and miniature golf course area to your left. Once you turn into the parking lot area, the Madrone Walkway can be accessed to your left. **GPS:** N29° 35.035' W99° 44.042'

The Hike

When the Spanish expeditioners arrived in the Garner State Park area in the 17th century, they named the Frio River "frio," which translates to cold. With a temperature that

The refreshing Frio River

ranges in the 60s, the Frio River is a crystal-clear delight to enjoy, especially during the warm Texas summers. It continues to be a life source today. Thanks to its riparian areas, many flora and fauna thrive in and along its waters. It also delivers water to aquifers, providing water for Texas residents.

The portion of the Frio River that flows from the town of Leakey to the town of Concan is the most free-flowing, and Garner State Park lies right along that region. Garner State Park was constructed by the Civilian Conservation Corps (CCC) and has been a place for entertainment since it opened in the summer of 1941. The CCC Pavilion, where most of these festivities began, is situated northeast of the Madrone Walkway and south of the Blinn River Trail. This guide begins with the Madrone Walkway, then connects with the Blinn River Trail for up-close views of the Frio River, and then circles back to the Madrone Walkway, providing a different perspective of the Frio River with a scenic overlook.

Begin the Madrone Walkway on the dirt path west of the miniature golf course near the parking lot entrance from State Park Road 29. At 560 feet, you will reach the aforementioned CCC Pavilion. The trail merges with an asphalt pathway and will eventually return to a dirt surface. Continue north on the Madrone Walkway. The entrance to the Blinn River Trail will occur at 0.15 miles. Take the right side of the fork to head onto the Blinn River Trail. The path surface starts to get uneven with intermittent rocks, so please watch your footing. Throughout the Blinn River Trail, the Frio River will be to your right and there will be several side trails to the river. You will also descend 15 feet in elevation to the 0.18-mile mark.

You will go in between several boulders and fallen tree trunks from the 0.24-mile mark to the 0.33-mile mark. A noticeable lookout point for the Frio River will be to your right at 0.43 miles. The scene is refreshing. Its waters glide over smooth rocks and among aquatic plants swaying in the wind. When you reach the junction at the 0.45-mile mark, bear left to continue on the Blinn River Trail and to recon-

Blinn River Trail (entrance from Madrone Walkway), Garner State Park

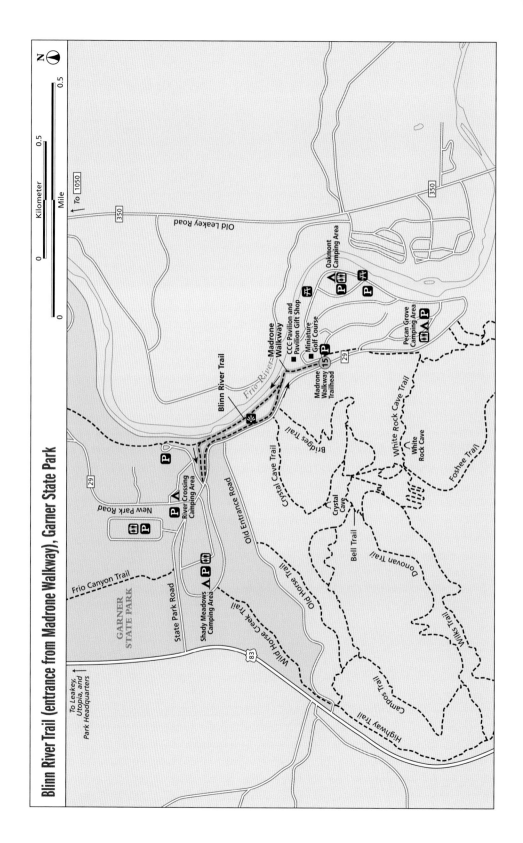

nect with the Madrone Walkway. Heading straight leads to a picnic area and another Blinn River Trail entrance. To the right is an offshoot.

The Blinn River Trail ends at the 0.58-mile mark. Curve around State Park Road 29 to head south back onto the Madrone Walkway. Be alert for vehicles. Once you get back on the Madrone Walkway, the path surface returns to asphalt. There will be an ascent of 80 feet in elevation from this point to the scenic overlook at the 0.78-mile mark. The scenic overlook with a small parking area will be to your left. A panoramic vista above the Frio River can be enjoyed from this viewpoint.

There will be a descent of 30 feet in elevation from the 0.86-mile mark to the 0.89-mile mark, the latter is when the Crystal Cave Trailhead will be to your right. At 0.92 miles, you will see the Bridges Trailhead to your right. Bypass the steep side trail to the Frio River to your left at 0.95 miles, as well as the Blinn River Trail entrance to

Vegetation thriving in the riparian area

your left at 0.97 miles that you originally took at the 0.15-mile mark. Return the way you came from the Madrone Walkway Trailhead.

Miles and Directions

0.0 The trail begins west of the miniature golf course and at the parking lot entrance.

0.11 Merge with the pathway from the CCC Pavilion to continue north on the Madrone Walkway.

0.15 Reach a fork. Take the right side to head onto the Blinn River Trail. Make a 15-foot descent to the 0.18-mile mark. The path surface turns uneven and rocky.

0.24 Watch for rocks and fallen tree trunks from here to the 0.28-mile mark.

0.43 Reach a lookout point for the Frio River to your right.

0.45 Reach a junction. Bear left.

0.58 The Blinn River Trail ends. Curve around State Park Road 29 to head south back onto the Madrone Walkway. Watch for passing vehicles. Make an ascent of 80 feet in elevation to the 0.78-mile mark.

0.78 Reach a scenic overlook to your left.

0.86 Make a 30-foot descent to the 0.89-mile mark.

0.89 Bypass the Crystal Cave Trailhead to your right.

0.92 Bypass the Bridges Trailhead to your right.

0.95 Bypass the off-shoot to the Frio River to your left.

0.97 Bypass the Blinn River Trail entrance to your left.

1.13 Arrive back at the trailhead.

16 Tie Slide Trail (combined with Gorman Falls Trail), Colorado Bend State Park

The sight of the mighty Colorado River meandering through the limestone ridges of Colorado Bend State Park is quite a display. The river, however, is not the only icon in the park—the 70-foot Gorman Falls and its irreplaceable ecosystem enchants hikers as well. Those taking the Tie Slide Trail and the Gorman Falls Trail will get to experience both.

Lake or river: Colorado River
Photogenic factor: 5
Start: Tie Slide Trailhead/Gorman Falls Trailhead
Elevation gain: 1,014 to 1,319 feet
Distance: 4.57-mile lollipop
Difficulty: Moderate to difficult due to the steep ascent and descent near Gorman Falls
Hiking time: 3–4 hours
Seasons/schedule: Open year-round, 6 a.m. to 10 p.m.
Fees and permits: $5 per person 13 years and older (subject to change), free for Texas State Parks Pass holders
Trail contacts: Colorado Bend State Park Headquarters, 1201 Colorado Park Road, Bend 76824; (325) 628-3240

Dog-friendly: Leashed dogs permitted
Trail surface: Dirt and rock
Land status: Texas Parks and Wildlife Department
Nearest town: San Saba (northwest), Lampasas (east), Burnet (southeast), Cherokee (west), Llano (southwest)
Other trail users: Mountain bikers/cyclists on Tie Slide Trail only
Maps: USGS Bend; Colorado Bend State Park map (available online at www.tpwd.texas.gov/state-parks/parks-map and via the TX State Parks mobile app)
Special considerations: Blue markers serve as guides for the Tie Slide Trail. Yellow and orange markers serve as guides for the Gorman Falls Trail.

Finding the trailhead: From downtown Austin, get onto I-35 N/US 290 E. Continue on I-35 N for 29.2 miles, and then take exit 266 for TX 195 N. Turn left onto TX 195 W and stay on it for 14.2 miles. Take the exit for TX 138 when you reach the town of Florence. Go left onto TX 138 and continue on it for 6.9 miles. Turn right onto US 183 N. Stay on US 183 N for 24.5 miles. When you reach the town of Lampasas, turn left onto W North Avenue. After 0.7 miles, turn right onto N Porter Street. Quickly merge onto FM 580/Nix Road by veering left. Continue on FM 580 for 22.7 miles. Turn left onto CR 436 in the town of Bend. After 0.3 miles, turn right onto CR 440. Go right onto CR 436/CR 442 after half a mile. In 2.9 miles, you will enter Colorado Bend State Park. Continue straight on Colorado Park Road for 0.4 miles. Turn right onto Gorman Road. The Tie Slide and Gorman Falls Trailheads will be at the eastern end of the parking lot. **GPS:** N31° 03.499' W98° 30.073'

The Hike

This guide starts with hiking the Tie Slide Trail and then eventually the Gorman Falls Trail. Hiking both trails allows hikers to see the Colorado River and also Gorman

Falls. The two trails commence at the same place east of the Gorman Falls parking lot. Within 60 feet of the trailhead, bear left at the sign onto the Tie Slide Trail. The right side is the Gorman Falls Trail, which will be the return route. Look for blue markers along the Tie Slide Trail to direct you where to go. The beginning portion of the Tie Slide Trail can be overgrown before you head into the wooded area. The scenery opens up into a prairie. At 0.35 miles, cross over huge slabs of rock and then enter a wooded area. The landscape alternates between wooded areas and arid prairie until the 1.21-mile mark. The route can be overgrown in the prairie portions. Go across a seasonal creek bed at 0.44 miles, and then you will reach an overlook to a small pond to your left a little over half a mile into the trail. The trail begins to head primarily east

Colorado River from the Tie Slide Trail

from the 0.65-mile mark. The trail surface turns rocky from the 1.45-mile mark to the 1.55-mile mark.

When you reach the fork at 1.55 miles, continue straight toward an overlook of the Colorado River. The right leads toward the Gorman Falls Trail. This guide will eventually take this route on the way back from the Colorado River overlook. From 1.58 miles to 1.60 miles, you will descend about 45 feet. Continue heading northeast onto the dirt path. The path returns to a rocky surface at 1.62 miles. Shortly after, you will come upon the Rusty's Roost platform for an overlook of the Colorado River. Enjoy the panoramic view, 200 feet above the winding Colorado River. The seemingly endless river courses through Ashe juniper–dotted limestone hills. Once you are done taking a break on one of the platform benches, turn around and return to the Gorman Falls Trail connection that was at the 1.55-mile mark.

You will return to the Gorman Falls Trail connection when the mileage reads as 1.7 miles. Take the left side of the fork to head onto the Gorman Falls Trail. The path gets rocky close to two miles into the trail. Continue heading southwest at the fork at 2.16 miles, and then at 2.34 miles, you will reach a junction and a bench. Bear left to head toward Gorman Falls. The right side goes back to the trailhead and parking

The incredible Gorman Falls

lot. This guide will take this route on the way back from Gorman Falls. It can get rocky and muddy at certain portions of the Gorman Falls Trail, and the route primarily heads east. Look for yellow and orange markers along the Gorman Falls Trail to direct you where to go. Prior to reaching Gorman Falls, the path splits and eventually merges. There might be a fallen tree trunk in the path to watch out for, and there will be brief shade on the path while in the wooded area.

Bear east to Gorman Falls when you get to the fork at 2.98 miles. The right side is a designated bicycle route to Gorman Falls, since the Gorman Falls Trail is for hikers only. You will make a descent of 55 feet to the fork at the 3.04-mile mark. At the final fork in the trail, bear left to head toward Gorman Falls. Heading right will lead you to Gorman Creek, Gorman Spring, and the conference center. Cross over a seasonal creek bed at 3.06 miles. You will make another descent, this time much steeper, starting at 3.13 miles. It will be a descent of 50 feet to the observation deck at 3.19 miles. Make sure to hang on to the handrail for extra support. When you reach the observation deck, take time to admire the spring-fed 70-foot waterfall, thundering down travertines to your northeast. After taking in the sights and reading the informational plaques, turn around and return to the Gorman Falls Trail and Tie Slide Trail connection from the 2.34-mile mark. Remember to use the handrail when heading back up the rocks.

The mileage will clock at 4.05 miles when you return to the Gorman Falls Trail and Tie Slide Trail connection. Continue straight on the Gorman Falls Trail toward the trailhead and parking lot. The route back to the trailhead for the most part is shaded, and the surface is less rocky. You will cross over an old access road at the 4.22- and 4.55-mile marks. The trail concludes back at the trailhead and parking lot at 4.57 miles.

Tie Slide Trail (combined with Gorman Falls Trail), Colorado Bend State Park

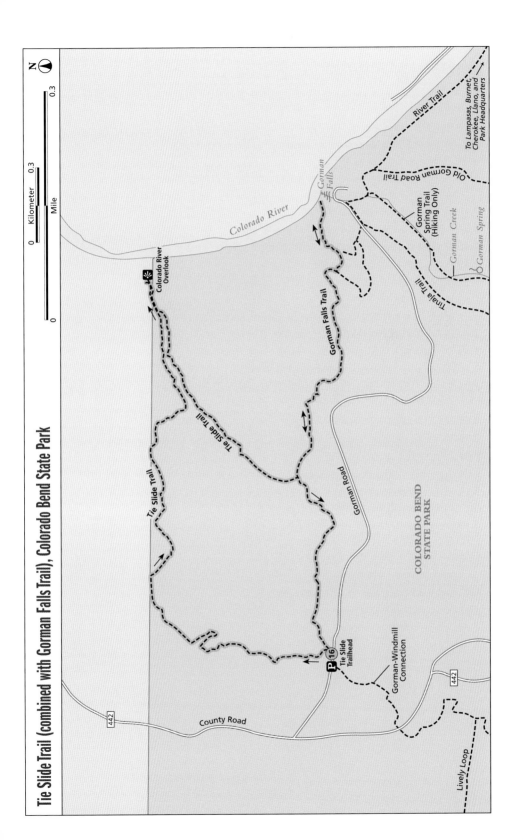

N

0   Kilometer   0.3

0   Mile   0.3

Colorado River

Colorado River Overlook

Gorman Falls

Tie Slide Trail

Tie Slide Trail

Gorman Falls Trail

River Trail

Old Gorman Road Trail

Gorman Spring Trail (Hiking Only)

Gorman Creek

Gorman Spring

Tinaja Trail

To Lampasas, Burnet, Cherokee, Llano, and Park Headquarters

Gorman Road

COLORADO BEND STATE PARK

P 16

Tie Slide Trailhead

Gorman-Windmill Connection

County Road

442

442

Lively Loop

Miles and Directions

0.0 The Tie Slide Trail and the Gorman Falls Trail both start east of the Gorman Falls parking lot.

0.01 Reach a fork next to the sign. Bear left onto the Tie Slide Trail. The path can be overgrown in the beginning portion before heading into the wooded area.

0.35 Cross over huge slabs of rock and enter a wooded area. The landscape alternates between wooded areas and arid prairie until the 1.21-mile mark. The route can be overgrown in the arid prairie portions.

0.44 Cross a seasonal creek bed.

0.52 Reach an overlook to a small pond to your left.

1.45 The trail surface turns rocky from here to the 1.55-mile mark.

1.55 Reach a fork. Continue straight.

1.58 Make a slight descent of 45 feet to 1.60 miles.

1.63 Reach the Rusty's Roost platform for an overlook of the Colorado River. Enjoy the view. Turn around and return to the Gorman Falls Trail connection from the 1.55-mile mark.

1.7 Reach the Gorman Falls Trail connection. Bear left onto the Gorman Falls Trail.

1.99 The path gets rocky.

2.16 Reach a fork. Continue southwest.

2.34 Reach a junction and a bench. Bear left to head toward Gorman Falls. It can get rocky and muddy at certain portions of the Gorman Falls Trail.

2.59 The path splits and eventually merges.

2.98 Reach a fork. Bear east. Make a descent of 55 feet to the 3.04-mile mark.

3.04 Reach a fork. Bear left.

3.06 Cross over a seasonal creek bed.

3.13 Make a descent of 50 feet to the observation deck at 3.19 miles. Make sure to hold on to the handrail for support.

3.19 Reach the observation deck. Enjoy the waterfall. Turn around and return to the Gorman Falls Trail and Tie Slide Trail connection from the 2.34-mile mark.

4.05 Reach the Gorman Falls Trail and Tie Slide Trail connection. Continue straight toward the trailhead and parking lot.

4.22 and 4.55 Cross over an old access road.

4.57 Arrive back at the trailhead.

17 Devil's Backbone Nature Trail (entrance from Devil's Waterhole Nature Trail), Inks Lake State Park

The smallest lake of the "Highland Lakes Chain," the photo-worthy Inks Lake, continues to be incredibly resourceful. From providing water and fish to the Indigenous peoples 8,000 years ago to housing rare vegetation such as rock quillwort and basin corn salad in its vernal pools, Inks Lake has been a sanctuary for many. Hiking the Devil's Backbone Nature Trail will take hikers along the roseate cliffs that flank the lake, allowing for up-close sights of the magnificent body of water.

Lake or river: Inks Lake
Photogenic factor: 5
Start: Devil's Waterhole Nature Trailhead
Elevation gain: 886 to 945 feet
Distance: 3.15 miles out and back
Difficulty: Moderate
Hiking time: 2–3 hours
Seasons/schedule: Open year-round, 8 a.m. to 10 p.m.
Fees and permits: $7 per person 13 years and older (subject to change), free for Texas State Parks Pass holders
Trail contacts: Inks Lake State Park Headquarters, 3630 Park Road 4 West, Burnet 78611; (512) 793-2223
Dog-friendly: Leashed dogs permitted (not permitted at the Wildlife Viewing Station/bird blind)

Trail surface: Dirt and gravel, with a portion of the trail on slabs of rock
Land status: Texas Parks and Wildlife Department
Nearest town: Burnet (east), Marble Falls (southeast)
Other trail users: None
Maps: USGS Longhorn Cavern; Inks Lake State Park map (available online at www.tpwd.texas .gov/state-parks/parks-map and via the TX State Parks mobile app)
Special considerations: Arrow markers serve as guides for this trail. Portions of this trail can get overgrown after a decent rainfall or during the spring and summer.

Finding the trailhead: From downtown Austin, travel on TX 1 Loop S for 3.8 miles, before exiting for US 290 E/TX 71 E/Southwest Parkway. After traveling on Southwest Parkway for 7.1 miles, turn right onto TX 71 W. Stay on TX 71 W for 29.8 miles. Keep to the right lane to merge onto US 281 N. Continue on US 281 N for 13.2 miles. Turn left onto Park Road 4. After 12.5 miles, turn left into Inks Lake State Park. Go for 0.9 miles into the park, and at each fork (four forks total) take the right side in order to reach the northernmost parking lot. The Devil's Waterhole Nature Trailhead will be northeast of the parking lot. **GPS:** N30° 44.741' W98° 21.635'

The Hike

Inks Lake is as useful as it is scenic. The original intent for Inks Lake was to use it to control the powerful Colorado River, which was prone to massive floods. It was

View of the Devil's Waterhole

constructed during the Great Depression by the Lower Colorado River Authority (LCRA) and then gifted to the Texas State Parks Board in 1940.

There will be several opportunities on your left to see Inks Lake right when you start on the Devil's Waterhole Nature Trail. Head northeast on the gravel path. Bear right at the "Caution" sign 245 feet into the trail to head across the footbridge. The trail eventually heads back northeast. There will be several more side trails on your left to view the infamous Devil's Waterhole until you reach the Valley Spring Creek Trail. The Devil's Waterhole is a popular swimming hole formed from the convergence of Spring Creek and Inks Lake. For any "daredevils" who would like to swim in the Devil's Waterhole, you will be able to access it from this route. Exercise caution while swimming in Inks Lake, as there are no lifeguards on duty.

You will encounter the entrance and exit to the Valley Spring Creek Trail at 0.18 miles. The Valley Spring Creek Trail is a loop. If taken in a clockwise direction, the entrance to the Valley Spring Creek Trail is to your left and the exit is through the woodlands to your right. Take the left side up the rosy-hued Valley Spring Gneiss rocks. Make a 10-foot ascent in elevation to the 0.22-mile mark where you then connect with a dirt path. The Valley Spring Gneiss rocks are signature to the Inks Lake landscape; they are some of the oldest rocks in all of Texas, formed almost 1.2 billion years ago. You will see these metamorphic rock outcrops throughout the park thrust up by two convergent plate tectonics events after being buried in the mantle of the earth. While Town Mountain Granite rocks are also dispersed throughout the park, they must not be confused with the Valley Spring Gneiss rocks, as they are igneous rocks. A great example of the two types of Precambrian Era rocks melded together is a segment along the shoreline of Devil's Waterhole.

There will be a few side trails before you reach the fork at 0.27 miles. You can bypass all of them by continuing straight—one that has value will be to your right at the 0.23-mile mark. It will be for an overlook of Devil's Waterhole and Inks Lake. Follow the arrow markers at the fork by bearing left to continue on the trail. The right leads to Park Road 4. Again, from the 0.28-mile mark until you reach the connection to the Devil's Backbone Nature Trail at the 0.55-mile mark, there will be several side trails to bypass. Follow the arrow markers and on the ground, green circles with white centers to keep you on the trail. There will be intermittent rocky ledges you will need to cross over before the path returns to dirt. These ledges will appear

Autumn in the Spring Creek Delta

at the 0.28-mile mark, the 0.34-mile mark, the 0.43-mile mark, and the 0.46-mile mark. At 0.41 miles, you will curve around a large rock formation.

The connection to the Devil's Backbone Nature Trail will occur a little over half a mile into the route. Follow the sign by bearing left to continue onto the Devil's Backbone Nature Trail. Heading right continues the loop route of the Valley Spring Creek Trail. At 0.58 miles, the trail curves, and heads north as you go down some rocks. Follow the red rectangular markers with yellow arrows. An "American Sycamore" interpretive wayside will be to your right at 0.63 miles. This portion of the trail up to the rocky riverbed and concrete overpass can get overgrown. Cross over the rocky riverbed and reconnect with the dirt path at the end of the concrete overpass at the 0.65-mile mark. The trail then heads west.

At 0.66 miles, a "Carving the Land" interpretive wayside will be to your left. From this point to the 1.52-mile mark, there will be several interpretive waysides along the trail. These interpretive waysides include information on the following: "Buckley's Yucca," "Ashe Juniper," "Valley Spring Creek," "Catclaw Mimosa," "Plateau Live Oak," "Makings of a Lake," "Lichen," "Texas Persimmon," "Ball Moss," "Inland Sea Oats," "Honey Mesquite," "Tasajillo," and "Whitebrush." Head into a wooded area shortly after. Shade becomes sparse after the 0.7-mile mark.

Devil's Backbone Nature Trail (entrance from Devil's Waterhole Nature Trail), Inks Lake State Park

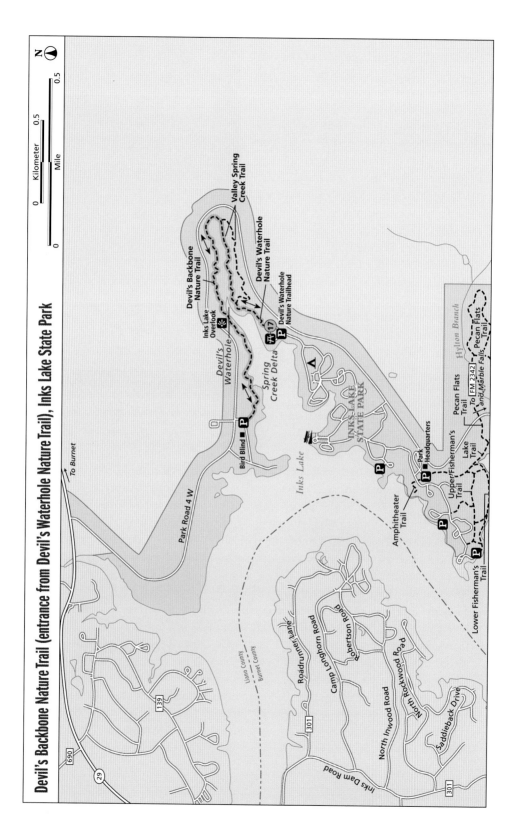

Bypass the side trail to your left at 0.85 miles, and then cross over a small footbridge at 0.98 miles. This portion of the trail can get overgrown. A noteworthy vista of Inks Lake and the Spring Creek Delta will be to your left a little over a mile into the trail. The "Plateau Live Oak" interpretive wayside will be to the right of the vista. Take time to sit on the viewing bench and bask in the stunning scene before you. This area of the lake that the vista overlooks is very popular among kayakers and anglers, so you might catch a glimpse of a few. After relishing the view, return west onto the trail.

At 1.06 miles, you will make a rocky descent of about 10 feet in elevation to the 1.08-mile mark. Go across the rocky ledge at 1.14 miles and head toward the "Lichen" interpretive wayside to reconnect with the dirt path. The trail curves north for a brief moment at the 1.5-mile mark and then heads back west. When you reach the access road to the Wildlife Viewing Station/bird blind at 1.59 miles, the Devil's Backbone Nature Trail ends. This area also serves as an entrance to the Devil's Backbone Nature Trail, but the gate to it is locked and gate access must be obtained from the park headquarters. At this point, turn around and return the way you came.

Miles and Directions

0.0 Begin at the Devil's Waterhole Nature Trailhead.

0.05 Bear right at the "Caution" sign to head across the footbridge. Bypass several side trails to your left.

0.18 Reach the entrance and exit to Valley Spring Creek Trail. Take the left side up the Valley Spring Gneiss rocks. Make a 10-foot ascent in elevation to the 0.22-mile mark where you then connect with a dirt path.

0.23 An offshoot to an overlook will be to your right.

0.25 to 0.55 Bypass the offshoots on both sides of the trail. Continue straight. Follow the in-ground arrow markers and green circles with white centers on the path to keep you on the trail. There will also be intermittent rocky ledges you will need to cross over.

0.27 Reach a fork. Follow the arrow markers. Bear left.

0.41 Curve around the large rock formation.

0.55 Reach the connection to the Devil's Backbone Nature Trail. Follow the sign by bearing left to start the Devil's Backbone Nature Trail.

0.58 Follow the red rectangular markers with yellow arrows and head down some rocks.

0.64 Cross over the rocky riverbed along the concrete overpass.

0.85 Bypass the side trail to your left.

0.98 Cross over a small footbridge.

1.02 Reach a worthwhile vista of Inks Lake with a viewing bench to your left.

1.06 Make a rocky descent of about 10 feet to the 1.08-mile mark.

1.14 Go across the rocky ledge and reconnect with the dirt path.

1.59 The Devil's Backbone Nature Trail ends at an access road to the Wildlife Viewing Station/bird blind area. Return the way you came.

3.15 Arrive back at the trailhead.

18 Hackenburg Loop, Pedernales Falls State Park

The impressive Pedernales River winds through bluffs etched with so much history—evidenced by the layers of limestone and sediment covered with Hill Country's signature junipers and shrubbery. The Hackenburg Loop allows hikers to have up-close views of the river, and also provides the opportunity to reach an overlook of the magnificent Pedernales Falls.

Lake or river: Pedernales River, Deep Lake, and Cypress Pool
Photogenic factor: 5
Start: Hackenburg Loop Trailhead
Elevation gain: 787 to 949 feet
Distance: 1.68-mile lollipop
Difficulty: Easy
Hiking time: About 1 hour
Seasons/schedule: Open year-round, 8 a.m. to 10 p.m.
Fees and permits: $6 per person 13 years and older (subject to change), free for Texas State Parks Pass holders
Trail contacts: Pedernales Falls State Park Headquarters, 2585 Park Road 6026, Johnson City 78636; (830) 868-7304
Dog-friendly: Leashed dogs permitted

Trail surface: Mixture of dirt, mowed grass, and asphalt
Land status: Texas Parks and Wildlife Department
Nearest town: Johnson City (west), Dripping Springs (southeast)
Other trail users: Mountain bikers/cyclists
Maps: USGS Pedernales Falls; Pedernales Falls State Park map (available online at www.tpwd.texas.gov/state-parks/parks-map and via the TX State Parks mobile app)
Special considerations: The portion of the Pedernales River that the Hackenburg Loop parallels is private property. No swimming, wading, or tubing is allowed. Possible flash flooding occurs in the area.

Finding the trailhead: From downtown Austin, travel on TX 1 Loop S for 4.6 miles until merging onto US 290 W/TX 71 W. Stay on US 290 W for 26.5 miles. When you reach the town of Henly, turn right onto Ranch Road 3232. After traveling on Ranch Road 3232 for 6.4 miles, turn right onto Pedernales Falls Road. Close to 200 feet, turn left onto Park Road 6026. Continue on Park Road 6026 for 4.6 miles until you reach the Pedernales Falls Trail system parking area. The non-vehicle access road that leads to the Hackenburg Loop Trailhead will be 120 feet southeast of the parking area entrance. Hike 205 feet on the non-vehicle access path and you will reach a fork. The right side of the fork is the Hackenburg Loop. **GPS:** N30° 19.979' W98° 15.072'

The Hike

Beautiful and seemingly calm, the Pedernales River can also be mighty. With a decent amount of rainfall, it can cause flash floods with little warning. Via water erosion, it carves its way through Marble Falls limestone carpeted with cedar forests.

Pedernales River in the fall

The Hackenburg Loop parallels the Pedernales River for the majority of its route, as rows of bald cypress trees interrupt congregations of Ashe juniper in the area.

The Hackenburg Loop starts on the right side of the fork, 205 feet into the non-vehicle path near the entrance of the Pedernales Falls Trail System parking area. The dirt path primarily heads in an easterly direction. At 0.12 miles, the trail surface turns to mowed grass. Cedars nestled among a mixture of prairie and prickly pears greet you as well. The trail surface turns to asphalt at 0.45 miles. At 0.55 miles, you will descend about 15 feet in elevation to the 0.57-mile mark where the path surface returns to dirt. The trail then heads north. Views of the Pedernales River open up to your right. From the 0.65-mile mark to the 0.72-mile mark, you will need to bypass several offshoots to the Pedernales River to your right. At 0.72 miles, take note of the protected area sign that states, "no recreational activities within 200 feet of posted sign." The trail begins to narrow shortly after.

You will then enter an area populated with large succulents. The landscape returns to the typical Hill Country scenery of cedar trees and shrubs at 0.90 miles. You will make a slight rocky descent of 10 feet elevation shortly after to the 0.92 mile-mark. A side trail to the Deep Lake area will be to your right. Continue straight on the "Lower Hackenburg" when you come upon the fork. The left side takes you to the "Upper Hackenburg." Be aware of intermittent unearthed tree roots and fallen tree branches in the path. You will encounter an overlook of Deep Lake to your right at 0.98 miles. Shortly after, bear left at the fork to continue on the

"Lower Hackenburg." The right side is an offshoot. There will also be an ascent in elevation through a narrow slot of rocks when the mileage reads 1 mile. At the fork at 1.01 miles, continue northwest on the Lower Hackenburg. You will come upon another fork at 1.04 miles, where the side trail from the 0.99-mile mark connects from the right. Bear left. There will be an ascent of 15 feet in elevation from this point to the 1.06-mile mark. The trail then widens back up. From the 1.09-mile mark to the 1.16-mile mark, bypass another round of offshoots, this time to your right. The path surface turns to gravel shortly after, all the way to the fork at the 1.23-mile mark.

At the fork, you will see a Hackenburg Loop sign that indicates its entrance/exit. By bearing right, you will then connect with the Pedernales Falls Trail System. When you reach the junction at 1.27 miles, continue straight to the Pedernales Falls/Cypress Pool Overlook. To your right is a bench that faces Cypress Pool. To your left is one of the trails in

View of the Pedernales River from the Hackenburg Loop

the Pedernales Falls Trail System. You will encounter several interpretive waysides at 1.32 miles. The route to the Pedernales Falls/Cypress Pool Overlook will be the stone steps to your right. Pedernales Falls is incredible to see, especially after decent rainfall. The base layers of limestone of the falls date back to nearly 300 million years ago. After taking in the view, turn around and return to the Hackenburg Loop connection from the 1.23-mile mark. At the Hackenburg Loop connection, continue straight. The trail will start to wind in a southwest direction at 1.57 miles, before you return to the trailhead. Take the non-vehicle path back to the parking area.

Hackenburg Loop, Pedernales Falls State Park

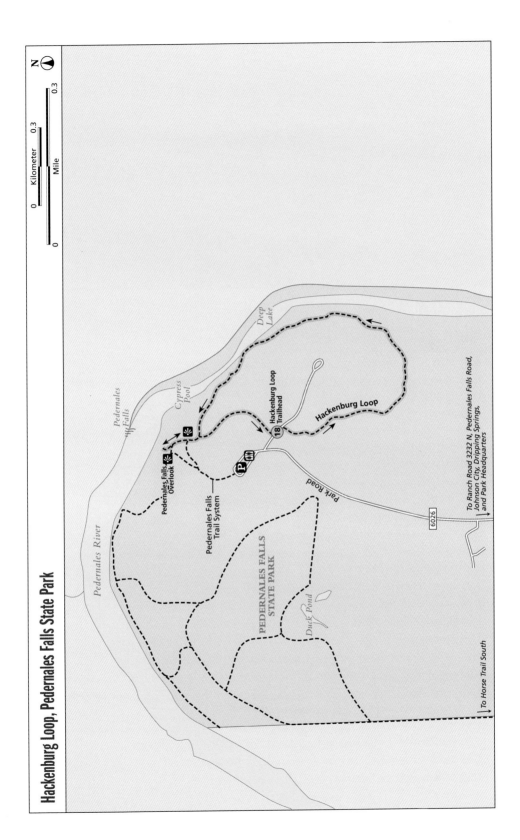

View of Cypress Pool

Miles and Directions

0.0 Start on the Hackenburg Loop Trailhead on the right side of the fork.

0.55 Make a 15-foot descent to the 0.57-mile mark. Views of the Pedernales River will be to your right.

0.65 Bypass several offshoots to your right from here to the 0.72-mile mark.

0.72 Take note of the protected area sign that states, "No recreational activities within 200 feet of posted sign."

0.91 Make a slight rocky descent of 10 feet to the 0.92-mile mark. Deep Lake will be to your right.

0.93 Reach a fork. Continue straight on the "Lower Hackenburg."

0.96 Watch for unearthed tree roots and fallen tree branches in the path.

0.98 Reach an overlook of Deep Lake to your right.

0.99 Reach a fork. Take the left side to continue on the "Lower Hackenburg." Ascend through a narrow slot of rocks to the 1-mile mark.

1.01 Reach a fork. Continue northwest.

1.04 Reach a fork. Bear left. Make an ascent of 15 feet from this point to the 1.06-mile mark.

1.09 Bypass the side trails to your right from this point to the 1.16-mile mark.

1.18 Continue onto the gravel path until you reach the fork at the 1.23-mile mark.

1.23 Reach a fork. Connect with the Pedernales Falls Trail System by bearing right.

1.27 Reach a junction. Continue straight to the Pedernales Falls/Cypress Pool Overlook.

1.32 Come upon several interpretive waysides. The route to the Pedernales Falls/Cypress Pool Overlook will be the stone steps to your right.

1.35 Reach the Pedernales Falls/Cypress Pool Overlook. After taking in the view, turn around and return to the Hackenburg Loop connection from the 1.23-mile mark.

1.45 Reach the connection to the Hackenburg Loop. Continue straight.

1.68 Arrive back at the trailhead.

19 Lake Loop (Lower) Trail, Lakeway City Park

Especially rewarding at sunset, the view of Lake Travis and Hurst Creek Cove from the relaxing Lake Loop (Lower) Trail is the perfect way to end the day. The cheerful wildflower meadow and Butterfly Garden along the trail serve as extra treats for hikers.

Lake or river: Lake Travis
Photogenic factor: 4+
Start: Lake Loop (Lower) Trailhead
Elevation gain: 668 to 756 feet
Distance: 1.41-mile lollipop
Difficulty: Easy
Hiking time: About 1 hour
Seasons/schedule: Open year-round, 6 a.m. to 10 p.m. (Daylight Savings Time) and 6 a.m. to 8 p.m. (Standard Time)
Fees and permits: None (subject to change)

Trail contacts: Lakeway Parks and Recreation Department, 105 Cross Creek, Lakeway 78734; (512) 314-7530
Dog-friendly: Leashed dogs permitted
Trail surface: Paved
Land status: City of Lakeway
Nearest town: Within Lakeway city limits
Other trail users: Cyclists, anglers, paddlers
Maps: USGS Mansfield Dam; Lakeway City Park Trail System map (available online at https://www.lakeway-tx.gov/125/Parks-Trails)

Finding the trailhead: From downtown Austin, take TX 1 Loop S to exit toward RM 2244/Rollingwood/W Lake Hills for Bee Caves Road. Turn right on Bee Caves Road. Stay on it for 10.9 miles. Turn right on Bee Cave Parkway. After 1.4 miles, turn right onto Ranch Road 620. Continue on Ranch Road 620 for 2.2 miles, and then turn left onto Lohmans Crossing Road. After traveling on Lohmans Crossing Road for 1.9 miles, turn right onto Hurst Creek Road. In 1.3 miles, the entrance to Lakeway City Park will be to your right. Turn right into Lakeway City Park and the Lake Loop (Lower) Trailhead starts to the right of the Huser Memorial pavilion. **GPS:** N30° 22.769' W97° 58.094'

The Hike

One of Lake Travis's protected harbors, Hurst Creek Cove, sits adjacent to Lakeway City Park. Its waters feed into Hurst Creek and nourish the landscape along the Hamilton Greenbelt. The Lake Loop (Lower) Trail in Lakeway City Park bestows panoramas of the cove and Lake Travis, while delighting hikers and their furry companions with wildflowers and fun amenities, such as the "Bark Park."

From the first parking lot you encounter at the Lakeway City Park entrance, start on the Lake Loop (Lower) Trail, west of the Huser Memorial pavilion. Take the paved path as it curves around the restroom building. When you reach a fork shortly after, take the left side to continue on the trail. The right side connects to the Challenge Trail. At 530 feet, you will reach a junction. The Butterfly Garden will be

A peaceful moment on the Lake Loop (Lower) Trail

to your right. This guide will take the loop in a clockwise direction. Bear left. There will be several offshoots to bypass from 0.2 miles until the trail heads east at 0.32 miles. Stay on the paved path.

A few benches overlooking Lake Travis will be along the trail. The trail heads south, and then west, before heading back south at the 0.55-mile mark. A series of picnic bench areas will occur shortly after on your right. Bypass the side trails to your left from this point to the 0.64-mile mark.

You will reach the second parking lot for the park to your right, just shy of three-quarters of a mile into the trail. Bypass the path to the playground to your right shortly after and continue straight. The most pivotal scenic overlook of Lake Travis and the Hurst Creek Cove will be available to your left at 0.84 miles. Take some time to enjoy the view from this spot as Lake Travis winds through the hills. This is a popular vantage point for people to reflect and be inspired, especially at sunrise and sunset. The trail curves around a wildflower meadow and heads north after the vista. Bypass the connections to the Challenge Trail to your left at 1.12 miles and 1.16 miles. When you reach the pedestrian crosswalk in the parking lot at 1.2 miles, watch for vehicles before going across. After the crosswalk, the Bark Park (dog park) will be to your left. One more highlight of the Lake Loop (Lower) Trail is the Butterfly Garden to your left at 1.30 miles. The Butterfly Garden is a beautiful tribute to Bernard M. Jacobson, the husband of a former Lakeway Parks and Recreation Commission member. Take note of the flourishing zinnias, lantanas, and daisies that

Lake Loop (Lower) Trail, Lakeway City Park

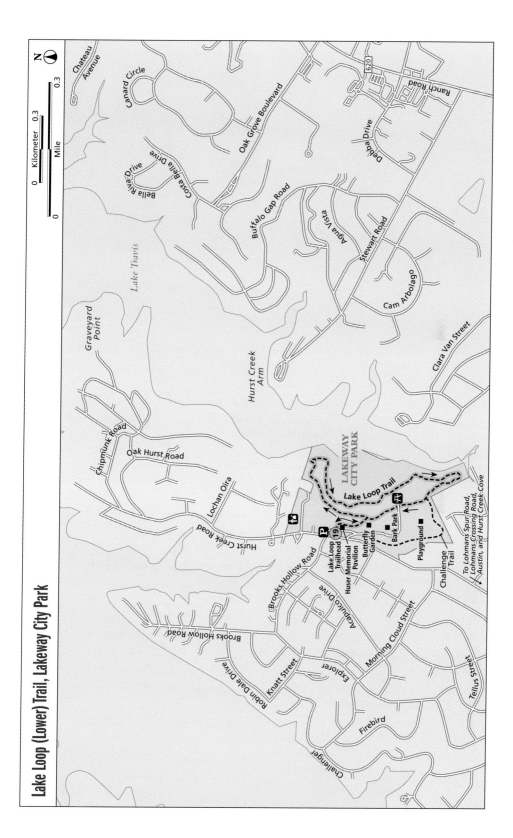

Vista of Lake Travis

Butterfly Garden by the trail

attract the butterflies to this garden. The junction from the original 530-foot mark will be shortly after. Bear left to return to the trailhead.

Miles and Directions

0.0 Start on the Lake Loop (Lower) Trail west of the Huser Memorial pavilion. Head south on the paved path around the restroom building shortly after.

0.03 Reach a fork. Take the left side to continue on the trail.

0.1 Reach a junction. Bear left to take the loop in clockwise direction.

0.2 Bypass the offshoot to your left at this point and at 0.24 miles.

0.55 A series of picnic benches will occur shortly after on your right. Bypass the offshoots to your left from this point to 0.64 miles.

0.73 Reach the second parking lot for the park to your right.

0.79 Bypass the path to the playground to your right.

0.84 Reach a scenic overlook of Lake Travis and the Hurst Creek Cove to your left.

0.97 Reach a wildflower meadow.

1.12 Bypass the entrance to the Challenge Trail to your left at this point and at 1.16 miles.

1.2 Watch for vehicles before going across the pedestrian crosswalk. After the crosswalk, the Bark Park (dog park) will be to your left.

1.3 Reach the Butterfly Garden to your left. The junction from the 0.1-mile mark will be shortly after. Bear left to return to the trailhead.

1.41 Arrive back at the trailhead.

20 Creekside Trail (combined with Prairie Loop), Commons Ford Ranch Metropolitan Park

The portion of Lake Austin that borders Commons Ford Ranch Metropolitan Park is a fun place to go paddling and swimming in. Visitors can also have a picnic on the lawn area and revel in the lake views with rocky bluffs as a backdrop. The trails within the park are just as leisurely—the Creekside Trail leading you to the shores of Lake Austin, and the Prairie Loop providing you with a plethora of wild scenery.

Lake or river: Lake Austin (formerly Lake McDonald) and Commons Ford Creek
Photogenic factor: 4+
Start: Creekside Trailhead
Elevation gain: 486 to 551 feet
Distance: 1.54-mile lollipop
Difficulty: Easy
Hiking time: About 1 hour
Seasons/schedule: Open year-round, 5 a.m. to 10 p.m.
Fees and permits: None (subject to change)

Trail contacts: Austin Parks and Recreation Department, 200 S Lamar Boulevard, Austin 78704; (512) 974-6700
Dog-friendly: Leashed dogs permitted
Trail surface: Dirt and mowed grass
Land status: City of Austin (managed in partnership with Travis Audubon)
Nearest town: Within Austin city limits
Other trail users: Cyclists, anglers, paddlers
Maps: USGS Mountain Springs; Commons Ford Ranch Metropolitan Park Trail System map (available at the Prairie Loop and Canyon Trailheads)

Finding the trailhead: From downtown Austin, take TX 1 Loop S to exit toward RM 2244/Rollingwood/W Lake Hills for Bee Caves Road. Turn right on Bee Caves Road. Stay on it for 7 miles. Turn right on S Cuernavaca Drive. After half a mile, turn left on Commons Ford Road. Stay on Commons Ford Road for 1.6 miles. At the fork for N Commons Ford Road, go left toward the sign. The Creekside Trailhead will be to your right in 0.4 miles, across from the parking area and west of Commons Ford Creek. **GPS:** N30° 20.291' W97° 53.437'

The Hike

Lake Austin is popular for its fishing and boating prospects, but it is also just as enjoyable for scenic hiking. This freshwater reservoir is especially alluring in the spring and summer. Visitors can enjoy the refreshing waters and the vivid landscape surrounding the lake. The Creekside Trail and the Prairie Loop both extend opportunities to enjoy the lake and the enchanting tranquility of the recently restored 40-acre prairie adjacent to it.

After starting at the Creekside Trailhead, you will notice that Commons Ford Creek parallels the trail to the east. About 600 feet into the trail, an overlook will be

Tranquil riparian area

to your left. At 0.17 miles, bypass the footbridge and the first connection to the East Trail will be to your right. Continue straight. Shortly after, there will be a side trail to your left that connects with a bird viewing trail and the Prairie Loop. Another side trail to your right will be a second connection to the East Trail.

A quarter of a mile into the trail, you will reach the lawn, dock, riparian area, and Lake Austin. After taking a break in this area, head west to continue on the Prairie Loop. The trail merges with the bird viewing trail coming from the south. Several benches will be available to your left along the path through the pecan grove. At 0.64 miles, the trail heads south through the prairie, and its surface changes to mowed grass. The prairie is a marvel. Through

Black Swallowtail seen from the Prairie Loop

impressive restoration efforts of the Commons Ford Prairie Restoration Organization and Travis Audubon, native species have returned to almost 90 percent, and any invasive species have dwindled significantly. Several interpretive waysides are displayed throughout the prairie from the 0.68-mile mark to the 1.18-mile mark. These interpretive waysides include topics such as the "Prairie Connection," "Commons Ford Prairie Restoration," "Commons Ford Ranch Metro Park," and "Birds of Commons

Creekside Trail (combined with Prairie Loop), Commons Ford Ranch Metropolitan Park

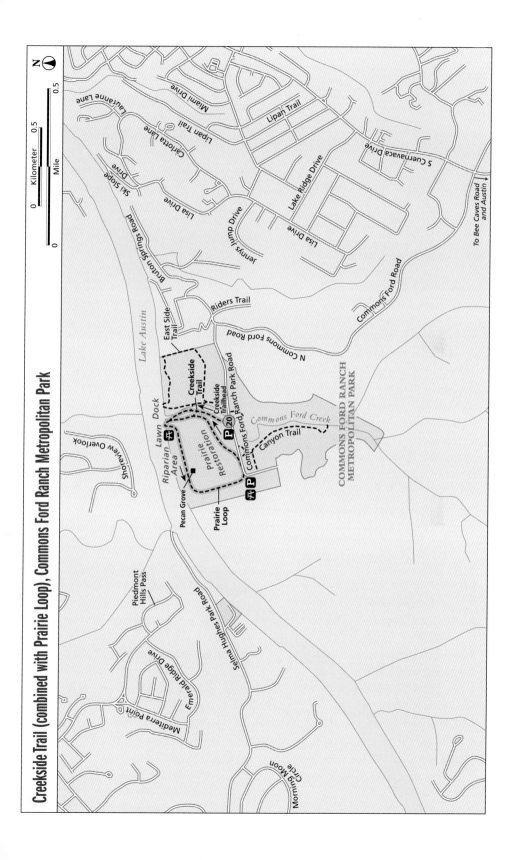

N

0   Kilometer   0.5
0   Mile   0.5

Lauranne Lane
Carlotta Lane
Lipan Trail
Miami Drive
Lipan Trail
Lake Ridge Drive
S Cuernavaca Drive
To Bee Caves Road
and Austin
Ski Slope Drive
Lisa Drive
Jennys Jump Drive
Lisa Drive
Commons Ford Road
Bruton Springs Road
Lake Austin
East Side Trail
Riders Trail
N Commons Ford Road
Creekside Trail
Creekside Trailhead
P 20
Commons Ford Ranch Park Road
Commons Ford Creek
Canyon Trail
COMMONS FORD RANCH
METROPOLITAN PARK
Lawn
Dock
Riparian Area
Prairie Restoration
Pecan Grove
Prairie Loop
P
Shoreview Overlook
Piedmont Hills Pass
Selma Hughes Park Road
Emerald Ridge Drive
Mediterra Point
Morning Moon Circle

Shores of Lake Austin

Ford Prairie." If you happen to hike through the colorful prairie during the spring and summer, note that it is lush with a myriad of butterflies waltzing among Texas thistles, purple coneflowers, antelope horn milkweed, and Texas paintbrushes. This area is also a delight for bird-watchers, thus the bird blind to your right at 0.7 miles. At 0.85 miles, continue east across the small dirt parking lot and grassy area along the fence to continue on the Prairie Loop. You will reconnect with the Prairie Loop to your left at the 0.93-mile mark. The path surface returns to mowed grass.

The trail winds north at 1.18 miles. There will also be the previously mentioned bird viewing trail that connects to the Creekside Trail to your right. Bypass the side trail and continue straight for additional mileage and to complete the Prairie Loop. You will return to the lakeshore and riparian area when the mileage clocks at 1.29 miles. Bear right back onto the Creekside Trail and head south to the trailhead.

Miles and Directions

0.0 Start at Creekside Trailhead north of the parking area and west of Commons Ford Creek.

0.11 An overlook will be to your left.

0.17 Reach a footbridge and the connection to the East Trail will be to your right. Continue straight.

0.25 Reach the lawn, dock, riparian area, and lake. Head west to continue on the Prairie Loop.

0.7 A bird blind will be to your right.

0.85 Continue east across the small dirt parking lot and grassy area along the fence to continue on the Prairie Loop.

0.93 Reconnect with the Prairie Loop to your left.

1.18 Bypass the bird viewing trail that connects to the Creekside Trail to your right.

1.29 Return to the lake and riparian area. Bear right back onto the Creekside Trail.

1.54 Arrive back at the trailhead.

21 San Marcos Riverwalk, San Marcos River Parks

While most of the area where the San Marcos River begins is protected, visitors can enjoy numerous recreational activities along the river in the area between City Park and J. J. Stokes Park. This guide takes visitors along the segment of the San Marcos River that is open to the public with a trail complete with pleasing views and direct access to the water.

Lake or river: San Marcos River
Photogenic factor: 5
Start: Trail has multiple entrances; this guide begins at Ramon Lucio Park.
Elevation gain: 545 to 617 feet
Distance: 2.06 miles out and back
Difficulty: Easy
Hiking time: About 1 hour
Seasons/schedule: Open year-round, 6 a.m. to 11 p.m.
Fees and permits: None (subject to change)

Trail contacts: San Marcos Parks and Recreation Department, 401 E Hopkins Street, San Marcos 78666; (512) 393-8400
Dog-friendly: Leashed dogs permitted
Trail surface: Paved
Land status: City of San Marcos Parks and Recreation Department
Nearest town: Within San Marcos city limits
Other trail users: Cyclists, anglers, paddlers
Maps: USGS San Marcos North; San Marcos River Parks map (available online at https://www.sanmarcostx.gov/1364/San-Marcos-River-Parks)

Finding the trailhead: Head east on Hopkins Street for 0.2 miles from the Square in San Marcos. Turn right on N C M Allen Parkway. Stay on N C M Allen Parkway for 0.7 miles. Turn left into Ramon Lucio Park. Close to 400 feet, go left toward the parking lot. The San Marcos Riverwalk has several entrance points; this guide starts the trail at the yellow metal pole and paved path where the parking lot ends. **GPS:** N29° 52.524' W97° 55.945'

The Hike

Emerging from the San Marcos Springs and Spring Lake (both fed by the Edwards Aquifer) in the heart of San Marcos is the delightful San Marcos River. It flows through the center of San Marcos before eventually joining the Blanco River just a few miles south. The San Marcos River is a refuge to several endangered species, which is the reason why most of the Spring Lake and San Marcos Springs areas have restricted public access. These endemic species include salamanders such as the Texas blind salamander and the San Marcos salamander, insects such as the Comal Springs dryopid beetle and the Peck's Cave amphipod, fish such as the fountain darter and San Marcos gambusia, and aquatic grasses such as the Texas wild rice plant.

View of the San Marcos River

The San Marcos Riverwalk covers most of the portion of the San Marcos River that is accessible to the public. It parallels the river for the majority of its route, offering excellent views and river access. It has several entrance points from each of the river parks; this guide begins at Ramon Lucio Park. Starting from the yellow metal pole northeast of the Ramon Lucio Park parking lot, you will come upon two forks. At each fork, take the left side of the fork away from the pavilion heading north. The trail will parallel the baseball fields. The trail starts to wind east at the 0.16-mile mark, and you will reach a fork once again. Take the right side of the fork toward the San Marcos River. Shy of a quarter of a mile into the trail, a river access point will be to your right. River access

Kayakers having fun on the river

San Marcos Riverwalk, San Marcos River Parks

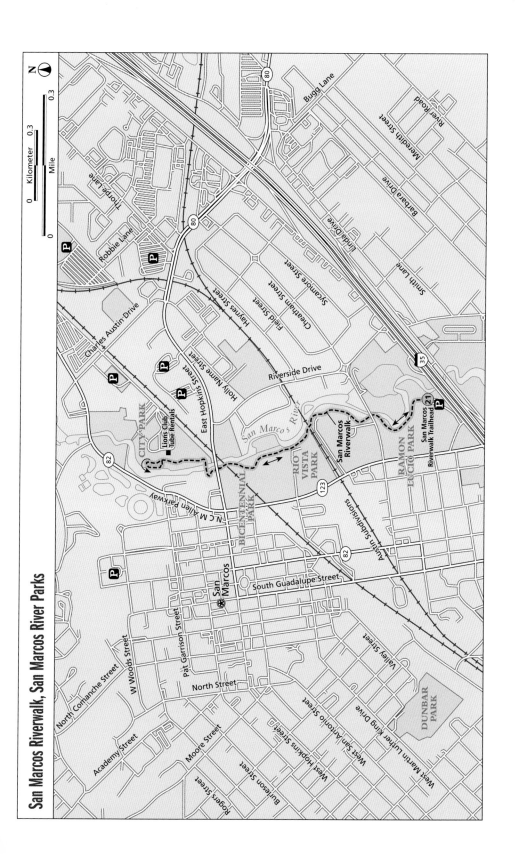

Waterfall feature near Rio Vista Park

points will continue to be available to your right at 0.32, 0.4, 0.61, and 0.72 miles. The San Marcos River is a favorite for paddlers as well. You will likely see people on the river as you meander along its banks. Prior to crossing the footbridge at the 0.64-mile mark, you will pass through several river parks—Rio Vista Park, Children's Park, and Bicentennial Park. There will be some interesting sights to stop and marvel at, including the small waterfall near Rio Vista Park, and the one-of-a-kind, Australian-made Liberty Swing at the Children's Park playscape.

Bear right across the footbridge at 0.64 miles. Bear right again across the footbridge at 0.81 miles. After going across the second footbridge, bear left at the fork at 0.93 miles. Going right will take you across the railroad tracks. At a little less than a mile, you will reach City Park and the Lions Club tube rentals building. Take the lollipop route to your left in a counterclockwise direction. You will go right along the banks of the San Marcos River on a stone ledge. After resting on the bench for a little while, head up the stairs toward the Lions Club tube rentals building. Reach the entrance to the lollipop route and then return to Ramon Lucio Park.

Miles and Directions

0.0 This guide begins at the yellow metal pole northeast of the parking lot. At both forks, take the left side, heading away from the pavilion.

0.16 Reach a fork. Bear right toward the San Marcos River.

0.24 A river access point will be to your right at this point and at 0.32, 0.4, 0.61, and 0.72 miles.

0.64 and 0.81 Bear right across the footbridge.

0.93 Reach a fork. Bear left.

0.98 Reach City Park and the Lions Club tube rentals building. Go down the stairs and bear left to take the lollipop route in a counterclockwise direction. Return the way you came.

2.06 Arrive back at the trailhead.

Honorable Mentions (Hill Country)

D Granite Trail (combined with Nature Trail), Milton Reimers Ranch Park

Milton Reimers Ranch Park is renowned for its rock-climbing opportunities, but it offers incredible hiking trails as well. Walled by rocky escarpments, the emerald-hued waters of the Pedernales River flow over a riverbed composed of flint rock. There are quite a few places along the Granite Trail where you can witness this visual. With access to the riverbanks, and river views up top, the Granite Trail is sure to please any outdoor enthusiast.

Lake or river: Pedernales River
Photogenic factor: 4+
Start: Granite Trailhead
Elevation gain: 656 to 832 feet

Distance: 4.74 miles out and back, with an optional spur down an access road to the beach
Difficulty: Moderate

View of the Pedernales River

Hiking time: 2–3 hours
Seasons/schedule: Open year-round, 7 a.m. to civil twilight
Fees and permits: $5 per person 13 years and older and $3 per senior 62 years and older (subject to change), free for Travis County Resident Annual Permit and Lifetime Senior Permit holders, cash only
Trail contacts: Milton Reimers Ranch Park Office, 23610 Hamilton Pool Road, Dripping Springs 78620; (512) 264-1923
Dog-friendly: Leashed dogs permitted
Trail surface: Granite
Land status: Travis County Parks
Nearest town: Within Dripping Springs city limits
Other trail users: Cyclists, anglers, rappelers
Maps: USGS Shingle Hills; Milton Reimers Ranch Park map (available online at https://parks.traviscountytx.gov/parks/reimers-ranch)
Special considerations: There is minimal shade on this trail. Start your hike early and bring adequate amounts of water. For additional hikes along the Pedernales River, check out the Upper River Trail and the Lower River Trail.

Finding the trailhead: Head west from downtown Austin on Bee Caves Road for 11.2 miles. Turn right onto TX 71 W. Travel on TX 71 W for 1.8 miles, and then turn left onto Hamilton Pool Road. After traveling 11.8 miles on Hamilton Pool Road, turn right onto Milton Reimers Ranch Road to enter Milton Reimers Ranch Park. Stay on Milton Reimers Ranch Road for 2.6 miles and the parking lot and trailhead will be to your left. **GPS:** N30° 21.845' W98° 07.431'

E Sandy Creek Park Trail, Sandy Creek Park

The short and sweet Sandy Creek Park Trail takes you along bluffs overlooking a secluded cove within Lake Travis. The view from the trail is stunning all day, but especially at sunset.

Lake or river: Lake Travis
Photogenic factor: 4
Start: Sandy Creek Trailhead, south of parking lot
Elevation gain: 620 to 697 feet
Distance: 0.4 miles out and back
Difficulty: Easy
Hiking time: 30 minutes
Seasons/schedule: Open year-round, sunrise to 8 p.m.
Fees and permits: $5 per person 13 years and older and $3 per senior 62 years and older (subject to change), free for Travis County
Resident Annual Permit and Lifetime Senior Permit holders
Trail contacts: Sandy Creek Park Office, 9500 Lime Creek Road, Leander 78641; (512) 854-7275
Dog-friendly: Leashed dogs permitted
Trail surface: Dirt
Land status: Travis County Parks
Nearest town: Within Austin city limits
Other trail users: None
Maps: USGS Mansfield Dam; Sandy Creek Park map (available online at https://parks.traviscountytx.gov/parks)

Finding the trailhead: Head north from downtown Austin on TX 1 Loop N for 6.4 miles. Take the exit for US 183 and Research Boulevard. Merge onto US 183 N after 0.2 miles, and then stay on US 183 N for 5 miles. Exit off US 183 N for Anderson Mill Road. Stay on Research Boulevard for 1.2 miles. Turn left on Anderson Mill Road. Continue on Anderson Mill Road for 6 miles. Go

Sunset on Lake Travis

left on Lime Creek Road. After 4.8 miles on Lime Creek Road, turn right into Sandy Creek Park. After 170 feet and passing by the park entrance booth, turn left. The Sandy Creek Trail has several entrance points; this guide starts at the trailhead at the very end of the parking lot about 400 feet into the road after you turn left. **GPS:** N30°28.156' W97°54.444'

F Lake View Lake Loop, Brushy Creek Lake Park

Brushy Creek Lake Park is a popular urban destination during the spring because of the incredible number of bluebonnets that bloom in concentration there. With Brushy Creek Lake as a backdrop and connections to the Brushy Creek Regional Trail for extra mileage, the loop around the lake is perfect for photo opportunities and exercise.

Lake or river: Brushy Creek Lake
Photogenic factor: 4+
Start: Lake View Lake Loop Trailhead
Elevation gain: 797 to 833 feet
Distance: 0.94-mile loop
Difficulty: Easy
Hiking time: 30 minutes
Seasons/schedule: Open year-round, 5 a.m. to 10 p.m.

Fees and permits: None (subject to change)
Trail contacts: City of Cedar Park Parks and Recreation Department Office, 1435 Main Street, Cedar Park 78613; (512) 401-5500
Dog-friendly: Leashed dogs permitted
Trail surface: Paved
Land status: City of Cedar Park Parks and Recreation Department
Nearest town: Within Cedar Park city limits

Blooming bluebonnets at Brushy Creek Lake

Other trail users: Mountain bikers/cyclists
Maps: USGS Leander; Brushy Creek Lake Park map (stationed at the park)

Special considerations: To add mileage, this trail connects with the Brushy Creek Regional Trail.

Finding the trailhead: From downtown Austin, travel on TX 1 Loop N for 10 miles and then take the exit for Palmer Lane. Merge onto Mopac Service Road. In half a mile, go left onto Palmer Lane. Travel on Palmer Lane for 7.9 miles. Turn right onto Brushy Creek Road. After 0.2 miles, head south into Brushy Creek Lake Park. The trail can be accessed anywhere from the parking lot. **GPS:** N30° 30.470' W97° 46.327'

G Overlook Trail, Overlook Park

The 8,240-acre Canyon Lake is a recreational destination within Hill Country. With its limestone shores and cliffs and clear waters, residents and tourists flock to the lake for the leisure it offers. Hikers who go on the Overlook Trail at Overlook Park will be able to enjoy the scenery of Canyon Lake and its shoreline.

Lake or river: Canyon Lake
Photogenic factor: 4
Start: Overlook Trailhead
Elevation gain: 909 to 993 feet
Distance: 0.84 miles out and back

Difficulty: Easy
Hiking time: 30 minutes–1 hour
Seasons/schedule: Open year-round, 8 a.m. to 7 p.m.
Fees and permits: None (subject to change)

Trail contacts: US Army Corps of Engineers Canyon Lake Office, 601 Corps of Engineers Road, Canyon Lake 78133; (830) 964-3341
Dog-friendly: Leashed dogs permitted
Trail surface: Dirt and gravel
Land status: US Army Corps of Engineers

Nearest town: San Marcos (east), New Braunfels (southeast)
Other trail users: Anglers
Maps: USGS Sattler; Overlook Park map (available online at https://www.canyonlake guide.com/helpful_info/park_information/ OverlookPark.pdf)

Finding the trailhead: From downtown San Antonio, get onto I-35 N by taking the I-35/US 281 N/I-37 N on-ramp. Stay on I-35 N for close to 33 miles before taking exit 191 for FM 306/ Canyon Lake. Once you reach the intersection for FM 306, go left. Continue on FM 306 for 14.3 miles. Turn left onto S Access Road. After 0.7 miles, turn right onto Corps of Engineers Road. The trailhead will be 0.6 miles north of the second parking lot. **GPS:** N29° 51.662' W98° 11.887'

View of Canyon Lake

South Texas Plains

Daybreak at Lake Casa Blanca (Hike 23)

22 Elmendorf Lake Loop, Elmendorf Lake Park

The serenity of Elmendorf Lake makes it a scenic treasure in the heart of West San Antonio. The astounding twin-spired Gothic chapel of Our Lady of the Lake University is distinguishable south of the lake. Ducks and egrets traverse under the lake's scenic bridges and find respite on Bird Island or under the swaying branches of the bald cypress trees along the shore.

Lake or river: Elmendorf Lake
Photogenic factor: 5
Start: Trail has multiple trailheads; guide begins at the parking lot at the southeast corner of SW 24th Street and W Commerce Street
Elevation gain: 623 to 669 feet
Distance: 1.2-mile loop
Difficulty: Easy
Hiking time: About 1 hour
Seasons/schedule: Open year-round, 5 a.m. to 11 p.m.
Fees and permits: None (subject to change)

Trail contacts: San Antonio Parks and Recreation Department, 5800 Old Highway 90, San Antonio 78227; (210) 207-8480
Dog-friendly: Leashed dogs permitted
Trail surface: Paved
Land status: City of San Antonio
Nearest town: Within San Antonio city limits
Other trail users: Cyclists, anglers, kayakers
Maps: USGS San Antonio West; City of San Antonio Elmendorf Lake Park trail accessibility map (available online at https://www.sanantonio.gov/Portals/0/Files/Parks/pdf/Elmendorf_map.pdf)

Finding the trailhead: From 3rd Street/E Martin Street and the N Colorado Street intersection in downtown San Antonio, travel on E Martin Street for 1.4 miles. Turn left on N Colorado Street. After 0.3 miles, turn right onto W Commerce Street. Continue west on Commerce Street for 1.8 miles. The Elmendorf Lake Park parking area will be to your left before the SW 24th Street intersection. The Elmendorf Lake Loop can be accessed from several points; this guide begins at the Biofiltration plaque. **GPS:** N29° 25.745' W98° 32.472'

The Hike

Elmendorf Lake is situated in an area that was once called "Lake View" in the late 19th century. The landowner, Amalie Elmendorf, had a vision for this region to be one of the most desirable neighborhoods in San Antonio. However, this vision never came to fruition due to a nationwide recession. The area ended up being sold to the city of San Antonio in the spring of 1917 with the following conditions: that the city rebuild the dam, continue to upkeep the area, and further the beautification of the land. Fast-forward to the year 2017, when Elmendorf Lake Park reopened with restorations and new amenities, thanks to the combination of a bond that was approved by voters in 2012 and funds provided by the city of San Antonio and the county. San

Elmendorf Lake in the autumn

Antonians and visitors alike can now enjoy the beauty of Elmendorf Lake with the stunning Our Lady of the Lake University in the background.

The trail can be accessed from multiple points along its route, as it loops around Elmendorf Lake. This guide begins at the "Biofiltration" plaque east of the main parking area and takes the loop in a clockwise direction, heading east. Take note of

ENVIRONMENTAL SUSTAINABILITY

Various landscape features were added to Elmendorf Lake Park that not only add to its beauty, but also help preserve and protect its ecosystem. Pollutants and stormwater runoff are blocked from entering the lake by various bioswales. Any stormwater that flows through the park is filtered within the rain gardens composed of particularly chosen dense vegetation and grasses. In addition to the carefully designed landscape, the park has three aeration fountains that contribute oxygen to the water, promoting a balanced and healthy environment for wildlife. The use of fertilizer on the landscape is also limited, reducing the number of pollutants entering the lake.

the many informational plaques along the Elmendorf Lake Park Trail. Not only do they describe the unique wildlife of Elmendorf Lake, but they also reveal the many eco-friendly features that have been incorporated. Within a couple hundred feet, you will come upon a picnic area with benches, one of several similar areas along the trail. A "Restoring Water Quality" plaque will be to your right. Before you reach Lake Plaza at 580 feet, you will come upon another picnic area with benches. An "Oscar Alvarado" plaque will be to your right. The vibrant benches within Lake Plaza feature mosaic tiles handlaid by artist Oscar Alvarado. Both the colors of the mosaics used and the abstract designs created by Alvarado were inspired by the flora and fauna of the lake.

At the 0.20-mile mark, a "Bald Cypress" plaque will be to your right. This sign explains the characteristics of the deciduous conifers that line the lake shoreline. In the fall, Elmendorf Lake is graced by the fiery cinnamon and golden hues of these grand trees. You will bear right across the first of three steel bridges shortly after a quarter of a mile on the trail. The bridge ends at 0.30 miles, and then you will bear left to go across the second steel bridge. Right before the second bridge, you will see a "Water Cycle" plaque. Bear right across the bridge. The second bridge ends at the 0.36-mile mark. Bear right to continue on the loop. A little over half a mile on the trail, you will see Bird Island to your right. Bird Island is a sanctuary and nesting area for many types of birds, including herons, ducks, egrets, and cormorants.

You will go under the SW 24th Street overpass at 0.61 miles. The trail eventually curves and heads north before you reach the third steel bridge at the 0.88-mile mark. The bridge ends at 0.92 miles where you will then bear right to continue on the loop. (Be aware that the waysides of this trail to the 1-mile mark can be covered in refuse.) You will go back under the SW 24th Street overpass at 1.08 miles. You will reach another picnic area with benches shortly after, as well as the "Life Above the Lake" and "Life on Bird Island" plaques. Make sure to enjoy the breathtaking views of the lake, most spectacularly at sunset, before returning to the parking area at 1.20 miles.

Elmendorf Lake Loop, Elmendorf Lake Park

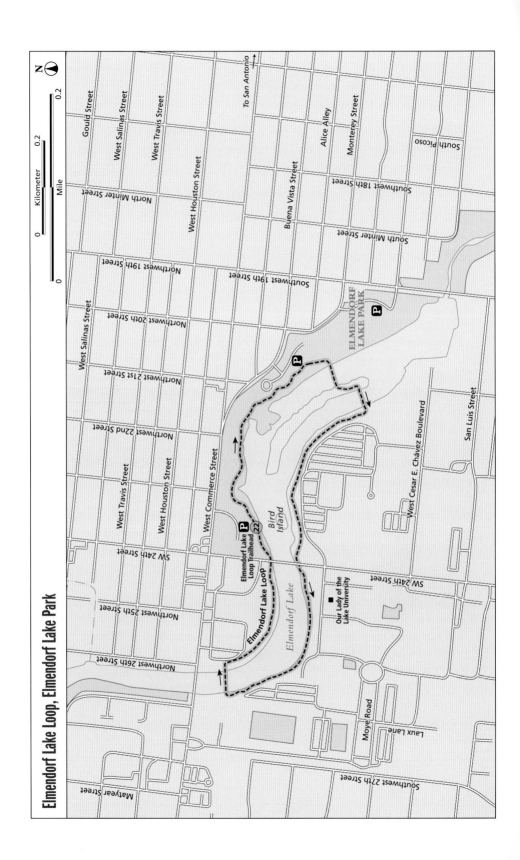

Pedestrian bridge on the Elmendorf Lake Loop

Miles and Directions

0.0 Begin at the "Biofiltration" plaque east of the parking area. This guide takes the loop in a clockwise direction.

0.04 and 0.08 Reach benches and a picnic area.

0.11 Reach Lake Plaza.

0.26 Bear right across the steel bridge.

0.3 The bridge ends. Bear left to go across another bridge.

0.32 Reach the second steel bridge. Bear right across the bridge.

0.36 The bridge ends. Bear right to continue the loop.

0.55 Bird Island will be to your right.

0.61 Head under the SW 24th Street overpass.

0.88 Head east across the third steel bridge.

0.92 The bridge ends. Bear right.

1.08 Return under the SW 24th Street overpass.

1.13 Reach benches and a picnic area.

1.2 The trail ends at the parking area.

23 Roadrunner Trail, Lake Casa Blanca International State Park

Situated in an arid landscape, the 1,600-plus acre Lake Casa Blanca provides refuge and sustenance to many flora and fauna. The mesquite-lined Roadrunner Trail is a lovely and easy route paralleling the lake. The trail is especially mesmerizing at sunrise, when hikers can have the chance to observe numerous flocks of birds delighting in the waters of Lake Casa Blanca.

Lake or river: Lake Casa Blanca
Photogenic factor: 4+
Start: Roadrunner Trailhead
Elevation gain: 446 to 473 feet
Distance: 1.92 miles out and back
Difficulty: Easy
Hiking time: 30 minutes–1 hour
Seasons/schedule: Open year-round, 7 a.m. to 10 p.m.
Fees and permits: $4 (non-peak season) and $5 (peak season) per person 13 years and older (subject to change), free for Texas State Parks Pass holders
Trail contacts: Lake Casa Blanca International State Park Headquarters, 5102 Bob Bullock Loop, Laredo 78041; (956) 725-3826

Dog-friendly: Leashed dogs permitted
Trail surface: Dirt and gravel
Land status: Texas Parks and Wildlife Department
Nearest town: Within Laredo city limits
Other trail users: Mountain bikers/cyclists
Maps: USGS Laredo East; Lake Casa Blanca International State Park map (available online at www.tpwd.texas.gov/state-parks/parks-map and via the TX State Parks mobile app)
Special considerations: There is no shade on the trail. Start your hike early and bring adequate amounts of water. At times, thorns from the mesquite trees can fall onto the trail. Make sure to wear closed-toe shoes.

Finding the trailhead: Head north on I-35 N from downtown Laredo and take exit 2. Merge onto San Dario Avenue. After 0.3 miles, turn right onto Lafayette Street. Lafayette Street eventually changes into W Saunders Street. Continue on W Saunders Street for 3.4 miles. Turn left to merge onto TX 20 Loop N/Bob Bullock Loop. After traveling on Bob Bullock Loop for 0.7 miles, turn right into Lake Casa Blanca International State Park. After 0.1 miles, turn right onto State Senator Judith Zaffirini Road. The Roadrunner Trailhead will be to your right (south of the parking area) after 1 mile. There is another entrance point for the Roadrunner Trail near the Recreation Hall Day-Use Area; this guide starts from the entrance with the Mesquite Bend Trail. The Mesquite Bend Trailhead is at the same location as the Roadrunner Trailhead but heads east. **GPS:** N27° 31.982' W99° 26.321'

The Hike

The topography where Lake Casa Blanca now lies was very different from the dry Western Rio Grande Plain it has now become. Over 40 million years ago, it used to be a swampy area along the Gulf of Mexico, shrouded by mangrove palm forests. In the entirety of North America, mangrove palms were only to be found here.

Sunrise at Lake Casa Blanca

Oysters made their home in this area as well, where the salt water from the ocean mixed with the fresh water of the river. Fast-forward to today—the coastline of the Gulf of Mexico is now hundreds of miles away, and what remains of those days are fossils of marine life. Lake Casa Blanca provides nourishment and refuge as its former landscape. As a haven for many migratory and wading birds, its most distinguishing service is that it serves as a breeding ground for the Morelet's seedeater. The Morelet's seedeater has not been seen in recent decades in the United States, except for Lake Casa Blanca International State Park and the Falcon Dam area. Visitors to Lake Casa Blanca International State Park may have the opportunity to catch a glimpse of this species. Javelina, white-tailed deer, and armadillos are also inhabitants of the park.

The Roadrunner Trail meanders along the top of the earthen Lake Casa Blanca Dam. Finished in 1951, the dam sits on Chacon Creek, impounding the water that forms Lake Casa Blanca. The height of the dam provides hikers with bird's-eye views of the lake. The trail begins south of the parking lot and at the same location as the Mesquite Bend Trailhead. The Roadrunner Trail heads west, while the Mesquite Bend Trail heads east. At about 200 feet onto the trail, you will pass through a fence gate. Views of Lake Casa Blanca will be to your right and mesquite trees will border the majority of the trail.

At 0.36 miles, there will be a "Small Animals, Big Impact" interpretive wayside and an overlook for a bat roosting site will be on your left. Nowadays, bats are less common. Make sure to check with the park headquarters about the best possibilities

Roadrunner Trail, Lake Casa Blanca International State Park

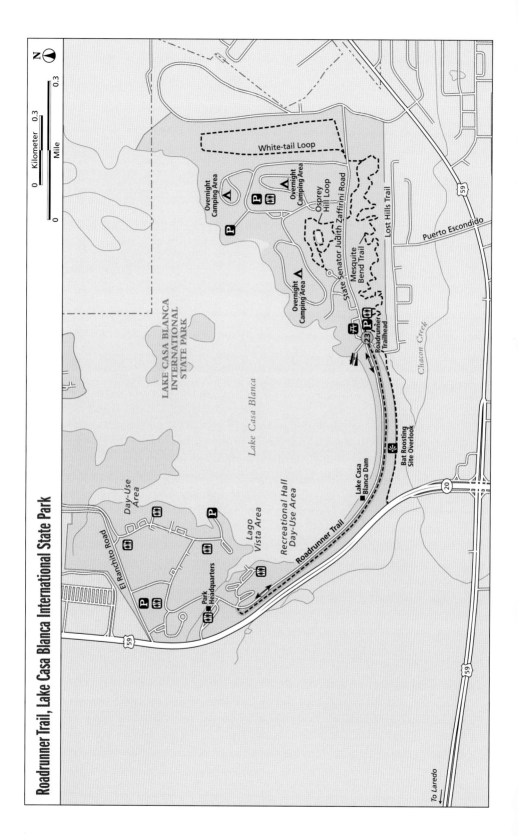

N

0   Kilometer   0.3

0   Mile   0.3

White-tail Loop

Overnight Camping Area

Overnight Camping Area

Overnight Camping Area

Osprey Hill Loop

State Senator Judith Zaffirini Road

Mesquite Bend Trail

Lost Hills Trail

Puerto Escondido

59

LAKE CASA BLANCA INTERNATIONAL STATE PARK

Lake Casa Blanca

Roadrunner Trailhead

23

Chacon Creek

Day-Use Area

El Ranchito Road

Lago Vista Area

Recreational Hall Day-Use Area

Roadrunner Trail

Lake Casa Blanca Dam

Bat Roosting Site Overlook

Park Headquarters

59

20

59

To Laredo

Birds who call Lake Casa Blanca home   *Mesquite trees along the Roadrunner Trail*

to view the bats from the overlook and other places within the park if you are interested. The trail curves northwest at 0.4 miles. TX 20 Loop N/Bob Bullock Loop will parallel the park boundary to your left. It can be a bit noisy depending on the time of the day, but not overpowering. Views of Lake Casa Blanca will continue to your right. At the 0.96-mile mark, you will reach the other entrance/exit for the Roadrunner Trail. The Recreation Hall Day-Use Area and Lago Vista Area will be to your right. At this point, turn around and return the way you came.

Miles and Directions

0.0 The trailhead begins south of the parking lot. Bear right to start on the Roadrunner Trail.

0.04 Pass through a fence gate. Views of Lake Casa Blanca will be to your right.

0.36 An overlook for a bat roosting site will be to your left.

0.4 TX 20 Loop N/Bob Bullock Loop will parallel the park boundary to your left. Views of Lake Casa Blanca will continue to your right.

0.96 Reach the other entrance/exit for Roadrunner Trail. The Recreation Hall Day-Use Area and Lago Vista Area will be to your right. Return the way you came.

1.92 Arrive back at the trailhead.

24 Falcon State Park Hiking Trail Loop, Falcon State Park

Although not nearly as wide as it was when it was built in the 1950s, the Falcon International Reservoir still continues to attract hikers and fishermen. Texas Lantana bloom within Tamaulipan scrub brush, and butterflies waltz among the varied florae and cacti on the hilly landscape. The Hiking Trail Loop takes hikers through the sundry landscapes within Falcon State Park, with views of Falcon International Reservoir along the way.

Lake or river: Falcon International Reservoir
Photogenic factor: 4
Start: Whitebrush Trailhead
Elevation gain: 243 to 344 feet
Distance: 2.52-mile loop
Difficulty: Easy
Hiking time: 1–2 hours
Seasons/schedule: Open year-round, 6 a.m. to 10 p.m.
Fees and permits: $3 (non-holiday) and $5 (holiday) per person 13 years and older (subject to change), free for Texas State Parks Pass holders
Trail contacts: Falcon State Park Headquarters, 146 Park Road 46, Falcon Heights 78545; (956) 848-5327
Dog-friendly: Leashed dogs permitted
Trail surface: Dirt and gravel

Land status: Texas Parks and Wildlife Department
Nearest town: Falcon Heights (southeast), Zapata and Laredo (north)
Other trail users: Mountain bikers/cyclists
Maps: USGS Falcon Village; Falcon State Park map (available online at www.tpwd.texas.gov/state-parks/parks-map and via the TX State Parks mobile app)
Special considerations: This route combines multiple trails to make it a loop. Trails are hiked in this order: Whitebrush Trail, Woodlands Trail, Desert Trail, Verdin Trail, and the Roadrunner Trail. There is minimal shade on this trail. Start your hike early and bring adequate amounts of water. During dry spells and summers, lake water levels can be low. Contact the park headquarters to check on current lake water levels.

Finding the trailhead: Head east on US 83 from downtown Laredo. US 83 eventually heads south. Close to 76 miles, turn right onto FM 2098/Ranch Road 2098. Continue on FM 2098/Ranch Road 2098 for 2.7 miles. Turn right onto Park Road 46. After 1 mile, you will reach the Falcon State Park Headquarters. The Whitebrush Trailhead will be north of the parking lot next to the park headquarters. **GPS:** N26° 34.991' W99° 08.566'

The Hike

This guide combines several connecting trails in Falcon State Park to comprise the Hiking Trail Loop. Several benches will be available along the route. The Hiking Trail Loop begins with the Whitebrush Trail and ends with the Roadrunner Trail. Within 100 feet on the trail, the trail heads west and its surface turns rocky. At the 265-foot

Falcon State Park Hiking Trail Loop, Falcon State Park

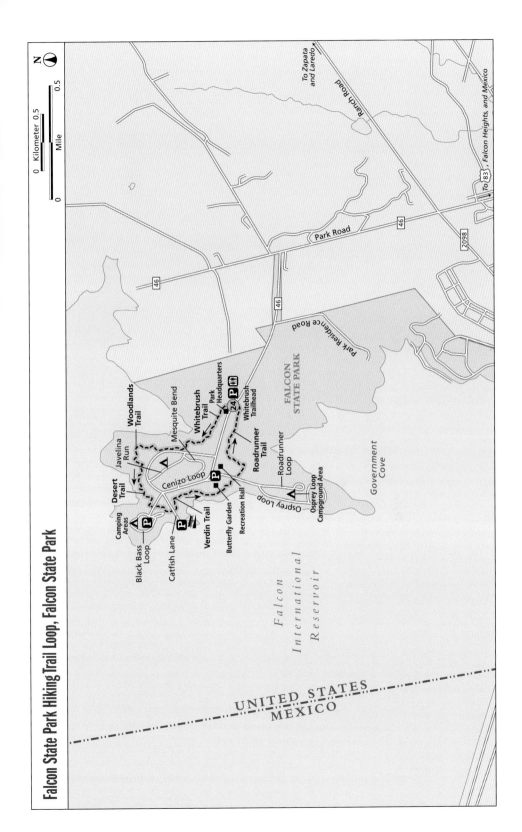

View of Falcon International Reservoir from the trail

mark, you will make a 10-foot descent to the 445-foot mark. Continue straight when you reach the fork. The left side leads to a helicopter crash commemoration site. In January 2003, two AH1W Super Cobra helicopters that were part of an evening counter-drug patrol with Joint Task Force Six in support of the U.S. Border Patrol, accidentally crashed into each other near the Falcon State Park headquarters. Tragically, all four members of the Marines onboard the helicopters passed away in the fiery crash.

The trail heads northwest at 0.28 miles. At 0.45 miles, bypass the offshoot to your left. Continue straight toward the benches and onto the Woodlands Trail. The Woodlands Trail interchanges from heading west and south a couple times before you connect with the Desert Trail. Bear right at the fork at 0.97 miles to continue onto the Desert Trail. The left side is an offshoot. Shy of a mile onto the trail, the trail heads southwest. The surface turns rocky until the 1.04-mile mark.

At 1.07 miles, views of the Falcon International Reservoir will open up to your right. In times of drought and during the summer, water levels can be low. Even at lower water levels, the reservoir provides a beautiful, calming scene. The trail then heads southwest. You will reach the road to the Black Bass Loop at the 1.26-mile mark. Watch for vehicles before crossing the road and then look for the brown sign at

the 1.27-mile mark to reconnect with the Desert Trail. The trail heads south shortly after. Views of the Falcon International Reservoir will be available again to your right at 1.31 miles. When you reach the fork at 1.37 miles, bear left to head toward Catfish Lane and the boat ramp area. The right leads to the Black Bass Loop. You will come upon Catfish Lane and the boat ramp parking area at 1.39 miles. Views of Falcon International Reservoir and, on a clear day, the Picachos Mountains in Mexico can be seen from here and at the Verdin Trailhead. Connect with the Verdin Trailhead at the 1.42-mile mark by heading east toward the boat ramp parking area. A brown sign will help you to stay on the trail. The trail heads south and then views of the Falcon International Reservoir will become available to your right once again, and this time the view is more panoramic.

You will come upon a covered picnic table area at 1.59 miles. Several of them will be dispersed to your right. Take the opportunity to have a snack or a meal with some relief from the sun. Once you are finished, begin to head across the picnic area parking lot at 1.62 miles. Continue straight and you will pass more covered picnic benches to your right. Views of the Falcon International Reservoir continue on your right. You will reconnect with the Verdin Trail at 1.67 miles. The last covered picnic table will be available at 1.77 miles, where you will reach a fork. Continue straight on the Verdin Trail.

The trail heads southeast at the 1.88-mile mark and then you will reach the road to Osprey Loop/Roadrunner Loop shortly after. Watch for vehicles when crossing the road. Connect with the Roadrunner Trailhead by looking for the brown sign at the 1.92-mile mark. Bypass the offshoot to your right at 1.96 miles and then the trail curves northeast and then east. Follow the sign with an arrow to continue heading east on the trail. The trail eventually curves northwest at 2.44 miles, before concluding southeast of the park headquarters and parking lot at 2.52 miles. If you have extra time to explore Falcon State Park, stop by the lovely butterfly garden that is adjacent to the recreation hall, north of the Verdin Trail segment.

Miles and Directions

0.0 The Hiking Trail Loop begins with the Whitebrush Trail, north of the parking lot for the park headquarters.

0.02 The path gets rocky.

0.05 Make a 10-foot descent from here to the 0.08-mile mark.

0.08 Reach a fork. Continue straight.

0.45 Bypass the offshoot to your left. Continue straight onto the Woodlands Trail.

0.97 Reach a fork. Bear right to continue onto the Desert Trail.

0.99 The path gets a bit rocky until the 1.04-mile mark.

1.07 Views of the Falcon International Reservoir open up to your right.

1.26 Reach the road that goes to the Black Bass Loop. Watch for vehicles before crossing the road. Reconnect with the Desert Trail at the 1.27-mile mark.

1.31 Views of the Falcon International Reservoir will be available to your right.

1.37 Reach a fork. Bear left to head toward Catfish Lane and the boat ramp area.

1.39 Reach Catfish Lane and the boat ramp parking area. Views of Falcon International Reservoir and the Picachos Mountains in Mexico can be seen from here as well as at the Verdin Trailhead. Connect with the Verdin Trailhead by heading toward the boat ramp parking area.

1.42 Look for the brown sign to stay on the trail. Head east.

1.56 Views of the Falcon International Reservoir will be to your right.

1.62 Go across the picnic area parking lot. Views of the Falcon International Reservoir continue on your right. You will reconnect with the Verdin Trail at 1.67 miles.

1.77 Reach a fork. Continue straight on the Verdin Trail. Bypass the offshoot to the left.

1.9 Reach the road to the Osprey Loop/Roadrunner Loop. Watch for vehicles when crossing the road. Connect with the Roadrunner Trailhead at the 1.92-mile mark.

1.96 Bypass the offshoot to your right.

2.02 Follow the sign with an arrow to continue heading east.

2.52 Arrive back at the trailhead.

Lantana blooming at Falcon State Park

25 Wader's Trail (with Alligator Lake and Llano Grande Lake), Estero Llano Grande State Park

Situated along the corridor of a major avian migration route, Estero Llano Grande State Park treats hikers to sights of all sorts of stunning birds. Several bodies of water were developed by biologists within the park to restore the area to its original ecosystem. These bodies of water not only draw migratory birds, but also other animals, such as the American alligator.

Lake or river: Alligator Lake, Llano Grande Lake, Kiskadee Pond, Ibis Pond, and Dowitcher Pond

Photogenic factor: 4+

Start: Wader's Trailhead

Elevation gain: 39 to 75 feet

Distance: 3-mile lollipop with 2 additional spurs

Difficulty: Easy

Hiking time: 1–2 hours

Seasons/schedule: Open year-round; headquarters hours are 8 a.m. to 5 p.m.

Fees and permits: $5 per person 13 years and older (subject to change), free for Texas State Parks Pass holders

Trail contacts: Estero Llano Grande State Park Headquarters, 3301 S International Boulevard (FM 1015), Weslaco 78596; (956) 565-3919

Dog-friendly: Leashed dogs permitted

Trail surface: Dirt and gravel; majority of the Wader's Trail segment is ADA accessible

Land status: Texas Parks and Wildlife Department

Nearest town: Located between Weslaco and Mercedes City, McAllen (west), Harlingen (east)

Other trail users: Mountain bikers/cyclists

Maps: USGS Mercedes; Estero Llano Grande State Park map (available online at www.tpwd.texas.gov/state-parks/parks-map and via the TX State Parks mobile app)

Special considerations: There is no shade on the Llano Grande Hiking Trail portion of the route. Start your hike early and bring adequate amounts of water. Ibis Pond and Dowitcher Pond are dry in the summer (and anytime there is a drought). Allowing the ponds to be dry in the summer helps with vegetation management and the opportunity to add logs to the ponds for the birds to perch on. Both ponds usually are restocked with water in late August or September. Check with the park headquarters for current water level conditions. Alligators live in the waters of Alligator Lake. Exercise caution and maintain a distance of at least 30 feet if an alligator is sighted.

Finding the trailhead: From the Commerce Street/Harrison Avenue intersection in Harlingen, head west on Harrison Avenue for 1.8 miles before merging onto I-2 W/US 83. Continue west on I-2/US 83 for 14.3 miles and then take exit 160. After a mile, go left onto N International Boulevard/Mile 3 Road W. After traveling on N International Boulevard/Mile 3 Road W for 2.3 miles, turn left onto Lakeview Drive and enter Estero Llano Grande State Park. No vehicles are allowed in the park. Park in the parking lot. The Wader's Trail starts south of the parking lot. **GPS:** N26° 07.607' W97° 57.473'

View of Alligator Lake from the trail

The Hike

The Wader's Trail begins south of the parking lot. In about 85 feet, bear left down the pavers to head toward the park headquarters. The trail heads south toward the park headquarters at about 425 feet into the trail. You will reach the park headquarters to your right at 0.1 miles. Head east curving through the hallway for the restrooms to connect with the concrete path. The trail heads primarily east until the 0.31-mile mark. At 0.13 miles, a "Gardening for Wildlife and You" interpretive wayside will be to your right. The path changes to a dirt and gravel surface shortly after.

Ibis Pond and an "Incredible Insects" interpretive wayside will be to your right at 0.15 miles. Bypass the connection to the Spoonbill Trail to your right. During the summer and in times of drought, Ibis Pond will likely be dried up. Make sure to check with the park headquarters about current water levels. When there is water in the ponds, you might catch a glimpse of the beautiful white ibis with their reddish-pink bills and legs or even the stunning roseate spoonbill. At 0.23 miles, continue straight at the fork. The right side of the fork is the Llano Grande Hiking Trail. Dowitcher Pond will be to your right at 0.27 miles. It suffers a similar fate to Ibis Pond, so again please check with the park headquarters for current water levels. Both Ibis Pond and Dowitcher Pond are generally restocked around late August or September on an annual basis.

When you come upon the fork at 0.31 miles, bear left to curve toward the boardwalk and bridge. Heading this way will lead you to Alligator Lake. The right side is a continuation of the Wader's Trail. This guide will return to this fork and have you complete the Wader's Trail after you hike to Alligator's Lake and the Llano Grande Hiking Trail. The bridge ends at the 0.32-mile mark. Bear right toward Alligator Lake. The left is part of the Camino de Aves trail. When you encounter another fork shortly after, do the same as you did at the other fork. Continue straight onto the Connector Trail toward Alligator Lake. The left side is again part of the Camino de Aves trail.

Grebe Marsh will appear to your left at 0.36 miles, with a couple benches shortly after. When you reach the fork at 0.43 miles, bear left toward Alligator Lake. Straight ahead is a continuation of the Connector Trail. This guide will take this route to the Llano Grande

A raft of ducks at Alligator Lake

Hiking Trail after you visit Alligator Lake. A picnic area will be to your left and a bench to your right just short of half a mile. A "Woodland Wonders" interpretive wayside will be to your right shortly after. You will reach the observation deck for the Alligator Lake Scenic Overlook at the 0.52-mile mark. A "Teeming with Life" interpretive wayside will also be at this point. In the mornings, you might be able to spot an alligator. Return the way you came to the original 0.43-mile mark.

The mileage clocks at 0.64 miles when you reach the fork from the original 0.43-mile mark. Bear left to continue on the Connector Trail to the Llano Grande Hiking Trail. Shy of three-quarters of a mile into the trail, the surface becomes no longer ADA accessible. You will make a 5-foot ascent from this point to the 0.77-mile mark. At 0.77 miles, you will reach a fork and an embankment to Llano Grande Lake. Bear left to head toward Kiskadee Pond. Lake views will be to your right. One mile into the trail, you will reach another fork. Continue straight on the Llano Grande Hiking Trail. The left is an additional connection to the Camino de Aves trail. Kiskadee Pond will appear to your left at 1.23 miles, and then the trail curves east until you reach the park boundary at 1.33 miles. A maintenance road will be to your left. Turn around and return to the fork at the 0.77-mile mark. The mileage will read as 1.89

Birds find refuge at Llano Grande Lake

miles when you get back to that fork. Bear right back onto the Connector Trail to return to the Wader's Trail connection at the original 0.31-mile mark.

It will be 2.16 miles into the hike when you reach the fork from the original 0.31-mile mark. Bear left to continue on the Wader's Trail. The trail surface becomes ADA accessible once again. There will be several times where you will need to continue straight on the Wader's Trail when you encounter forks from the 2.31-mile mark to the 2.48-mile mark. There will be connections to the Spoonbill Trail and the Llano Grande Hiking Trails that you will need to bypass as the trail heads west. At two and a half miles into the trail, you will need to bear left to continue on the Wader's Trail. Straight is the Llano Grande Hiking Trail. When you reach the "Sit and Enjoy" interpretive wayside and Ibis Pond at 2.6 miles, the path can get a bit tricky. Bear left toward the fork at the 2.71-mile mark to take the right side for the Wader's Trail. Paths to the north and south are part of the Spoonbill Trail.

You will reach the final fork of the trail at 2.78 miles. Continue straight on the Wader's Trail. The left is the Flycatcher Trail. When you come upon the west side of the park headquarters at 2.9 miles, the trail surface becomes non-ADA accessible. Continue straight along the northern wall of the park headquarters. There will be a side trail to the west that goes to a Park Host area. When you reach the familiar pavers leading to the park headquarters at 2.95 miles, bear right to return to the trailhead.

Wader's Trail (with Alligator Lake and Llano Grande Lake), Estero Llano Grande State Park

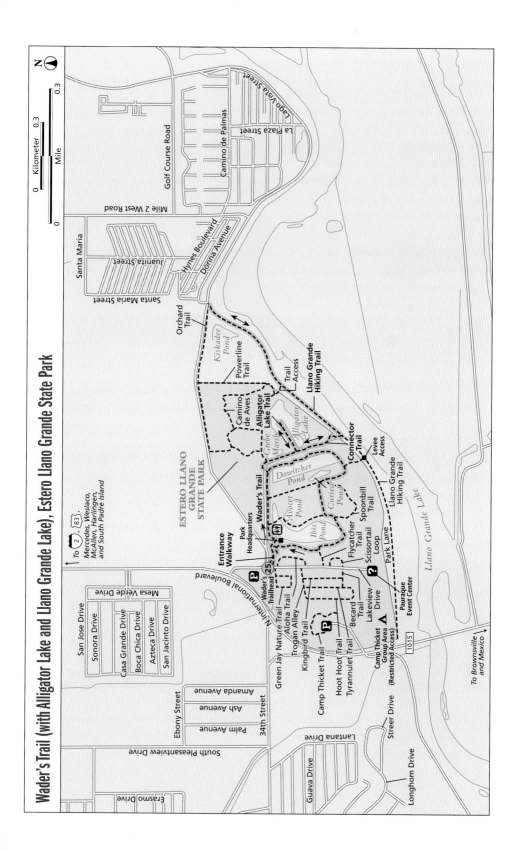

Miles and Directions

0.0 The Wader's Trail starts south of the parking lot.

0.02 Bear left down pavers to head toward the park headquarters.

0.1 Reach the park headquarters to your right. Head east curving through the hallway for the restrooms to connect with the concrete path.

0.13 The path changes to a gravel surface shortly after.

0.15 Ibis Pond will be to your right. Bypass the connection to the Spoonbill Trail to your right.

0.23 Reach a fork. Continue straight.

0.27 Dowitcher Pond will be to your right.

0.31 Reach a fork. Bear left toward the boardwalk and bridge to head to Alligator Lake.

0.32 The bridge ends. Bear right toward Alligator Lake.

0.34 Reach a fork. Continue straight onto the Connector Trail toward Alligator Lake.

0.36 Grebe Marsh will be to your left.

0.43 Reach a fork. Bear left toward Alligator Lake.

0.52 Reach the observation deck for the Alligator Lake Scenic Overlook. Return to the original 0.43-mile mark.

0.64 Reach the fork from the original 0.43-mile mark. Bear left to continue on the Connector Trail.

0.74 The surface is no longer ADA accessible. Make a 5-foot ascent to the 0.77-mile mark.

0.77 Reach Llano Grande Lake. Bear left to take the Llano Grande Hiking Trail to Kiskadee Pond. Lake views will be to your right.

1.0 Reach a fork. Continue straight.

1.23 Partial views of Kiskadee Pond will be to your left.

1.33 Reach the park boundary. Return to the fork at the 0.77-mile mark.

1.89 Reach the fork from the original 0.77-mile mark. Bear right to return to the Wader's Trail connection at the original 0.31-mile mark.

2.16 Reach the fork from the original 0.31-mile mark. Bear left to complete the Wader's Trail. The trail surface becomes ADA accessible again.

2.31 Reach a fork. Continue straight.

2.41 Reach a fork. Continue straight.

2.48 Reach a junction. Continue straight.

2.5 Reach a fork. Bear left.

2.6 Reach a fork. Ibis Pond will be straight ahead. Bear left toward the fork at the 2.71-mile mark to take the right side for the Wader's Trail.

2.78 Reach a fork. Continue straight.

2.9 Reach the west side of the park headquarters. The trail surface becomes non-ADA accessible. Continue straight along the northern wall of the park headquarters.

2.95 Reach the pavers leading to the park headquarters. Bear right to return to the trailhead.

3.0 Arrive back at the trailhead.

Prairies and Lakes

Sunflowers in full bloom at Attwater Prairie Chicken National Wildlife Refuge (Honorable Mention Hike I)

26 Blue Waterfront Trail, Lake Mineral Wells State Park

True to its title, the Blue Waterfront Trail takes hikers along the waterfront of Lake Mineral Wells. Views of the Cross Timber forested ravines cascading into the 646-acre lake and sights of Civic League Island are advantages of the hike.

Lake or river: Lake Mineral Wells
Photogenic factor: 5
Start: Blue Waterfront Trailhead
Elevation gain: 820 to 896 feet
Distance: 2.96 miles out and back
Difficulty: Moderate
Hiking time: 1–2 hours
Seasons/schedule: Open year-round, 6 a.m. to 10 p.m.
Fees and permits: $7 per person 13 years and older (subject to change), free for Texas State Parks Pass holders
Trail contacts: Lake Mineral Wells State Park Headquarters, 100 Park Road 71, Mineral Wells 76067; (940) 328-1171

Dog-friendly: Leashed dogs permitted
Trail surface: Dirt and rocky path
Land status: Texas Parks and Wildlife Department
Nearest town: Within Mineral Wells city limits
Other trail users: Anglers
Maps: USGS Mineral Wells East; Lake Mineral Wells State Park map (available online at www.tpwd.texas.gov/state-parks/parks-map and via the TX State Parks mobile app)
Special considerations: There will be numerous offshoots on this trail. Follow the blue markers to stay on the trail.

Finding the trailhead: From the US 180 and US 281 intersection in Mineral Wells, travel on US 180 E for 4 miles. Turn left onto Park Road 71. After 0.7 miles, go left to curve around the southern end of Lake Mineral Wells to head toward the Post Oak and Live Oak Camping Areas. After 1.1 miles, bypassing the two camping areas, continue on to Park Road 71 B for 0.2 miles. Turn right toward the canoe and kayak launch area at the Plateau Camping Area. The trail begins south of the canoe and kayak launch area. There will be five parking spaces near the trailhead.
GPS: N32° 49.514' W98° 02.140'

The Hike

The Blue Waterfront Trail begins south of the canoe and kayak launch area. At 225 feet into the trail, bear right toward the blue marker to continue on the trail. The left is an offshoot. You will repeat this process 270 feet into the trail. Afterward, the trail heads east, and then back south. At 0.21 miles, bear left toward the blue marker. The path to the south goes to the Live Oak Camping Area. The trail then curves north shortly after. Head toward the blue marker, and then the trail winds primarily northeast until the 0.36-mile mark. Meanwhile, partial views of Lake Mineral Wells appear to your north and a view of the cove shows up to your left at 0.31 miles. As

Mornings at Lake Mineral Wells

the trail begins to head south at 0.36 miles, follow the blue marker. Views of Lake Mineral Wells will reappear to your left.

Take the left side along the shoreline at the fork at the 0.38-mile mark. The right is an offshoot to the Live Oak Camping Area. You will have access to the lake shore from this point to the 0.48-mile mark. From the 0.48-mile mark to the 0.52-mile mark, you will make a 10-foot ascent and cross a wooden footbridge. Soon after, the first of four fishing piers will be to the left. Bypass the offshoot to your right and continue to hug the shoreline. You will come upon a beautiful overlook of Lake Mineral Wells to your left at 0.6 miles. From this point, the trail begins to head southwest away from the lakeshore and prickly pears will border the path.

The trail heads west when the mileage clocks at three-quarters of a mile. You will make a rocky 5-foot descent from 0.77 miles to the 0.8-mile mark. Soon after, bypass an offshoot from a parking area to your left and continue heading west on the trail. You will make another rocky 5-foot descent, this time from the 0.82-mile mark to the 0.84-mile mark. A beautiful overlook for Civic League Island will be afforded to you to your left after the descent. When you are ready to leave the view, bypass the offshoot to your right. The second fishing pier will be to your right.

Shortly after going over a seasonal streambed, bypass the offshoot to your left to the Post Oak Camping Area at 1.1 miles. Continue straight. At the 1.13-mile mark, follow the blue marker and curve around the barricaded water supply structure. You

Vista point from the Blue Waterfront Trail

will pass through some Post Oak Camping Area sites at the 1.22-mile mark, and then the third fishing pier will be to your left. The fourth and last fishing pier will be to your left at 1.31 miles. A cove will come into view at 1.35 miles, as well as a screened shelter area. When you head south across a wooden footbridge, you will have a fantastic view of the cove. Turtles and geese can be seen in this cove at times. The trail then curves southeast. Once you reach the parking lot for the screen shelters, turn around and return to the trailhead.

Blue Waterfront Trail, Lake Mineral Wells State Park

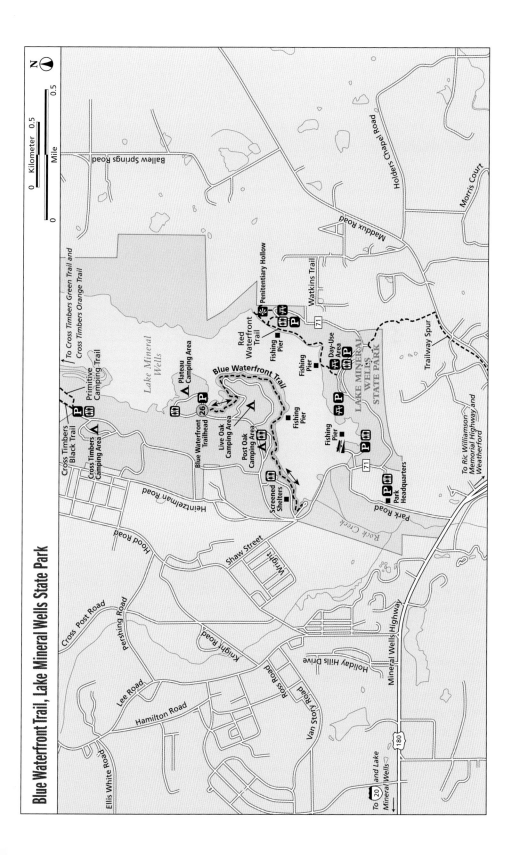

CRAZY WATER

The town of Mineral Wells is known for its medicinal well water. Hailed as a cure for all sorts of ailments back in the late 1800s, the water from the mineral wells was bathed in and imbibed. Mineral spas grew in massive popularity and resort hotels with them sprang up all throughout Texas. The use of mineral water is not as common as it was back then, but there is still a great deal of interest. Specifically for Mineral Wells, the local mineral water is bottled commercially by the famous Crazy Water company and sold in grocery stores. The Crazy Water company owns the Crazy Well, which when it was dug, caused the town of Mineral Wells to grow rapidly. While Lake Mineral Wells does not contain any mineral springs water, its waters are still resourceful for the residents of Mineral Wells.

Miles and Directions

0.0 The trail starts at the canoe and kayak launch area.

0.04 and 0.05 Bear right.

0.21 Bear left.

0.27 Partial lake views will be to your north.

0.31 A view of the cove opens up to your left.

0.36 Go along the lakeshore. Views of Lake Mineral Wells will be to your left.

0.38 Reach a fork. Bear left along the shoreline. There will be lakeshore access from this point to the 0.48-mile mark.

0.48 Make a 10-foot ascent to the 0.52-mile mark.

0.55 Cross a wooden footbridge. A fishing pier will be to your left.

0.57 Bypass the offshoot to your right.

0.6 Reach a vista of Lake Mineral Wells to your left.

0.77 Make a 5-foot rocky descent from here to the 0.8-mile mark.

0.81 Bypass an offshoot to a parking area to your left.

0.82 Make a 5-foot rocky descent from here to the 0.84-mile mark.

0.89 Reach an overlook for Civic League Island to your left. Bypass the offshoot to your right. Another fishing pier will be to your right.

1.08 Cross a seasonal streambed.

1.1 Bypass the offshoot to the Post Oak Camping Area to your left.

1.13 Curve around the barricaded water supply structure.

1.22 Pass through some Post Oak Camping Area sites.

1.25 and 1.31 A fishing pier will be to your left.

1.35 Reach a cove and screened shelter area.

1.43 Cross a wooden footbridge. A view of the cove occurs at this point.

1.48 Reach a parking lot for the screen shelters. Return the way you came.

2.96 Arrive back at the trailhead.

27 Paluxy River Trail (entrance from Cedar Brake Outer Loop), Dinosaur Valley State Park

The Paluxy River flows over limestone bedrock where dinosaurs once roamed. It has carved through the Glen Rose Formation, showcasing rock from an ancient sea. Those who hike on the Paluxy River Trail will get to see dinosaur tracks up close, experience the river, and admire the Ashe juniper and hardwood forest that embellish the limestone walls of the Paluxy River Valley surrounding them.

Lake or river: Paluxy River
Photogenic factor: 5
Start: Cedar Brake Outer Loop Trailhead
Elevation gain: 643 to 867 feet
Distance: 3.55 miles out and back
Difficulty: Easy
Hiking time: About 2 hours
Seasons/schedule: Open year-round, 6 a.m. to 10 p.m.
Fees and permits: $8 per person 13 years and older (subject to change), free for Texas State Parks Pass holders
Trail contacts: Dinosaur Valley State Park Headquarters, 1629 Park Road 59, Glen Rose 76043; (254) 897-4588
Dog-friendly: Leashed dogs permitted
Trail surface: Mixture of dirt, asphalt, and gravel

Land status: Texas Parks and Wildlife Department
Nearest town: Granbury (northeast), Glen Rose (southeast)
Other trail users: Mountain bikers/cyclists, anglers
Maps: USGS Glen Rose West; Dinosaur Valley State Park map (available online at www.tpwd.texas.gov/state-parks/parks-map and via the TX State Parks mobile app)
Special considerations: Orange markers with white arrows serve as guides for this trail. The best season to view dinosaur tracks is during the summer when the Paluxy River is low. There is minimal shade on this trail. Start your hike early and bring adequate amounts of water.

Finding the trailhead: From the FM 205 and Elm Street intersection in Glen Rose, travel on FM 205 N for 4.4 miles. When you see the Dinosaur World Museum to your left, make a slight right onto Park Road 59. In 0.8 miles, take the Park 59 loop in a counterclockwise direction. After 0.2 miles on the loop, turn right toward the Theropod and Sauropod Group Sites. In 495 feet, turn right into the parking lot. The Cedar Brake Outer Loop Trailhead will be at the farthest southeast end of the parking lot. **GPS:** N32° 14.969' W97° 48.736'

The Hike

Not too many places in Texas do hikers have the opportunity to observe dinosaur tracks. There are several dinosaur track sites to see along the beautiful Paluxy River Trail, in addition to the Paluxy River itself and the infamous Blue Hole. To hike the Paluxy River Trail, you will need to access it from the Cedar Brake

The Paluxy River   *Sunset at the Blue Hole*

Dinosaur tracks

Outer Loop Trailhead. About 290 feet from the trailhead, you will reach a fork. Bear left. Bypass the side trail to your left before passing by the Theropod Group Sites. At 600 feet, you will encounter a junction. Bear left onto the Paluxy River Trail. To your right is also the Paluxy River Trail; however, this guide does not include that part of the route. Continuing straight will lead you onto the Cedar Brake Outer Loop Trail.

Bypass the side trail to your right prior to reaching the campground road a quarter of a mile into the trail. This portion of the route through the campground is undefined. Watch for passing vehicles as you head north on the campground road. You will reconnect with the Paluxy River Trail at campsite #17. Follow the campsite numbers in consecutive order to reach campsite #17.

Once you reconnect with the Paluxy River Trail, the trail surface changes to asphalt. Continue north in the shade as the river parallels to your right. You will resume bypassing several offshoots until 0.79 miles. The shade dissipates at the 0.58-mile mark as the landscape opens up into a bluestem prairie and the trail heads northwest. Once you reach the first of three parking lots along the trail, look for vehicles before going through the parking lot. You will reconnect with the Paluxy River Trail at the Rock Beach entrance sign. The trail surface returns to dirt. Prior to reaching the second parking lot at 0.93 miles, the trail curves and heads south. You will need to bypass another entrance to Rock Beach to your right and you will come upon an interpretive wayside on the topic of "Oceans of Grass" to your left.

At the second parking lot, stay to your right along the asphalt. Going this way will lead to the Main Track Site. Head down the stairs to the interpretive waysides detailing the topics of "Fossil Tracks" and "Sign of the Ancient Times." Head west across the river to the Main Track Site. Use caution when crossing—this area might be slippery. If the river is too high, do not cross. You will reach the Main Track Site when the mileage clocks at a mile. The Main Track Site is where fossil collector Ronald T. Bird discovered sauropod tracks in 1940. This finding was the first of its kind to provide evidence that sauropods had existed. Theropod tracks can also be found at the Main Track Site. Once you have finished surveying the tracks, return across the river and up the stairs. At the top of the stairs, bear right. Look for the orange marker to the south of you at the 1.05-mile mark to reconnect to the Paluxy River Trail. The path surface will return to dirt.

The third parking lot will be at the 1.11-mile mark. Continue south on the dirt path. Bypass the offshoot to the river to your right shortly after and continue south toward the pavilion. Go up the four wooden steps and continue south on the wide gravel path. The pavilion will be to your right just shy of a mile and a quarter into the trail. You will reach the entrance to the Blue Hole to your right at the 1.36-mile mark. Head west through an open area and down the stairs to the Blue Hole. The Blue Hole is a popular, age-old swimming hole with translucent water. During the summer, this area can be populated. At sunset when the crowds have left, the 20-foot Blue Hole is especially photo-worthy. After enjoying the view, turn around and return to the open area. Bear left to hike toward the Ballroom Tracks. The path surface returns to dirt. When you reach the fork at 1.46 miles, continue straight. The left side goes to another parking lot. Shortly after, access to the Ballroom Track Site will be to your right. Head west to the Ballroom Track Site. The Ballroom Track Site will appear when the mileage clocks a little over a mile and a half. The name of the site derives from the appearance of the tracks found in this area. Hundreds of theropod and sauropod tracks seem to be moving in different directions, as if the dinosaurs were dancing around on what is now the limestone riverbed. After marveling at the Ballroom Track Site, return to the Paluxy River Trail.

When you reconnect with the Paluxy River Trail, you have two options. You can either bear right or turn around and return the way you came. This guide continues through the South Primitive Camping Area just in case the Taylor Track Site is visible at the time of your hike. The Taylor Track Site will be southwest of South Primitive

Paluxy River Trail (entrance from Cedar Brake Outer Loop), Dinosaur Valley State Park

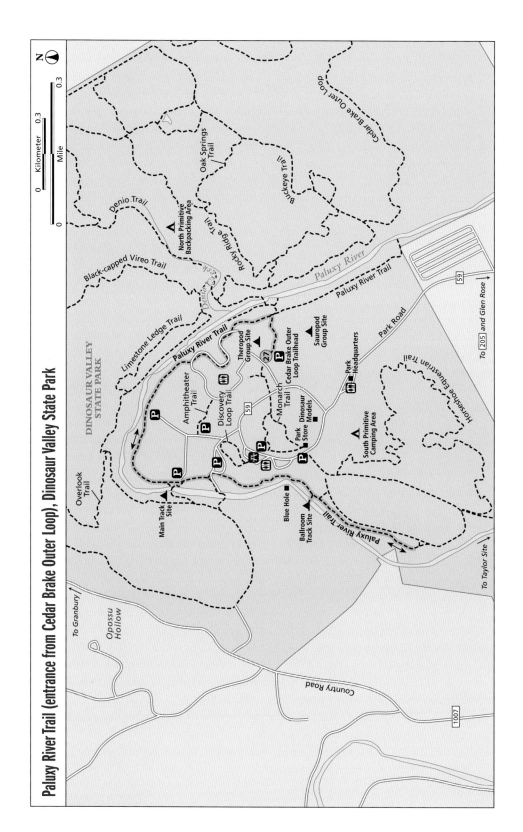

campsite #6. Note that the wide set of tracks is only visible during a drought or low river flow. The Paluxy River Trail ends at South Primitive campsite #8. At this point, turn around and return the way you came, bypassing the scenic spurs.

Miles and Directions

0.0 Start at the Cedar Brake Outer Loop Trailhead.

0.05 Reach a fork. Bear left and pass by the Theropod Group Sites.

0.11 Reach a junction. Bear left.

0.23 Bypass the side trail to your right.

0.25 Reach the campground road. The portion of the route through the campground is undefined. Watch for passing vehicles as you head north on the road. Reconnect with the Paluxy River Trail at campsite #17.

0.48 Reconnect with the Paluxy River Trail. Bypass several offshoots.

0.58 Bypass several offshoots to your right.

0.67 Reach a parking lot to your left. Watch for vehicles as you go through the parking lot and reconnect with the Paluxy River Trail at the 0.69-mile mark and Rock Beach entrance sign.

0.79 Bypass the offshoot to your right.

0.88 Another entrance to Rock Beach will be to your right.

0.93 Reach another parking lot. Stay on the asphalt to your right.

0.95 Head down the stairs to view the Main Track Site.

0.97 Head west across the river to the Main Track Site. This area might be slippery. If the river is too high, do not cross.

1.0 Reach the Main Track Site. Return across the river and up the stairs. At the top of the stairs, bear right. Look for the orange marker to the south of you at the 1.05-mile mark to reconnect to the Paluxy River Trail.

1.11 Reach another parking lot.

1.16 Bypass the path to the river to your right. Continue south toward the pavilion.

1.21 Go up the four wooden steps and continue south on the wide gravel path.

1.36 Reach the entrance to the Blue Hole to your right. Head west through an open area and down the stairs to the Blue Hole.

1.39 Reach the Blue Hole. Turn around and return to the open area. Bear left to the Ballroom Tracks.

1.46 Reach a fork. Continue straight.

1.48 Head west to the Ballroom Track Site.

1.51 Reach the Ballroom Track Site. Return to the Paluxy River Trail.

1.54 Reconnect with the trail. Bear right or turn around and return the way you came. This guide continues through the South Primitive Camping Area. The Taylor Track Site will be southwest of South Primitive campsite #6. It is only visible during a drought or when the river is low.

1.86 The Paluxy River Trail ends at South Primitive campsite #8. Turn around and return the way you came, bypassing the scenic spurs.

3.55 Arrive back at the trailhead.

28 Bosque Hiking Trail, Meridian State Park

Created by the Civilian Conservation Corps (CCC) during the Great Depression, the 72-acre Lake Meridian is surrounded by bluffs made of Edwards Limestone festooned with the area's signature cedars. On the Bosque Hiking Trail, hikers will be able to savor numerous lake views and be awed by the craftsmanship of other structures made by the CCC along the route.

Lake or river: Lake Meridian
Photogenic factor: 5
Start: Bosque Hiking Trailhead
Elevation gain: 935 to 1,044 feet
Distance: 2.41-mile loop
Difficulty: Moderate to difficult due to uneven, rocky trail with steep descents
Hiking time: 2-3 hours
Seasons/schedule: Open year-round, 6 a.m. to 10 p.m.
Fees and permits: $5 per person 13 years and older (subject to change), free for Texas State Parks Pass holders
Trail contacts: Meridian State Park Headquarters, 173 Park Road 7, Meridian 76665; (254) 435-2536

Dog-friendly: Leashed dogs permitted
Trail surface: Dirt and rocky path
Land status: Texas Parks and Wildlife Department
Nearest town: Meridian (northeast), Clifton (southeast)
Other trail users: Anglers
Maps: USGS Meridian; Meridian State Park map (available online at www.tpwd.texas.gov/state-parks/parks-map and via the TX State Parks mobile app)
Special considerations: Blue blazes on trees serve as guides for this trail.

Finding the trailhead: From the US 84 and TX 6 corridor in Waco, head north on TX 6 for 42.3 miles. Turn left onto TX 22 W. After 2.5 miles, turn right onto Park Road 7 N. In 423 feet, turn right toward Cedar Ridge Campground. In 1 mile, the Bosque Hiking Trailhead and "Carved in Time and Stone" sign will be to your right, opposite the parking area and Little Forest Junior Trailhead. Watch for passing vehicles before crossing the road. **GPS:** N31° 53.577' W97° 42.151'

The Hike

Lake Meridian is a no-wake lake, allowing it to be the perfect recreation spot with little disturbance. It is nestled in what used to be grassland, but now covered in Ashe juniper and other cedars due to the preclusion of fires necessary to restore the area to its original prairie landscape. The overwhelming presence of the invasive Ashe juniper does have one silver lining, however. It serves as a breeding ground for the endangered golden-cheeked warbler. If you come to hike the Bosque Hiking Trail in Meridian State Park in the spring, you might be fortunate to catch a glimpse of

Tranquil moment at Lake Meridian

one of these rare birds. Thanks to the lake being designated as no-wake, the quietness might even allow you to hear the golden-cheeked warblers' distinctive melody.

The Bosque Hiking Trail commences south of State Park Road 7, across from the Little Forest Junior Trailhead. Within 70 feet onto the trail, you will reach a fork. Blue blazes indicate the route of the Bosque Hiking Trail, so follow the blue blaze by continuing straight toward Bee Ledge. Heading right will connect you to the Little Forest Junior Trail. At 190 feet, you will reach the Bee Ledge overlook. This natural overlook provides a beautiful vista of Lake Meridian. After enjoying the view, bear right. The Little Forest Junior Trail will parallel to your right for a short distance. At 415 feet, make a slight rocky descent of 30 feet in elevation for the next 20 feet. You will come upon another overlook of Lake Meridian, and then bear right into a forested area of cedar elm, oak, and Ashe juniper. The trail winds in a northerly direction until curving south near the 0.44-mile mark. The path gets less rocky once you cross over a seasonal creek bed at 0.18 miles. At 0.27 miles, you will hike a series of stone steps. To your left, a creek will eventually parallel the trail. Watch for unearthed tree roots in the path. You will head west over a wooden bridge prior to the trail winding south.

A little more than half a mile into the trail, you will cross over a small footbridge. At 0.64 miles, go up the log steps and rocky ledge for a 30 feet ascent in elevation to the 0.66-mile mark. Following that, you will make a couple slight descents in elevation down some rocks, 25 feet from the 0.69-mile mark to the 0.72-mile mark, and 10 feet from the 0.91-mile mark to the 0.92-mile mark, respectively. After a mile into the trail, you will reach the parking area for Shinnery Ridge West campsites #30 and #31 and a scenic viewing point. Take some time to enjoy the view by the lakeshore before heading southwest to reconnect to the trail at the sign denoting the Bosque Hiking Trail.

Footbridge on the Bosque Hiking Trail

You will come upon the Shinnery Ridge West primitive campsites at 1.21 miles. Bear left and follow the blue arrows painted on State Park Road 7 going past campsites #24 and #25. Watch for vehicles before crossing over the stone bridge. Reconnect with the trail at the Bosque Hiking Trail sign at the 1.30-mile mark. You will head down some stone steps and then the trail heads east. Views of Lake Meridian will appear to your left a little over a mile and a half into the trail. Once you cross over a stone block at 1.56 miles, the forested area will end, and then you will bear left to head northeast across the dam. The dam was constructed on Bee Creek by World War I veterans, employed by the Civilian Conservation Corps (CCC) in the early 1930s. The dam is composed of rock and dirt and ends at 1.78 miles. At that point, you will reach a fork. Bear left toward Lake Meridian.

Soon after, you will reach a swimming area. Take the stone block steps to continue on the trail. The path becomes undefined in the grassy area. Go around the east side of the CCC refectory and pavilion. The CCC refectory and pavilion are also examples of the aforementioned World War I veterans' remarkable workmanship. The structures are made of trees and limestone cut from the Lake Meridian area. Once you reach the other end of the CCC structures, head down the ramp and stone steps to reconnect with the trail. The blue blazes on trees will indicate you are on the right path. Lake Meridian will be parallel to your left.

Please watch for vehicles when you go across the access road at 1.93 miles. Two miles into the trail, you will cross over a wooden bridge. Bypass the path to the day-use area to your left. Watch again for passing vehicles when using the pedestrian crosswalk to go across State Park Road 7 shortly after. Take caution for any fallen tree branches in the path after you head down the stone steps at 2.13 miles. The trail then curves west up some stone steps. At 2.16 miles, the trail heads northwest into a forested area. As you approach the 2.18-mile mark, head around the rocks and the tree with the blue blaze. A couple more blue blazes ahead will indicate you are on the right path. The trail surface will eventually level out to dirt, and at 2.21 miles a park bench will be to your left and a connection to the Little Forest Junior Trail will be to your right. Blazes on trees will now be both blue and yellow. The forested area eventually ends, but there will still be some scattered shade available. At 2.31 miles, the

Bosque Hiking Trail, Meridian State Park

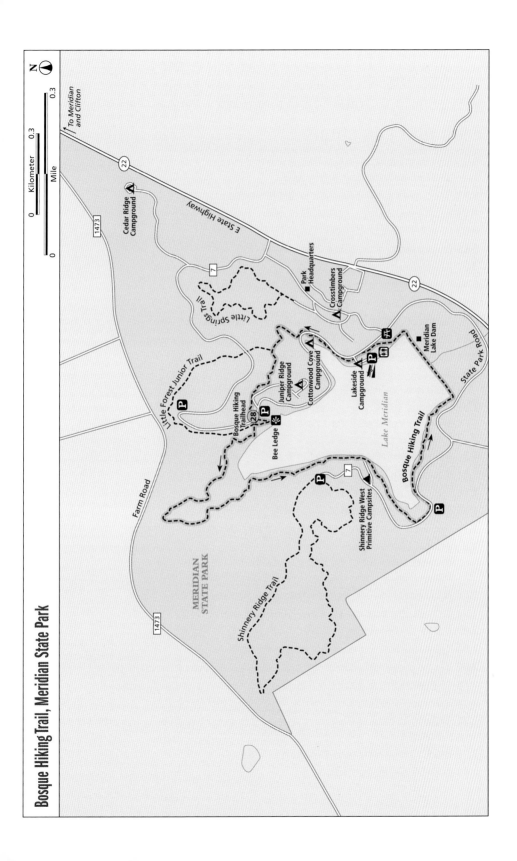

N

Kilometer
0   0.3
Mile
0   0.3

To Meridian
and Clifton

22

1473

Cedar Ridge
Campground

E State Highway

7

Little Springs Trail

Park
Headquarters

Crosstimbers
Campground

Little Forest Junior Trail

22

Bosque Hiking
Trailhead

Juniper Ridge
Campground

Cottonwood Cove
Campground

Lakeside
Campground

Meridian
Lake Dam

State Park Road

P

28

Bee Ledge

Lake Meridian

Bosque Hiking Trail

Farm Road

P

7

Shinnery Ridge West
Primitive Campsites

P

MERIDIAN
STATE PARK

Shinnery Ridge Trail

1473

trail winds northwest for a short distance and then heads back west. You will reach a bird viewing blind to your right at 2.36 miles. State Park Road 7 will be to your left. At 2.41 miles, the trail loops back to State Park Road 7 and the parking area.

Miles and Directions

0.0 Start on the Bosque Hiking Trail. You will need to cross State Park Road 7 to get to the trailhead. Watch for passing vehicles.

0.01 Reach a fork. Continue straight toward Bee Ledge.

0.04 Reach the Bee Ledge overlook. Bear right.

0.08 Make a descent of 30 feet for about 20 feet. Bear right.

0.18 Cross a seasonal creek bed.

0.27 Reach some stone steps.

0.42 A creek will parallel to your left. Watch for unearthed tree roots in the path.

0.44 and 0.55 Cross a small footbridge.

0.64 Ascend 30 feet up the log steps and rocky ledge to the 0.66-mile mark.

0.69 Make a descent of 25 feet down some rocks to the 0.72-mile mark.

0.91 Make a descent of 10 feet down some rocks to the 0.92-mile mark.

1.0 Reach parking areas for Shinnery Ridge campsites #30 and #31 and a scenic viewing point. Head southwest to reconnect to the Bosque Hiking Trail.

1.21 Reach the Shinnery Ridge West primitive campsites. Bear left following the painted blue arrows on State Park Road 7 past campsites #24 and #25. Watch for passing cars before crossing the stone bridge.

1.3 Reconnect with the trail at the Bosque Hiking Trail sign. Go down some stone steps.

1.51 Views of Lake Meridian will appear to your left.

1.56 Cross over a stone block.

1.58 Bear left across the dam.

1.78 Dam ends. Reach a fork. Bear left toward Lake Meridian.

1.8 Reach a swimming area. Take the stone block steps to continue on the trail. The path becomes undefined in the grassy area. Go around the east side of the CCC building and pavilion.

1.88 At the end of the CCC structure, head down the ramp and stone steps.

1.93 Go across the access road. Watch for passing vehicles.

2.0 Cross a wooden bridge.

2.04 Bypass the path to the day-use area to your left.

2.06 Use the pedestrian crosswalk to go across State Park Road 7. Watch for passing vehicles.

2.13 Go down some stone steps and then go back up some stone steps shortly after.

2.18 Head around the rocks and the tree with the blue blaze.

2.21 A bench will be to your left and the Little Forest Junior Trail will be to your right. Continue straight.

2.36 Reach a bird viewing blind to your right.

2.41 Arrive back at the trailhead.

29 Northwest Trail System (combined with Overlook Trail), Eagle Mountain Park

Eagle Mountain Park is a little oasis north of Fort Worth. It contains a mixture of cross-timber forests and prairie blanketing undulating hills, and an impressive lake for scenic views and respite. The Northwest Trail System courses through the varied landscape, as well as along and up above the Eagle Mountain Lake shoreline.

Lake or river: Eagle Mountain Lake

Photogenic factor: 5

Start: Main Park Trailhead

Elevation gain: 630 to 746 feet

Distance: 3.24-mile lollipop, with an additional lollipop to an overlook

Difficulty: Moderate to difficult due to steep inclines and declines

Hiking time: 1–2 hours

Seasons/schedule: Open year-round, sunrise to sunset

Fees and permits: None (subject to change)

Trail contacts: Tarrant Regional Water District, Eagle Mountain Lake Office, 10201 North Shore Drive, Fort Worth 76135; (817) 237-8585

Dog-friendly: Only service animals permitted

Trail surface: Paved on portions of the Main Park Trail, dirt and rocky path on the remainder of the route

Land status: Tarrant Regional Water District

Nearest town: Pecan Acres (north), Avondale (northeast), Eagle Mountain and Fort Worth (south)

Other trail users: Anglers, paddlers

Maps: USGS Avondale; Eagle Mountain Park map (available online at https://www.trwd.com/wp-content/uploads/2020/12/8.5X11_Eagle.Mountain.Park_flyer.pdf)

Special considerations: Eagle Mountain Park is extremely popular, and the parking lot fills up fast, especially on the weekends. Try to get to the park early when it opens at sunrise or at least before 8 a.m. The Northwest Trail System includes both the Northwest Trail and the Ridge Loop Trail.

Finding the trailhead: From the Commerce Street and W 4th Street intersection in downtown Fort Worth, head southeast on Commerce Street for a quick 0.1 miles. Turn left onto 7th Street. Merge onto TX 280 Spur shortly after. After less than half a mile on TX 280 Spur, take the I-35W N/US 287 N exit. Stay on I-35W N for 8.9 miles. Take the exit for US 81 N/US 287 N. Travel on US 81 N/US 287 N for 4 miles. Take the Bonds Ranch Road exit. Close to 430 feet after exiting, you will need to turn left onto Bonds Ranch Road going through two traffic circles. Continue on Bonds Ranch Road for 6.6 miles after the second traffic circle. Turn right onto Morris Dido Newark Road. The entrance and parking lot for Eagle Mountain Park will be to your left after 1.6 miles. **GPS:** N32° 56.122' W97° 28.815'

The Hike

Originally designated to become a Texas state park, Eagle Mountain Park was too small in acreage to fit the state criteria of a state park. An arrangement between

Windmill from Kay Kimble's ranch   *View from the Overlook Trail*

Eagle Mountain Lake shoreline

the Trust for Public Land and the Tarrant Regional Water District saved the park from urban development and allowed it to become a regional park. A pavilion with numerous exhibits on the geography and history of the area serves as the entrance to Eagle Mountain Park. To the north of the pavilion, a windmill belonging to the founder of the Kimble Art Foundation in Fort Worth, Kay Kimble, stands just as it did when it was built in 1938. The trails of Eagle Mountain Park all stem from the Main Park Trail, which starts north of the pavilion. The trail surface is paved until you reach the fence. Head southwest through the opening in the fence. When you reach the fork about 265 feet into the trail, bear left to continue on the Main Park Trail to connect with the Overlook Trail. The Overlook Trail is optional. This guide includes it for an additional scenic point. After completing the Overlook Trail, this guide will complete the two trails of the Northwest Trail System, the Northwest Trail and the Ridge Loop Trail. The Northwest Trail will begin to the right side of the fork.

The connection to the Overlook Trail will occur at 425 feet into the trail. Bear right to start on the Overlook Trail. The Overlook Trail is a lollipop route and there will be several picnic benches available on this route. You can take the route in either direction, but this guide takes it in a clockwise direction. When you reach the overlook, it will be to your left at the 0.22-mile mark. The view is particularly beautiful at sunrise and sunset, and also during the fall or winter when the view is less obscured by foliage. Once you are ready to return, head east to complete the loop. When the loop concludes at 0.34 miles, take the spur segment of the lollipop to the connection with the Northwest Trail System at the original 265-foot mark. The mileage will read as 0.4 miles when you reach the Northwest Trailhead. Bear left to start on the Northwest Trail.

The Northwest Trail initially heads northwest down a 10-foot rocky descent to the 0.46-mile mark. There will be several offshoots to bypass and a wooden footbridge to cross before you reach the fork at 0.65 miles. Bear left at the fork. The right connects to an access road. After bypassing another offshoot, you will come upon another fork. This time, bear right. The southern route leads to a closed-off boat launch area. A map exhibit will be to your left.

You will reach the day-use area at the 0.98-mile mark. There will be picnic benches, restrooms, and drinking fountains available at the day-use area. Feel free to take a break here before continuing on the trail. You will need to bypass an offshoot to your left and make a 10-foot descent from the 1.13-mile mark to the 1.14-mile mark prior to the trail heading west. Bear left when you come upon the junction with the access road at 1.23 miles.

The Ridge Loop Trail starts when the mileage clocks at 1.33 miles. This guide takes the loop in a clockwise direction. A map exhibit will be to your left. The trail curves northwest. There will be several offshoots to Eagle Mountain Lake to your left that you need to bypass before you encounter a vista of the lake at 1.65 miles. On a clear day, you will be able to see the neighborhood docks to your right and the popular boating hangout spot, "Party Cove," to your left. The waves of Eagle Mountain Lake gently roll up onto the ivory-hued, sandy shores bordering the trail. There will be a 5-foot hump with rock steps to cross from this point to the 1.68-mile mark, and then you will be rewarded with a few more shoreline lake vistas to your left. After you cross a wooden footbridge, the trail heads northeast away from the lake and then eventually southeast. A worthwhile feature of the Ridge Loop Trail is the overlook of Eagle Mountain Lake to your right at the 2.08-mile mark. A bench will be available for you to sit on while you are mesmerized by the bird's-eye view. Cross-timber shrouded hills slope into the seemingly unruffled lake, setting a very tranquil scene.

Northwest Trail System (combined with Overlook Trail), Eagle Mountain Park

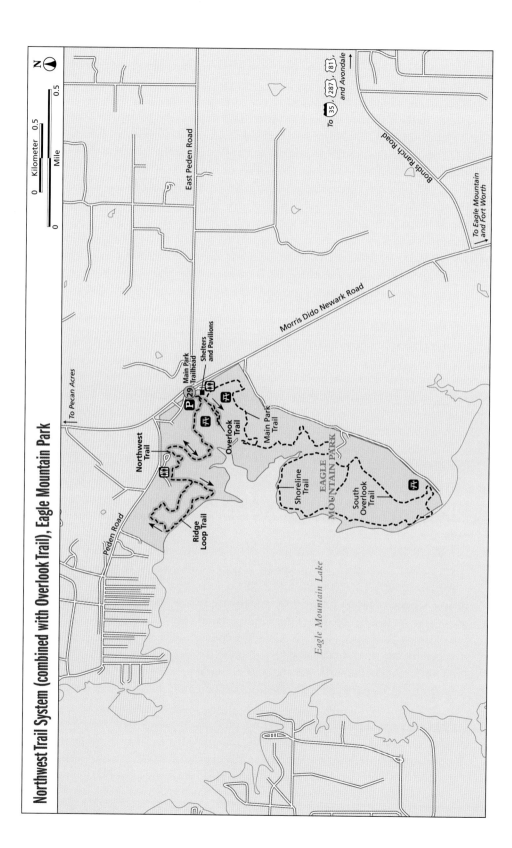

Continue straight at the fork at 2.18 miles. The left side of the fork connects to an access road. You will make a rocky 40-foot rocky descent from here to the 2.27-mile mark. When the mileage clocks at 2.27 miles, the Ridge Loop Trail concludes at the original 1.33-mile mark. Bear left to return to the pavilion and Main Park Trailhead, bypassing the Overlook Trail.

Miles and Directions

0.0 The trail starts north of the pavilion. Head southwest through the opening in the fence.

0.05 Reach a fork. Bear left to go on the Overlook Trail. This is optional; this guide includes the Overlook Trail.

0.08 Bear right to start on the Overlook Trail.

0.12 Reach the loop portion of the lollipop route. This guide takes the loop in a clockwise direction.

0.22 Reach the overlook to your left.

0.24 Head east to complete the loop.

0.34 The loop concludes. Take the spur segment of the lollipop to return to the connection with the Northwest Trail System.

0.4 Reach the connection to the Northwest Trail System. Bear left to start on the Northwest Trail.

0.44 Make a rocky descent of 10 feet to the 0.46-mile mark.

0.48 Bypass offshoots to your right and left.

0.52 Cross a wooden footbridge.

0.59 Bypass several offshoots to your right.

0.65 Reach a fork. Bear left.

0.68 Bypass an offshoot to your left.

0.72 Reach a fork. Bear right.

0.98 Reach the day-use area.

1.09 Bypass an offshoot to your left.

1.13 Make a 10-foot descent to the 1.14-mile mark.

1.23 Reach a junction. Bear left.

1.33 Reach the Ridge Loop Trail. This guide takes the loop in a clockwise direction.

1.47 to 1.61 Bypass several offshoots to the lake to your left.

1.65 A vista of the lake will be to your left. Go over a 5-foot hump with rock steps to the 1.68-mile mark.

1.68, 1.71, and 1.76 A vista of the lake will be to your left.

1.72 Cross a wooden footbridge.

2.08 Reach an overlook with a bench to your right.

2.18 Reach a fork. Continue straight. Make a rocky 40-foot rocky descent to the 2.27-mile mark.

2.27 The Ridge Loop Trail ends at the original 1.33-mile mark. Bear left and return the way you came, bypassing the Overlook Trail.

3.24 Arrive back at the trailhead.

30 Haller's Haven Nature Trail, Hagerman National Wildlife Refuge

The landscape of the Hagerman National Wildlife Refuge looks like a beautiful painting. Lake Texoma escapes into shallow marshes, and all kinds of spectacular birds find shelter around its waters. The scenery that can be experienced from the Haller's Haven Trail is a testament to the beauty of the refuge. With two tranquil ponds, lake access, and a mixture of bottomland forests and prairie, the Haller's Haven Trail has something that can be appreciated by any hiker.

Lake or river: Lake Texoma
Photogenic factor: 5
Start: Haller's Haven Nature Trailhead
Elevation gain: 617 to 676 feet
Distance: 3.38-mile lollipop, with an additional spur
Difficulty: Easy
Hiking time: 1–2 hours
Seasons/schedule: Open year-round, sunrise to sunset; visitor center hours are 9 a.m. to 4 p.m. Mon through Sat and 1 p.m. to 5 p.m. Sun
Fees and permits: None (subject to change)
Trail contacts: Hagerman National Wildlife Refuge Visitors Center, 6465 Refuge Road, Sherman 75092; (903) 786-2826
Dog-friendly: Leashed dogs permitted
Trail surface: Dirt, with a brief segment of mowed grass and gravel
Land status: US Fish and Wildlife Service

Nearest town: Pottsboro and Denison (east), Sherman (southeast), Whitesboro (southwest)
Other trail users: None
Maps: USGS Gordonville; Hagerman National Wildlife Refuge map (available online at https://www.fws.gov/refuge/hagerman/visit-us/trails)
Special considerations: There is no shade on this trail from Picnic Pond to the end of Dead Woman Pond and any wildflower areas. Start your hike early and bring adequate amounts of water. Seasonal hunting is permitted in some areas of the Hagerman National Wildlife Refuge. A "hunt in progress" sign will be posted at the refuge entrance during those times. At times, overflow from Lake Texoma can cause roads and trails within the refuge to become flooded. Check with the visitor center prior to visiting the refuge to check for road and trail conditions.

Finding the trailhead: From the US 82 and TX 91 corridor in Sherman, travel west on US 82 for 5.7 miles. Take exit 636 for TX 289. After 0.6 miles, turn right onto TX 289 N. Continue north on TX 289 for 5.5 miles. Turn left onto Hagerman Road. Stay on Hagerman Road for 4.5 miles. Turn right onto Refuge Road. Refuge Road changes into Hagerman Corp Road (no sign) in 0.1 miles. Travel on Hagerman Corp Road for 0.6 miles. At the fork, go right toward the picnic area and the Goode Day-Use Area. The Haller's Haven Nature Trailhead will be on the northern side of the loop. Parking is available in the Goode Day-Use Area. **GPS:** N33° 45.216' W96° 45.807'

The Hike

The scenic Haller's Haven Nature Trail begins at the northern end of the Goode Day-Use Area. It initially heads northeast into a wooded area. At 385 feet, you will bear left

Picnic Pond

onto the path that is a combination of gravel and mowed grass. Picnic Pond will be to your right. The pond ends at the 0.13-mile mark, and you will enter one of several wildflower areas on the trail.

The most noteworthy portion of the trail begins by heading northwest across the metal pedestrian bridge at 0.23 miles. Gorgeous views of Dead Woman Pond will become available to your right and expansive views of Lake Texoma to your left. At times, a wide variety of birds can be seen resting or gliding on the waters. These views continue until the 0.42-mile mark. In the meantime, there will be a path leading to a bench overlooking Dead Woman Pond to your right at 0.27 miles.

As you head away from Dead Woman Pond and Lake Texoma and have hiked half a mile into the trail, there will be an overlook with a bench for Lake Texoma to your left. The trail then heads northeast, and the path surface returns to dirt. You will encounter another wildflower area at 0.61

Hagerman National Wildlife Refuge is a haven for many birds

miles. The third wildflower area will greet you after you reach the loop portion of the lollipop route at 0.84 miles. Take the loop in a counterclockwise direction.

The trail begins to head west after you have gone 1 mile into the trail. From the 1.13-mile mark to the 1.15-mile mark, you will make a 10-foot descent. You will cross over a seasonal creek bed quickly after. The trail then heads south at 1.61 miles. This guide includes the optional spur to the lakeshore at 1.78 miles. Head straight onto the spur for lake access. The mileage will clock at 2.03 miles when you reach the lakeshore. Enjoy the expansive view before you, and then turn around and go back to the fork

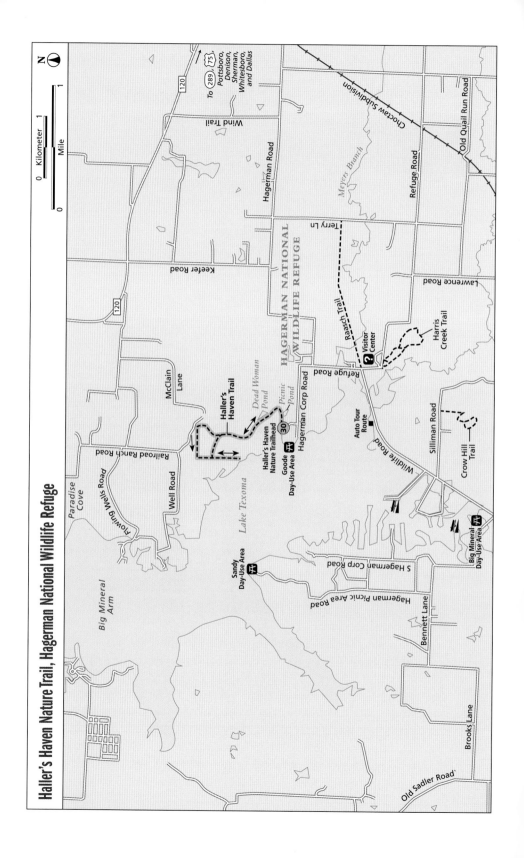

Haller's Haven Nature Trail, Hagerman National Wildlife Refuge

N

0   Kilometer   1

0   Mile

To 289 75
Pottsboro,
Denison,
Sherman,
Whitesboro,
and Dallas

120

Wind Trail

Hagerman Road

Choctaw Subdivision

Meyers Branch

Refuge Road

Old Quail Run Road

Keefer Road

120

Terry Ln

HAGERMAN NATIONAL
WILDLIFE REFUGE

McClain
Lane

Dead Woman
Pond

Raasch Trail

Visitor
Center

Lawrence Road

Haller's Haven Trail

Picnic
Pond

Harris
Creek Trail

Railroad Ranch Road

30

Refuge Road

Well Road

Haller's Haven
Nature Trailhead

Hagerman Corp Road

Goode
Day-Use Area

Silliman Road

Flowing Wells Road

Auto Tour
Route

Crow Hill
Trail

Paradise
Cove

Wildlife Road

Big Mineral
Arm

Lake Texoma

Sandy
Day-Use Area

S Hagerman Corp Road

Big Mineral
Day-Use Area

Hagerman Picnic Area Road

Bennett Lane

Brooks Lane

Old Sadler Road

THE ORIGIN OF DEAD WOMAN POND

On the dark evening of November 21, 1926, G. Dewey Ball and his pregnant wife, Annie Caddell, headed for the town of Hagerman to attend a church service. They never actually went to the church, and when G. Dewey Ball returned home without his wife, there was cause for concern. Ball claimed this wife had been mortally wounded from being thrown into a pond from their overturned buggy. When Annie Caddell was brought back home by a neighbor who owned an automobile, it was too late, and Annie Caddell passed away. It was determined that the young woman had not suffered injuries from a buggy accident but instead had been assaulted on the head several times with a blunt instrument (later concluded to be a 2-foot-long pipe). G. Dewey Ball eventually confessed to murdering his wife and was sentenced to life in prison. Dead Woman Pond is presumed to be the pond that Annie Caddell was thrown into.

from the original 1.78-mile mark. When you reach the fork from the original 1.78-mile mark, the mileage will read as 2.27 miles. Bear right to complete the loop. The loop portion of the lollipop route concludes at the 2.54-mile mark. From here, bear right back on the spur portion of the lollipop to return to the trailhead.

Miles and Directions

0.0 The trail starts at the northern end of the Goode Day-Use Area.

0.07 Bear left. Picnic Pond will be to your right.

0.13 Enter a wildflower area.

0.23 Cross a metal pedestrian bridge. Views of Dead Woman Pond will be to your right and views of Lake Texoma to will be to your left.

0.27 A path leading to a bench overlooking Dead Woman Pond will be to your right.

0.5 An overlook with a bench for Lake Texoma will be to your left. Head northeast.

0.61 Enter a wildflower area.

0.84 Reach the loop portion of the lollipop. This guide takes the loop in a counterclockwise direction. Reenter a wildflower area.

1.13 Make a 10-foot descent to the 1.15-mile mark.

1.15 Cross a seasonal creek bed.

1.78 Head straight onto the spur for lake access.

2.03 Reach the lakeshore. Enjoy the view. Return to the fork from the original 1.78-mile mark.

2.27 Reach the fork from the original 1.78-mile mark. Bear right to complete the loop.

2.54 The loop portion of the lollipop route ends. Bear right on the spur portion of the lollipop to return to the trailhead.

3.38 Arrive back at the trailhead.

Rabbit sighting along the trail

31 Ike's Hike and Bike Trail to Lover's Leap, Eisenhower State Park

Lover's Leap and Lake Texoma are some of Eisenhower State Park's crown jewels. Ike's Hike and Bike Trail traverses along soaring cliffs above the lake, leading hikers to entrancing coves, a beautiful swimming beach, and the aforementioned Lover's Leap.

Lake or river: Lake Texoma

Photogenic factor: 5

Start: Ike's Hike and Bike Trailhead Access Point #9

Elevation gain: 577 to 706 feet

Distance: 2.32 miles out and back

Difficulty: Moderate

Hiking time: 1–2 hours

Seasons/schedule: Open year-round; headquarters hours are Sun through Thurs 8 a.m. to 5 p.m., Fri 8 a.m. to 10 p.m., and Sat 8 a.m. to 7 p.m. (subject to change)

Fees and permits: $5 per person 13 years and older (subject to change), free for Texas State Parks Pass holders

Trail contacts: Eisenhower State Park Headquarters, 50 Park Road 20, Denison 75020; (903) 465-1956

Dog-friendly: Leashed dogs permitted

Trail surface: Dirt and rocky path

Land status: Texas Parks and Wildlife Department

Nearest town: Durant (northeast), Denison (southeast)

Other trail users: Mountain bikers/cyclists, anglers

Maps: USGS Denison Dam; Eisenhower State Park map (available online at www.tpwd.texas.gov/state-parks/parks-map and via the TX State Parks mobile app)

Special considerations: Pay attention to unearthed tree roots that occur intermittently throughout the trail. Ike's Hike and Bike Trail is 4 miles 1-way, with parking for 8 out of 14 of its access points.

Finding the trailhead: From the US 82 and US 75 corridor in Sherman, travel on US 75 N for 7.4 miles. Take exit 70 for FM 84. In 0.3 miles, turn left onto FM 84 W. Travel on FM 84 W for 1.6 miles, and then turn right onto Lil Old Road. After 0.5 miles on Lil Old Road, turn right onto Eisenhower Road. Stay on Eisenhower Road for 1.3 miles. Go left onto State Park Road 20 into Eisenhower State Park. After traveling on State Park Road 20 for 1.6 miles (bypassing the roads to the Bois D'Arc Ridge Camping Area and Cedar Hollow Group Area), turn right toward the Deer Haven Screen Shelters and Eisenhower Yacht Club. In about 270 feet, access point #9 for Ike's Hike and Bike Trail will be to your left, next to a parking area. **GPS:** N33° 49.331' W96° 36.788'

The Hike

Eisenhower State Park was built in honor of the World War II five-star general Dwight D. Eisenhower, who was born in nearby Denison. He would later become known as this country's 34th president. With breathtaking landscape along

Swimming beach at Eisenhower State Park

the shorelines of Lake Texoma, it is a real treat for hikers who visit the park. This guide begins at access point #9 for Ike's Hike and Bike Trail. Access point #9 can be found east of the parking area and west of the Deer Haven Screened Shelters and the Eisenhower Yacht Club. The trail starts off heading northwest. Close to 475 feet, you will make a rocky 40-foot descent. After bypassing the offshoot to a cove to your right, you will reach the wooden bridge and Ammonite Crossing point at 0.16 miles. A "Prehistoric Detectives" interpretive wayside will be to your right. Due to the geological Preston Anticline, oceanic ammonite fossils dating back to the Cretaceous period are exposed on the ravines of the cove below. Bypass another offshoot to the cove to your right at 0.21 miles and then cross over a seasonal creek bed shortly after. Partial views of Lake Texoma will open up to your right at the 0.41-mile mark.

You will come upon a spur to a fishing pier to your right at 0.45 miles. While optional, the spur takes you to some up-close views of Lake Texoma. If you choose to go down the stone steps, you will reach the fishing pier when the mileage reads 0.47 miles. In the mornings, you will likely see anglers on their boats fishing in the stunning cove. Once you have finished taking in the view, turn around and return to the junction at the original 0.45-mile mark. The mileage will clock at shy of half a mile when you return to that point. Bear right to continue on the trail.

View from Lover's Leap

Bench at Lover's Leap

You will need to bypass several offshoots to your left shortly after and then a vista of Lake Texoma will greet you to your right. The trail then heads west. When you bypass the side trail to the Fossil Ridge Camping Area to your left at 0.55 miles, be aware that this segment of the trail can get overgrown after a decent rainfall or during the spring and summer. At 0.58 miles, the trail curves south. You will also make an ascent of 10 feet from this to the 0.6-mile mark. Once you reach the 0.6-mile mark you will need to bypass the offshoot to your left. Soon, you will come upon a fork. Follow the brown wooden sign by bearing right. When the trail curves north at 0.67 miles, it splits but eventually merges.

You will come upon a picnic area at the 0.82-mile mark. Look ahead to the north for a brown wooden sign to help you stay on track. From the 0.94-mile mark to the 0.96-mile mark, you will make a 10-foot ascent. One of Eisenhower State Park's notable features, Lover's Leap, will be at the 1.04-mile mark. Feel free to take a break on the bench provided and enjoy the awe-inspiring view from this towering overlook of the lake. Once you are ready, curve around the bench and head south toward the swimming beach. You can also turn around and return to the trailhead, bypassing the spur to the fishing pier. This guide continues on to the swimming beach area for more scenic views.

Ike's Hike and Bike Trail to Lover's Leap, Eisenhower State Park

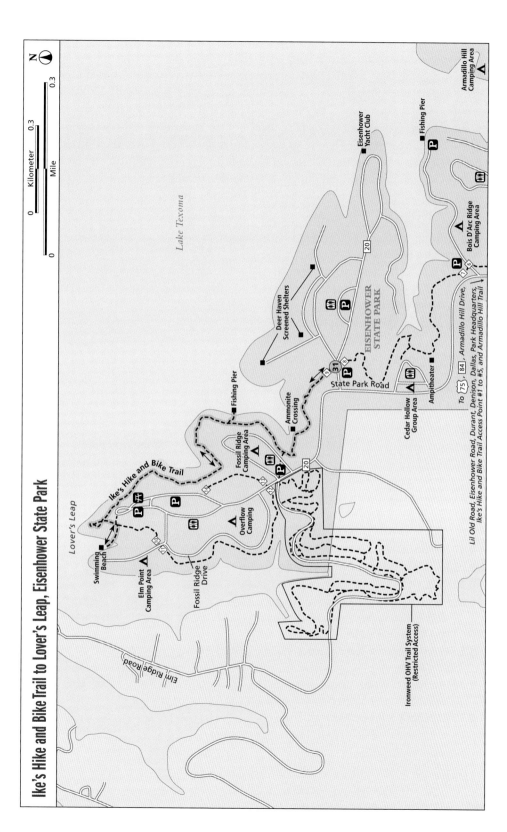

Lake Texoma

Lover's Leap

Ike's Hike and Bike Trail

Swimming Beach

Elm Point Camping Area

Fossil Ridge Drive

Elm Ridge Road

Overflow Camping

Fossil Ridge Camping Area

Fishing Pier

Ammonite Crossing

Deer Haven Screened Shelters

Eisenhower Yacht Club

EISENHOWER STATE PARK

State Park Road

Cedar Hollow Group Area

Ampitheater

Ironweed OHV Trail System (Restricted Access)

Fishing Pier

Bois D'Arc Ridge Camping Area

Armadillo Hill Camping Area

To 75, 84, Armadillo Hill Drive, Eisenhower Road, Durant, Denison, Dallas, Park Headquarters, Ike's Hike and Bike Trail Access Point #1 to #5, and Armadillo Hill Trail

Kilometer 0.3   0.3

Mile

N

To your right at the 1.1-mile mark, you will reach a wide gravel path that leads to the swimming beach. Ike's Hike and Bike Trail continues straight to access point #10. The path to the left heads to a parking lot for the day-use area. Bear right and go down several stone steps. The mileage will clock at 1.16 miles when you reach the swimming beach. Take a moment to reflect on the enchanting scenery (especially beautiful at sunrise) in front of you or take a dip in the waters. There is no lifeguard on duty so swim with caution. When you have finished your respite, turn around and return to the trailhead, bypassing the spur to the fishing pier.

Miles and Directions

0.0 The trail starts east of the parking area and west of the Deer Haven Screened Shelters and the Eisenhower Yacht Club.

0.09 to 0.16 Make a rocky 40-foot descent.

0.16 Bypass the offshoot to the cove to your right. Reach the wooden bridge and Ammonite Crossing point shortly after.

0.21 Bypass the offshoot to the cove to your right.

0.26 Cross a seasonal creek bed.

0.41 Partial lake views will be to your right.

0.45 Reach a junction. Bear right to go down the stone steps for an optional spur to the fishing pier.

0.47 Reach the fishing pier. Return to the trail.

0.49 Reach the original junction from the 0.45-mile mark. Bear right.

0.51 Bypass several offshoots to your left. A vista of Lake Texoma will be to your right.

0.55 This portion of the trail can get overgrown. Bypass the side trail to the Fossil Ridge Camping Area to your left.

0.58 Make an ascent of 10 feet to the 0.60-mile mark.

0.6 Bypass the offshoot to your left. Reach a fork. Follow the brown wooden sign by bearing right.

0.67 The trail splits and then merges.

0.82 Reach a picnic area. Follow the brown wooden sign to stay on track.

0.94 Make a 10-foot ascent to the 0.96-mile mark.

1.04 Reach Lover's Leap and a bench. Take in the view. Curve around the bench and head south toward the swimming beach. You can also turn around and return bypassing the spur to the fishing pier.

1.1 Reach a junction. Bear right down the wide gravel path and stone steps toward the swimming beach.

1.16 Reach the swimming beach. There is no lifeguard on duty so swim with caution. Turn around and return to the trailhead, bypassing the spur to the fishing pier.

2.32 Arrive back at the trailhead.

32 Cross Timbers Trail, Ray Roberts Lake State Park (Johnson Branch Unit)

The Cross Timbers Trail is aptly titled for the area it traverses, the Eastern Cross Timbers of Texas. In this region, the Grand Prairie and Blackland Prairie ecosystem meet, allowing for a landscape diverse in its flora and fauna. The Cross Timbers Trail also leads hikers to the gentle shores of Ray Roberts Lake. Hikers can soak up the lake views and learn new things from the interpretive waysides displayed throughout the trail.

Lake or river: Ray Roberts Lake (formerly known as Lake Aubrey)
Photogenic factor: 4
Start: Cross Timbers Trailhead can be accessed from any campground in the Johnson Ranch Unit; this guide starts from the Juniper Cove Campground
Elevation gain: 614 to 709 feet
Distance: 3.02-mile lollipop
Difficulty: Easy
Hiking time: 1–2 hours
Seasons/schedule: Open year-round, 6 a.m. to 10 p.m.
Fees and permits: $7 per person 13 years and older (subject to change), free for Texas State Parks Pass holders

Trail contacts: Ray Roberts Lake State Park Headquarters (Johnson Branch Unit), 100 PW 4153, Valley View 76272; (940) 637-2294
Dog-friendly: Leashed dogs permitted
Trail surface: Paved
Land status: Texas Parks and Wildlife Department
Nearest town: Valley View (northwest), Sanger (southwest)
Other trail users: Mountain bikers/cyclists, anglers
Maps: USGS Mountain Springs; Ray Roberts Lake State Park map (available online at www.tpwd.texas.gov/state-parks/parks-map and via the TX State Parks mobile app)
Special considerations: There will be several vehicle roads to cross during this route. Please watch for passing vehicles before crossing.

Finding the trailhead: From downtown Dallas, travel on I-35E N for 39.2 miles. Continue north onto I-35 N. Stay on I-35 N for 15.4 miles before exiting off exit 483 toward Lone Oak Road/FM 3002. Turn right onto E Lone Oak Road. Travel for 6.5 miles on E Lone Oak Road. Turn right onto PW 4153/State Park Road 4153. Continue on State Park Road 4153 for 1.3 miles. Go right into the Juniper Cove Campground. In 200 feet, turn right to go on the one-way loop through the Juniper Cove Campground. After 0.1 miles, the trailhead will be to your right at the pedestrian crosswalk near campsite #37. **GPS:** N33° 25.185' W97° 03.206'

The Hike

Renamed after one of Denton's beloved congressmen and conservationists, Ray Roberts, Ray Roberts Lake continues to supply water to Roberts's former constituents in Denton, as well as residents in Dallas. Ray Roberts Lake sources its water from Texas's largest watershed, the Trinity River Watershed. This massive body of water provides many recreational opportunities, including hiking along its shoreline via the Cross Timbers Trail.

The Cross Timbers Trail begins northeast of the crosswalk when you enter the one-way loop into the Juniper Cove Campground. At 0.17 miles, campsite #135 will be to your right. Continue northeast on the Cross Timbers Trail. When you reach the fork at 0.21 miles, bear right to continue on the trail. The left side goes to the DORBA Trail System. An "Along the Trail" interpretive wayside will be to your right shortly after. When you reach the crosswalk for State Park Road 4153 at 0.31 miles, watch for passing vehicles before continuing across. The trail then heads east. You will be surrounded by an abundance of wildflowers around the 0.43-mile mark during the spring and summer. In this area, you will be delighted by arrays of black-eyed Susans, prairie verbena, spotted beebalm, and antelope horn among the little bluestem grasses. A little over half a mile into the trail, a "Fire in the Cross Timber" interpretive wayside will be to your right. The trail starts to head south at the 0.62-mile mark, and you will reach a gravel access road. Watch for passing vehicles before crossing it to continue on the Cross Timbers Trail. Another interpretive wayside, "The Cross Timbers," will be to your left at 0.78 miles. Again, watch for passing vehicles before crossing State Park Road 4153 at 0.89 miles. Wild berries thrive to your right.

When you reach the fork at 1.32 miles, the Jones Family Corral and a "Hearth and Home" interpretive wayside will be to your right. The corral that was built in the 1930s is all that is left of a family farm from the 1850s. Before Ray Roberts Lake State Park came to be, the Jones family farm was passed down through generations for 120 years. Continue straight to complete the spur segment of the lollipop. To

Wildflowers along the Cross Timbers Trail

Shoreline of Ray Roberts Lake

your right will be the return route to complete the loop part of the lollipop. Continue straight at the fork at 1.41 miles. The left side of the fork goes to the Willow Cove Campground. At the 1.52-mile mark, you will come upon a junction. Both paths to your left lead to the Willow Cove Campground. The paths to your right lead to the Post Oak Beach picnic area and parking lot. There will continue to be several side paths after this junction. Continue south and you will encounter another junction at the 1.63-mile mark. Head east toward the swimming beach area. Once you reach the swimming beach area, bear right onto the paved trail. Feel free to go all the way toward the end of the beach. From this vista, you will be able to see Ray Roberts Lake, Wolf Island, and Ray Roberts Dam. When you are ready, return to the fork where the Jones Family Corral stands.

Deer sighting at Ray Roberts Lake State Park

When you have returned to the site of the Jones Family Corral, bear left to complete the loop portion of the lollipop route. Again, watch for passing vehicles before going across the crosswalk on Johnson Park State Road at 2.24 miles. Continue west

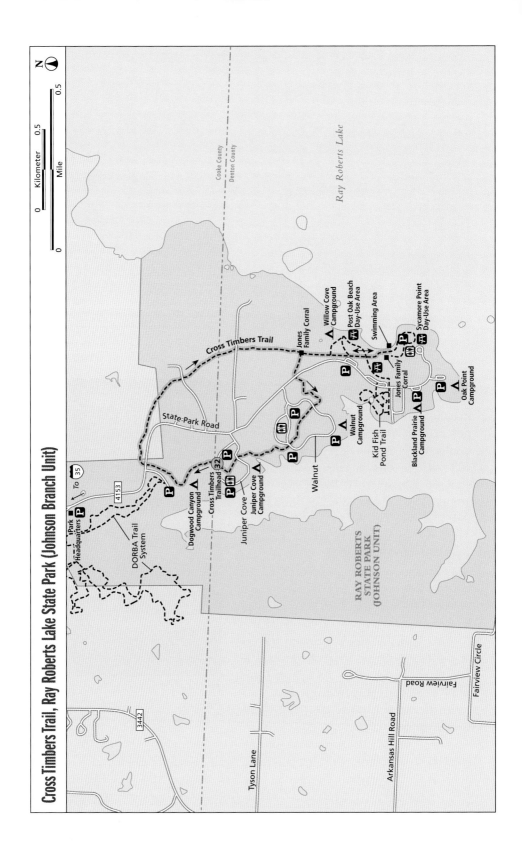

Cross Timbers Trail, Ray Roberts Lake State Park (Johnson Branch Unit)

on the Cross Timbers Trail. At 2.28 miles, there will be a small pond to your right and then a "Prairie Splendor" interpretive wayside to your right. The trail begins to wind south shortly after, and then curves north. When you reach the Walnut Campground parking area, you will need to cross another crosswalk. As always, watch for passing vehicles before going across. Continue heading northwest when you reach the playground and parking lot at 2.56 miles. Bypass the side trail to your left soon after.

As always, when you reach the other side of the Walnut Campground parking area, watch for vehicles before going across the crosswalk. A "Wild About Wetlands" interpretive wayside will be to your right at 2.84 miles. The final pedestrian crosswalk on the trail will be at the 2.89-mile mark when you reach the Juniper Cove Campground. Be alert for vehicles before going across the crosswalk. When you reach the junction at 2.96 miles, bear right. Going left will lead you to a playground, lakeshore, and another parking area for the Juniper Cove Campground. You will complete the trail at 3.02 miles when you arrive back at the trailhead.

Miles and Directions

0.0 Begin heading northeast on the paved trail that starts at the pedestrian crosswalk in the Juniper Cove Campground.

0.21 Reach a fork. Bear right.

0.31 Reach State Park Road 4153. Watch for vehicles before crossing.

0.64 Reach a gravel access road. Watch for vehicles before crossing.

0.89 Reach State Park Road 4153. Watch for vehicles before crossing.

1.32 Reach a fork. The Jones Family Corral will be to your right. Continue straight to do the spur segment of the lollipop.

1.41 Reach a fork. Continue straight.

1.52 Reach a junction. Continue straight.

1.63 Reach a junction. Head east toward the swimming beach area.

1.65 Reach the swimming beach area. Bear right onto the paved trail.

1.74 Views of Ray Roberts Lake, Wolf Island, and Ray Roberts Dam from this point. Return to the fork at the original 1.32-mile mark.

2.15 Reach the Jones Family Corral. Bear left to complete the loop portion of the lollipop.

2.24 Reach Johnson Park State Road. Watch for vehicles before crossing.

2.28 A small pond will be to your right.

2.45 Reach the Walnut Campground parking area. Watch for vehicles before crossing.

2.56 Reach a junction. Continue straight.

2.59 Bypass the side trail to your left.

2.64 Reach another Walnut Campground parking area. Watch for vehicles before crossing.

2.89 Reach Juniper Cove Campground. Watch for vehicles before crossing.

2.96 Reach a junction. Bear right.

3.02 Arrive back at the trailhead.

33 Cedar Creek South and North Loops, Cooper Lake State Park (Doctors Creek Unit)

On the Cedar Creek South and North Loops, hikers will be offered outlooks of the 19,305-acre Jim Chapman Lake and experience the landscapes and biodiversity of the Post Oak Savannah and Blackland Prairie ecoregions. In addition to its trails, the lake offers unspoiled wildlife viewing, fishing, and paddling for those looking for some reprieve from the daily grind.

Lake or River: Jim Chapman Lake (also known as Cooper Lake)

Photogenic Factor: 4

Start: Cedar Creek South Loop Trailhead

Elevation gain: 420 to 454 feet

Distance: 1.1-mile loop, with an optional spur

Difficulty: Easy

Hiking time: 30 minutes–1 hour

Seasons/schedule: Open year-round, 6 a.m. to 10 p.m.

Fees and permits: $5 per person 13 years and older (subject to change), free for Texas State Parks Pass holders

Trail contacts: Cooper Lake State Park Headquarters (Doctors Creek Unit), 95 Park Road 8154, Cooper 75432; (903) 395-3100

Dog-friendly: Leashed dogs permitted

Trail surface: Dirt and mowed grass

Land status: Texas Parks and Wildlife Department

Nearest town: Cooper (north), Sulphur Springs (southeast)

Other trail users: Mountain bikers

Maps: USGS Cooper South; Cooper Lake State Park Trails map (available online at www.tpwd.texas.gov/state-parks/parks-map and via the TX State Parks mobile app)

Finding the trailhead: From downtown Dallas, get onto I-30E. After traveling about 6 miles on I-30E, stay in the left lane to continue on I-30E. Stay on I-30E for 48.1 miles until you take exit 101 for TX-24 N toward FM1737. After traveling on TX-24 N for 25 miles, make a right on TX-24 BUS/W Dallas Avenue. Continue on TX-24 BUS for 2.2 miles, and then make a right on FM1529/Country Club Road. Travel on FM1529 for 1.7 miles before making a right onto Park Road 8154. The Cedar Creek South Loop Trailhead and parking lot (eight spaces and one disabled space) will be to your left after 1.1 miles. **GPS:** N33° 20.596' W95° 40.531'

The Hike

Where Jim Chapman Lake (also known as Cooper Lake) lies today used to be the Sulphur River floodplain. After the US Army Corp of Engineers dammed up the South Sulphur River, the lake was formed. It is now a body of water abundant with diverse aquatic life that provides water to several districts in North Texas and remains a place for recreation.

Shoreline of Jim Chapman Lake

The Cedar Creek trail system, having earned its title from a neighboring settlement from the 17th century, consists of four loops—North, South, East, and West. This guide will include both the South and North loops, allowing hikers to see and have access to the north shore of Jim Chapman Lake, while adding mileage. There are several interpretive waysides along the route, containing information on the following subjects: "Poison Ivy," "Pocket Prairie," "Honey Locust," "Winged Elm," "Common Persimmon," "Winged Sumac," "Mexican Plum," "Post Oak," and "Eastern Red Cedar." The route begins at the Cedar Creek South Loop Trailhead southeast of the parking area where you enter a wooded area. Watch for unearthed tree roots in the path about 625 feet into the trail. At 0.14 miles, the shade dissipates as you enter a prairie. The path surface turns from dirt to mowed grass. After a decent rainfall, this area can get muddy. The trail returns to a wooded area with partial shade at 0.23 miles and then into prairie landscape shortly after.

At 0.28 miles, the trail heads east. Lake views will be to your right. You will reach an optional spur to the Lake Cooper shoreline to your right at the 0.3-mile mark. If you'd like to see the lake up close, head down the spur to reach the shoreline. You will reach the Lake Cooper shoreline at 0.36 miles. Take some time to enjoy the view and then turn around and head back to the Cedar Creek South Loop trail. The mileage clocks at 0.24 miles when you reconnect with the trail. Bear right to continue on the Cedar Creek South Loop. You will once again enter a wooded area.

After crossing a seasonal streambed at 0.43 miles, a "Bois d'Arc" interpretive wayside will be to your right. At the 0.46-mile mark, bear left toward 7th Street to connect with the Cedar Creek North Loop and exit the wooded area. The right side of the fork heads toward the Pelican Point Day-Use Area and the leopard frog marsh.

Cedar Creek South and North Loops, Cooper Lake State Park (Doctors Creek Unit)

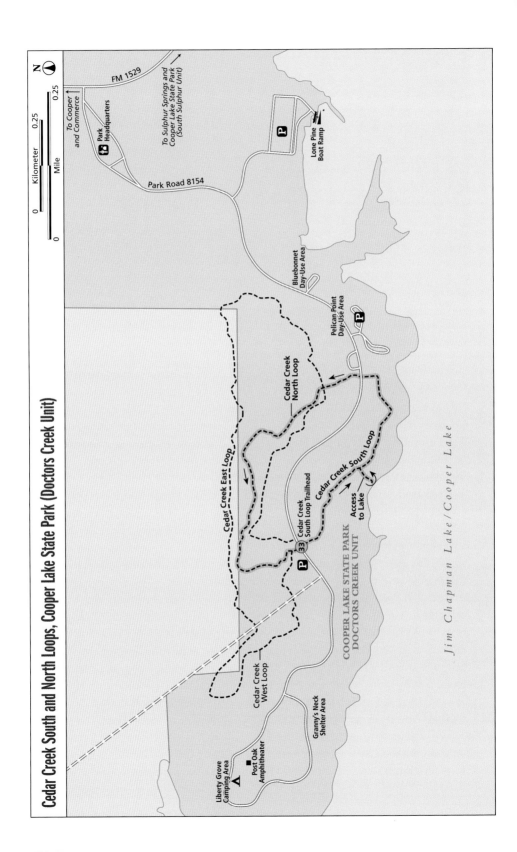

N

0   Kilometer   0.25

0   Mile   0.25

To Cooper
and Commerce

FM 1529

Park Headquarters

To Sulphur Springs and
Cooper Lake State Park
(South Sulphur Unit)

Park Road 8154

P

Lone Pine
Boat Ramp

Bluebonnet
Day-Use Area

Pelican Point
Day-Use Area

P

Cedar Creek
North Loop

Cedar Creek East Loop

Cedar Creek South Loop

Cedar Creek
South Loop Trailhead

33

P

Access
to Lake

COOPER LAKE STATE PARK
DOCTORS CREEK UNIT

Cedar Creek
West Loop

Granny's Neck
Shelter Area

Liberty Grove
Camping Area

Post Oak
Amphitheater

Jim Chapman Lake/Cooper Lake

Watch for passing vehicles before crossing 7th Street, as there is no pedestrian crosswalk. There will be a brown sign indicating the nature trail.

Prairie landscape along the Cedar Creek South Loop

Throughout the Cedar Creek North Loop, the landscape will continuously change between oak forests and prairie. A little more than half a mile into the route, the trail heads northwest. You will reach a connection to the Cedar Creek East Loop at 0.56 miles. Continue straight on the Cedar Creek North Loop. Follow the brown sign indicating the nature trail. The trail curves north and then eventually back northwest at 0.69 miles. Bear left at the fork at 0.92 miles. Northwest toward the bench is the Cedar Creek East Loop. The trail heads south shortly after. You will reach 7th Street once again at the 1.1-mile mark. Watch for passing vehicles before crossing (again, no pedestrian crosswalk) back to the parking area and the Cedar Creek South Loop trailhead.

Miles and Directions

0.0 Start at the Cedar Creek South Loop Trailhead southeast from parking area.

0.12 Watch for unearthed tree roots in the path.

0.28 Lake views will be to your right.

0.3 Reach a spur to the Lake Cooper shoreline to your right. Head down the spur to reach the shoreline.

0.36 Reach the Lake Cooper shoreline and enjoy the view. Turn around and head back to the Cedar Creek South Loop trail.

0.42 Reconnect with the trail. Bear right to continue on the Cedar Creek South Loop.

0.43 Cross over a seasonal streambed.

0.46 Reach a fork. Bear left toward 7th Street to connect with the Cedar Creek North Loop.

0.49 Watch for passing vehicles before crossing 7th Street (no pedestrian crosswalk).

0.56 Reach the Cedar Creek East Loop connection. Continue straight on the Cedar Creek North Loop.

0.92 Reach a fork. Bear left.

1.1 Watch for passing vehicles before crossing 7th Street again (no pedestrian crosswalk). Arrive back at the trailhead.

34 Shoreline Trail, Cedar Hill State Park

Staying true to its name, the Shoreline Trail parallels Joe Pool Lake, offering continuous views of the freshwater beauty. In the spring, hikers can spot multitudes of the Texas state flower, the bluebonnet, blooming along the shore. ADA accessible, this trail allows many to enjoy the lake and its surrounding scenery.

Lake or river: Joe Pool Lake
Photogenic factor: 4+
Start: Shoreline Trailhead
Elevation gain: 472 to 541 feet
Distance: 2.12 miles out and back
Difficulty: Easy
Hiking time: About 1 hour
Seasons/schedule: Open year-round, 6 a.m. to 10 p.m.
Fees and permits: $7 per person 13 years and older (subject to change), free for Texas State Parks Pass holders
Trail contacts: Cedar Hill State Park Headquarters, 1570 West FM 1382, Cedar Hill 75104; (972) 291-3900
Dog-friendly: Leashed dogs permitted
Trail surface: Paved, ADA accessible
Land status: Texas Parks and Wildlife Department

Nearest town: Dallas and Duncanville (northeast), Arlington (northwest), Cedar Hill (southeast), Mansfield (southwest)
Other trail users: None
Maps: USGS Duncanville; Cedar Hill State Park map (available online at www.tpwd.texas .gov/state-parks/parks-map and via the TX State Parks mobile app)
Special considerations: During the spring season with adequate rainfall, the Texas state flower, the bluebonnet, blooms vibrantly around Joe Pool Lake. Cedar Hill State Park is very popular due to its proximity to the Dallas–Fort Worth metro area, so make sure to reserve day passes ahead of time. There is no shade on this trail. Start your hike early and bring adequate amounts of water.

Finding the trailhead: From downtown Dallas, get onto I-35E N. Use I-35E N to merge onto I-35 N. Stay on I-35 N for 4.3 miles before continuing onto US 67 S. Travel for 9.6 miles on US 67 S. Take the exit for FM 1382/Grand Prairie/De Soto. Travel on N TX 67/N J Elmer Weaver Freeway for half a mile before turning right onto FM 1382/Belt Line Road. After traveling on FM 1382/Belt Line Road for 2.6 miles, turn right onto Penn Branch Parkway. Continue on Penn Branch Parkway for 0.4 miles (the park headquarters will be to your left) until you reach the stop sign and the road changes to W Spine Road. Travel on W Spine Road for half a mile. A parking lot for the boat ramp area will be to your left. The Shoreline Trailhead is west of the boat ramp parking area near the restrooms. The word "TRAIL" in all capital letters indicates a good starting point. **GPS:** N32° 37.694' W96° 58.943'

The Hike

Fed by both Mountain Creek and Walnut Creek, Joe Pool Lake is an immensely popular recreation area. Cedar Hill State Park is one of several parks that has access to Joe Pool Lake, and the portion of the lake that is within the park is surrounded

Sunrise at Joe Pool Lake

by limestone bluffs blanketed by cedar and Texas Blackland Prairie grassland. The Shoreline Trail is one of several trails in Cedar Hill State Park that has lake views. It also has a couple advantages—its ADA-accessibile surface and its continuous access to the shoreline.

The scenic Shoreline Trail begins west of the boat ramp parking area, near the restrooms. The word "TRAIL" in capital letters on the surface will indicate you are on the right path. The trail heads southwest for about 250 feet, before curving and heading northwest. At 0.1 miles, there will be a "Life along Mountain Creek" inter-pretive wayside to your left. The trail then heads northwest shy of a quarter of a mile into the trail. The "A Meadowlarks Message" interpretive wayside will be to your

Shoreline Trail, Cedar Hill State Park

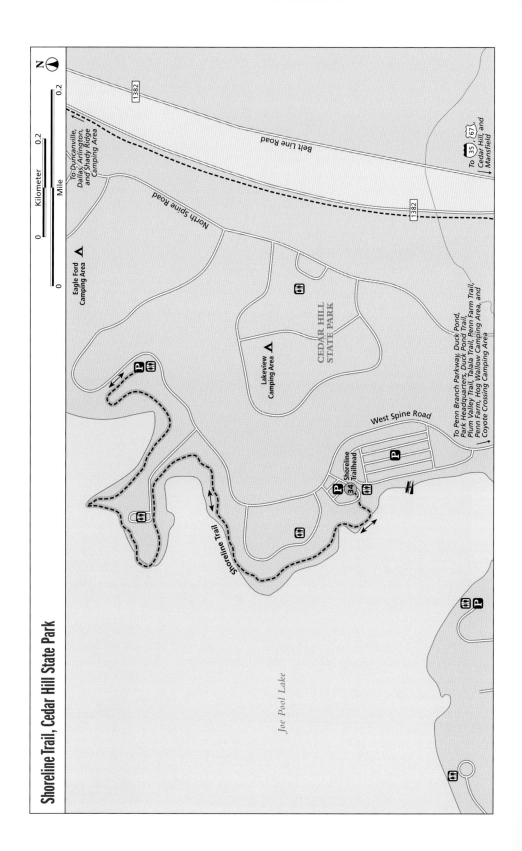

Picnic area around Joe Pool Lake

left at 0.36 miles. At the 0.41-mile mark, there will be a playground to your left, and then the trail begins to head northwest shortly after.

The trail changes between heading north and east in between 0.6 miles and 0.7 miles. Make sure to take some time to enjoy the view of Joe Pool Lake from the bench as the trail curves southeast at about the three-quarters of a mile mark. The trail then settles on heading east. In between all this, you will encounter the "Have You Heard?" interpretive wayside to the west. "Swim Smart" signs will be to your left at the 0.79- and 0.85-mile marks. The trail heads in a northeasterly direction at 0.9 miles, and then the "Keep Cedar Hill Wild" interpretive wayside will be to your left shortly after. Prior to reaching the end of the trail at 1.06 miles, the trail curves southeast. Similar to the beginning of the trail, the word "TRAIL" in capital letters on the surface at the 1.06-mile mark will indicate that the path ends and for you to turn around. At this point, turn around and return the way that you came. For a more rugged hiking experience (not ADA accessible) that has higher elevation views of Joe Pool Lake, the 2-plus-mile Talala Trail is another beautiful hike within Cedar Hill State Park to consider.

Miles and Directions

0.0 Begin at the Shoreline Trailhead. Start west of the boat ramp parking area. The word "TRAIL" in capital letters on the surface will indicate you are on the right path.

0.41 Reach a playground to your left.

1.06 Reach the end of the trail. The word "TRAIL" in capital letters on the surface will indicate that the path ends and for you to turn around. Return the way you came.

2.12 Arrive back at the trailhead.

35 White Rock Lake Trail, White Rock Lake Park

The calm scene of sailboats and sculls gently floating on top of White Rock Lake, especially against the pastel and faded skies of sunrise, is a picture-perfect moment. This is just one of the many photogenic scenes that can be seen from the White Rock Lake Trail. The trail meanders through dense forests and is flanked by historical buildings, making the trail a bucket-list hike.

Lake or river: White Rock Lake

Photogenic factor: 5

Start: Accessible from any of the parking lots surrounding White Rock Lake, this guide starts at the Big Thicket area

Elevation gain: 420 to 502 feet

Distance: 9.24-mile loop

Difficulty: Moderate due to length

Hiking time: 4–5 hours

Seasons/schedule: Open year-round, 6 a.m. to 11 p.m.

Fees and permits: None (subject to change)

Trail contacts: City of Dallas Parks and Recreation Department Main Office, 1500 Marilla Street Suite 6FN, Dallas 75201; (214) 670-4100

Dog-friendly: Leashed dogs permitted

Trail surface: Alternates between paved asphalt and concrete, ADA accessible

Land status: City of Dallas Parks and Recreation Department

Nearest town: Within Dallas city limits

Other trail users: Mountain bikers/cyclists, anglers

Maps: USGS White Rock Lake; White Rock Lake Park map (available online at https://www.dallascounty.org/departments/plandev/trails/maps/whiterock.php)

Special considerations: This trail is used frequently by cyclists. Be alert for cyclists headed your way or coming from behind you. There is partial shade on this trail. Due to the trail length, start your hike early and bring adequate amounts of water.

Finding the trailhead: From the I-345 and US 75 corridor in downtown Dallas, travel on US 75 N for 3.2 miles. Take exit 3 for Mockingbird Lane/SMU Boulevard. After 0.1 miles, turn right onto E Mockingbird Lane. Continue on E Mockingbird Lane for 3.7 miles. Turn right onto Scout Hill Drive. After 0.1 miles, turn left onto Lawther Drive. Close to 0.6 miles, you will see the Big Thicket area and parking lot to your left. **GPS:** N32° 50.815' W96° 42.979'

The Hike

White Rock Lake is a popular place for locals and visitors, and for a good reason. Anywhere you go on the lake, it serves as a beautiful, photographic backdrop. Ducks glide on the waters among boats, beautiful structures like the cultural bathhouse and the pumphouse offer glimpses into history, and the continuous canopy of trees provide solace from city life. The White Rock Trail circumnavigates the entire lake and can be accessed from any parking lot in the park. This guide starts the trail at

Daybreak at White Rock Lake   *A raft of ducks by the shoreline*

the Big Thicket area northeast of the parking lot and takes the loop in a clockwise direction. The trail heads primarily south with a few portions heading north and east for a brief period.

There will be several pedestrian crosswalks to cross while on the route. At 0.62 miles, you will come upon your first one. As for all crosswalks and anytime you have to cross a road, watch for vehicles before crossing. The Bath House Cultural Center will be to your right. It was originally built in 1930 as a bathhouse with an art deco design and later became Dallas's first-ever neighborhood cultural center. When you reach the access road at 0.77 miles, again please watch for vehicles before crossing. A view of the downtown skyline, particularly amazing at sunset, will be to your right at 0.83 miles.

There will be a couple of pedestrian crosswalks and pedestrian footbridges to cross from the 1.42-mile mark until you reach a parking lot at the 2.08-mile mark. At the 2.08-mile mark, the trail becomes undefined. Use the sidewalk to go east around the restrooms. Head toward the intersection where you will see the wide path barricaded with yellow metal poles. It will have two stone pillars with plaques stating "White Rock." Pelican Point will be to your right. Views of White Rock Lake will eventually return to your right.

Starting at 2.96 miles, the Dallas Arboretum spans to your left for about a quarter of a mile. You will cross a couple more pedestrian bridges as the trail curves south and parallels Garland Road. Once the spillway comes into view, the trail heads north

Boathouse near the trail

and you will reach a nice vista point of the spillway at 4.31 miles. When you reach the connection to the SoPAC Trail shortly after, bear right across the pedestrian bridge. After the trail heads north across the spillway, you will need to head down the ramp, and then you will come upon the stately pumphouse structure to your right, just shy of 5 miles into the trail. Continue straight past the pumphouse until you reach another parking lot. Watch for vehicles before heading toward the pole barriers to the left of the parking lot to reconnect with the trail. Bear right when you encounter another connection to the SoPAC Trail at 5.22 miles.

There will be another pedestrian bridge and pedestrian crosswalk to cross before you reach a road at 6.27 miles. This particular road does not have a crosswalk. As all the other times you need to cross the road, pay attention to passing vehicles before crossing. When you head across a boardwalk starting at 7.81 miles, a boathouse will be to your right. The trail then heads primarily east when the mileage reads at 8 miles. After crossing another pedestrian bridge and passing by a dog park to your left, you will cross the final pedestrian bridge at 8.48 miles. When the pedestrian bridge ends at 8.62 miles, bear right to return to the Big Thicket area. Cross the final pedestrian crosswalk of the route at 8.68 miles when it is safe to do so, and then bypass the path to your left that connects to Boy Scout Hill shortly after. The trail eventually heads south all the way back to the Big Thicket area, with views of sailboats and sculls belonging to the White Rock Boat Club and Dallas United Crew. You will have successfully completed the entire loop when the mileage clocks at 9.24 miles and you have returned to the Big Thicket area.

The historic pumphouse

White Rock Lake Trail, White Rock Lake Park

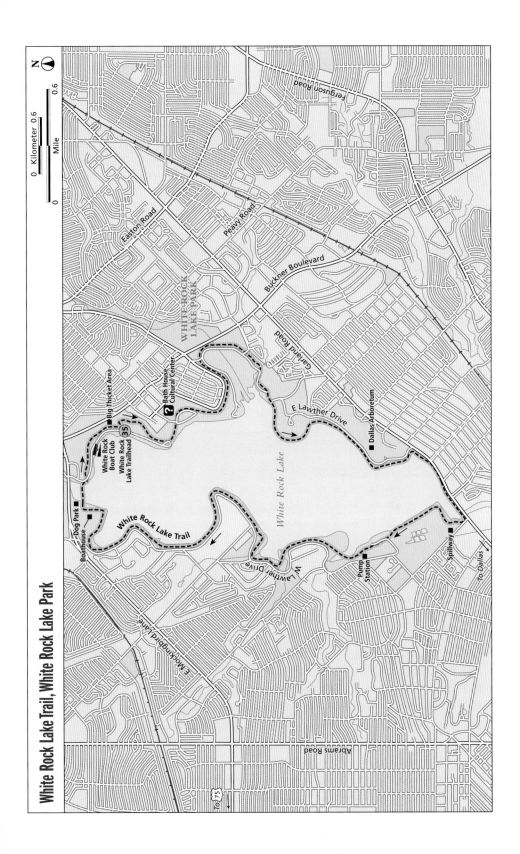

- Easton Road
- Peavy Road
- Ferguson Road
- WHITE ROCK LAKE PARK
- Buckner Boulevard
- Bath House Cultural Center
- Garland Road
- Big Thicket Area
- White Rock Boat Club
- White Rock Lake Trailhead
- 35
- E Lawther Drive
- Dallas Arboretum
- White Rock Lake
- Dog Park
- Boathouse
- White Rock Lake Trail
- W Lawther Drive
- Pump Station
- Spillway
- To Dallas
- E Mockingbird Lane
- Abrams Road
- To 75

N

0 Kilometer 0.6
0 Mile 0.6

Miles and Directions

0.0 Start the trail at the Big Thicket area northeast of the parking lot. This guide takes the loop in a clockwise direction.

0.62 Reach a pedestrian crosswalk. Watch for vehicles before crossing. The Bath House Cultural Center will be to your right.

0.77 Reach an access road. Watch for vehicles before crossing.

0.83 A view of the downtown skyline will be to your right.

1.35 A pavilion and playground will be to your right.

1.42 Reach a pedestrian crosswalk. Watch for vehicles before crossing.

1.59 Cross a pedestrian bridge.

1.79 Reach a pedestrian crosswalk. Watch for vehicles before crossing.

1.93 Cross a small pedestrian bridge.

2.08 Reach a parking lot. Pelican Point will be to your right. Use the sidewalk to go east around the restrooms until you reach the fork at 2.13 miles. Take the right side of the fork that is wider and barricaded with yellow metal poles. There will be two stone pillars with plaques with the words "White Rock."

2.29 Views of White Rock Lake will return to your right.

2.96 The Dallas Arboretum will be to your left.

3.59 and 4.16 Cross a pedestrian bridge.

4.31 Reach a vista point of the spillway.

4.35 Reach a fork. Bear right across the pedestrian bridge.

4.56 The trail heads north across the spillway.

4.86 Head down the ramp.

4.93 A pumphouse will be to your right.

4.95 Reach a fork. Continue straight.

5.06 Reach a parking lot. Watch for vehicles before heading toward the pole barriers to the left of the parking lot to reconnect with the trail.

5.22 Reach a fork. Bear right.

5.28 Cross a pedestrian bridge. The boathouse will be to your right.

5.35 Reach a pedestrian crosswalk. Watch for vehicles before crossing.

5.84 Continue north at the fork.

6.27 Watch for vehicles before crossing the road. There is no crosswalk.

7.81 Cross a boardwalk.

8.04 Cross a pedestrian bridge.

8.45 A dog park will be to your left.

8.48 Cross a pedestrian bridge and then bear right.

8.68 Reach a pedestrian crosswalk. Watch for vehicles before crossing.

8.75 Bypass the path to your left that connects to Boy Scout Hill.

9.24 Arrive back at the trailhead.

36 Trinity Forest Trail to Little Lemmon Lake, Joppa Preserve

A walk through the ethereal Trinity Forest and sights of the quaint Little Lemmon Lake are just a couple of the highlights of the Trinity Forest Trail segment that runs through the Joppa Preserve. A footbridge that was used for a scene in the film *Bonnie and Clyde* makes the trail notable.

Lake or river: Little Lemmon Lake
Photogenic factor: 4+
Start: Eco Park Trailhead
Elevation gain: 371 to 407 feet
Distance: 4.4 miles out and back
Difficulty: Easy
Hiking time: 1–2 hours
Seasons/schedule: Open year-round, 5 a.m. to 11 p.m.
Fees and permits: None (subject to change)
Trail contacts: City of Dallas Parks and Recreation Department Main Office, 1500

Marilla Street Suite 6FN, Dallas 75201; (214) 670-4100
Dog-friendly: Leashed dogs permitted
Trail surface: Paved asphalt and concrete, ADA accessible
Land status: City of Dallas Parks and Recreation Department
Nearest town: Within Dallas city limits
Other trail users: Mountain bikers/cyclists, anglers
Maps: USGS Hutchins; Trinity Forest Trails map (available online at https://trinityrivercorridor .com/recreation/trinity-trails-phase-1-and-2)

Finding the trailhead: From downtown Dallas, travel on I-45 S for 7.4 miles. Take exit 277. Turn left onto Simpson Stuart Road after 0.3 miles. Stay on Simpson Stuart Road for 1 mile, and then turn left onto Locust Drive. The Eco Park Trailhead will be to your right in about 450 feet. Parking for the trailhead will be available to your left at Eco Park. Use the pedestrian crosswalk to get to the trailhead from the parking lot. **GPS:** N32° 41.405' W96° 43.819'

The Hike

Although it's a leisurely hike, the stretch of the Trinity Forest Trail from the Eco Park Trailhead to Little Lemmon Lake is a worthwhile one. It includes a decent amount of mileage, and the view of Little Lemmon Lake at the end of the route makes a nice compensation. The trail begins on the sidewalk east of the Eco Park parking lot and pedestrian crosswalk. At 465 feet, bear left onto Simpson Stuart Road. There are barriers blocking vehicles from coming onto this segment of the road, but still watch for any vehicles entering the intersection. The trail is undefined for about 150 feet and then the surface changes to asphalt. At 0.39 miles, the trail surface changes to concrete and remains this way all the way through. A green sign indicating a point in the trail (reads TFT 200/TFT 104) will appear at the 0.45-mile mark. These types

Little Lemmon Lake

of signs will occur throughout the trail as helpful location pinpoints in the case of emergency.

Bear left at the TFT 200/TFT 104 sign. From this point, you will enter a portion of the Trinity Forest, and the trail becomes shaded. The dense foliage obscures any trace of Lake Lemmon to your right. However, you will be able to see Little Lemmon on this trail. Any shade on the trail dissipates at 1.28 miles when you reach a picnic area to your left and the Joppa Preserve Trailhead. A parking lot will be to your right at 1.41 miles and then the trail becomes shaded again. A lovely vista point of a small pond will be available to your left shortly after, and then the pond ends at the 1.66-mile mark. The landscape opens up at 1.76 miles and the trail heads northeast along some power lines.

There will be a short footbridge to cross close to the 2-mile mark. This bridge is called the Great Trinity Trail Bridge. Where it is situated is the very spot where the Texas Ranger shoot-out scene in *Bonnie and Clyde* was filmed. The trail heads north after you cross the notable footbridge. Bypass the offshoot to your left after crossing the bridge and then you will be back in a forested area. The pretty and peaceful Little Lemmon Lake will be to your left. You will likely see an egret or two residing on the shoreline. A couple benches will be by the side of the trail starting at 2.06 miles. Little Lemmon Lake ends when you bear right toward the Trinity Forest Trailhead and the parking lot. The mileage reads as 2.2 miles at the Trinity Forest Trailhead. Turn around and return the way you came.

Trinity Forest Trail to Little Lemmon Lake, Joppa Preserve

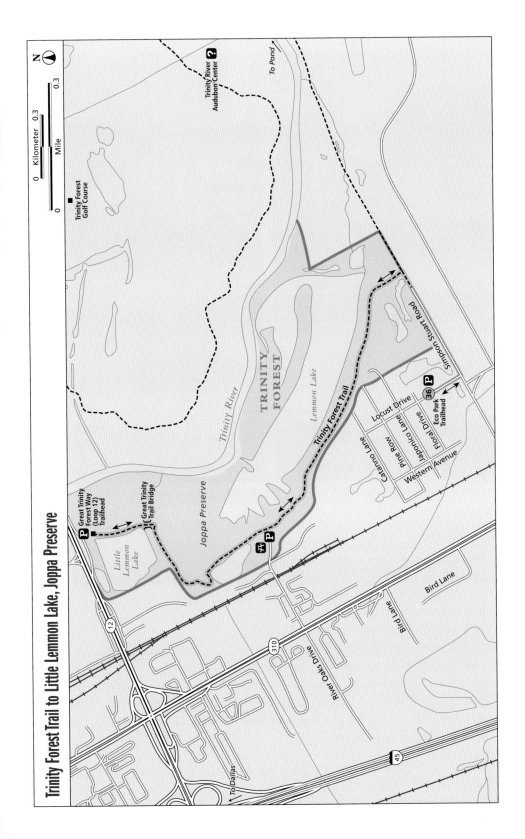

N

0   Kilometer   0.3

0   Mile   0.3

Trinity Forest Golf Course

Trinity River Audubon Center

To Pond

Trinity River

TRINITY FOREST

Lemmon Lake

Joppa Preserve

Great Trinity Forest Way (Loop 12) Trailhead

Little Lemmon Lake

Great Trinity Trail Bridge

Trinity Forest Trail

Locust Drive

Catarino Lane

Pine Row

Japonico Lane

Floral Drive

Western Avenue

Simpson Stuart Road

Eco Park Trailhead

36

To Dallas

River Oaks Drive

Bird Lane

Bird Lane

12

310

45

An egret waits by the shoreline

The Trinity Forest Trail

Miles and Directions

0.0 The trail begins east of the Eco Park parking lot and pedestrian crosswalk.

0.09 Bear left onto Simpson Stuart Road. There are barriers blocking vehicles from coming onto this segment of the road.

0.45 Reach the TFT 200/TFT 104 point. Bear left.

1.28 A picnic area will be to your left.

1.41 A parking lot will be to your right.

1.48 A vista point of a small pond will be to your left.

1.98 Cross the Great Trinity Trail Bridge.

2.01 Bypass the offshoot to your left. Little Lemmon Lake will be to your left.

2.2 Reach the Trinity Forest Trailhead and parking lot. Return the way you came.

4.4 Arrive back at the trailhead.

37 Twin Peaks Trail (combined with Dana Peak Hill Trail), Dana Peak Park

With nearly 60 miles of shoreline, Stillhouse Hollow Lake continues to serve multiple purposes—recreation, conservation, and flood control. The glistening waters of the lake, its peaceful inlets, and its surrounding wildflower dotted, rocky landscape, draws hikers, cyclists, and campers for an enjoyable getaway.

Lake or river: Stillhouse Hollow Lake
Photogenic factor: 4+
Start: Dana Peak Hill Trailhead
Elevation gain: 577 to 801 feet
Distance: 4.16-mile figure 8
Difficulty: Difficult due to steep inclines and declines
Hiking time: 2–3 hours
Seasons/schedule: Open year-round, sunrise to sunset
Fees and permits: $5 per vehicle (subject to change); pay at Stillhouse Lake office, no fee if hiking only and starting at the trailhead north of the park main entrance
Trail contacts: US Army Corps of Engineers Stillhouse Hollow Lake Office, 3740 FM 1670, Benton 76513; (254) 939-2461
Dog-friendly: Leashed dogs permitted
Trail surface: Dirt and rocky path
Land status: US Army Corps of Engineers

Nearest town: Harker Heights (northwest), Nolanville (north), Belton (northeast)
Other trail users: Mountain bikers/cyclists, except on the Dana Peak Hill Trail (hikers only)
Maps: USGS Nolanville; US Army Corps of Engineers Stillhouse Hollow Lake map (available online at https://www.swf-wc.usace.army .mil/stillhouse/Recreation/Trails/Hike.shtml)
Special considerations: Blue metal circles with arrows serve as trail guides for the Twin Peaks Trail. Red metal circles with arrows serve as guides for the Fire Line Trail (the connecting trail between the Dana Peak Hill Trail and the Twin Peaks Trail). This trail is used frequently by mountain bikers/cyclists. Be alert for those headed your way or coming from behind you. There is minimal shade on this trail. Start your hike early and bring adequate amounts of water.

Finding the trailhead: From the US 77 BUS N/La Salle Avenue and 3rd Street intersection south of Baylor University in Waco, head southwest on US 77 BUS N/La Salle Avenue for 1.7 miles. After going through the traffic circle, continue on La Salle Avenue for 0.4 miles. Turn right onto Primrose Drive, and then turn left onto N Interstate 35 Frontage Road. Travel on N Interstate 35 Frontage Road for 0.3 miles. Merge onto I-35 S. Stay on I-35 S for 39.5 miles. When you reach the town of Belton, continue on I-14/US 190 W. After 3.7 miles, take exit 297. Travel for 1.4 miles and then turn left onto Simmons Road. In 0.2 miles, turn right onto FM 2410. Stay on FM 2410 for 5.3 miles. Go left onto Comanche Gap Road. Continue on Comanche Gap Road for 2.4 miles. The parking area for the Dana Peak Trail System will be straight ahead to the east. The Dana Peak Hill Trailhead will be south of the main trailhead for the Dana Peak Trail System. **GPS:** N31° 01.908' W97° 36.499'

The Hike

This guide includes the Dana Peak Hill Trail with the Twin Peaks Trail for a different vantage point of Stillhouse Hollow Lake. It starts off at the Dana Peak Hill Trailhead, which will be south of the main trailhead for the Dana Peak Trail System. It heads southeast for a rocky 100-foot ascent to the high point at the 0.14-mile mark. After 120 feet into the trail, continue straight at the fork to continue on the Dana Peak Hill Trail. The right is the Highline Trail. A vista of Stillhouse Hollow Lake will welcome you straight ahead as a reward for the tough ascent. After the vista, the trail begins to narrow and begins to curve northwest. From the 0.35-mile mark, you will make a rocky 90-foot descent to the 0.45-mile mark. Bypass the offshoots to your left during the descent.

At 0.45 miles, you will reach the Fire Lane Trail and the trail widens. Bear right to head toward the Twin Peaks Trail. The markers for the Fire Lane Trail are red. The left heads back to the Dana Peak main trailhead and parking area. This guide will take that route on the way back. There will be several connections to other trails during your trek on the Fire Line Trail. This includes connections to the Fence Line Trail, Camel Back Trail, Cedar Cemetery Trail, Lagoon Loop, and Twister Trail. As long as you head northeast until you reach the Twin Peaks Trail connection at the 1.29-mile mark, you will stay on track. The trail will curve north after the second connection to the Lagoon Loop at the 0.87-mile mark, and then heads back northeast after the connection to the Twister Trail at the 1.1-mile mark. The trail splits and quickly merges at 1.12 miles, and then heads northeast.

View of Stillhouse Hollow Lake from the trail

Twin Peaks in the distance

You will encounter a connection to the Twin Peaks Trail at the 1.29-mile mark. Bear right to start on the Twin Peaks Trail. The path to the northeast will be the return route once you have completed the Twin Peaks Trail. The trail becomes narrow again. Watch for periodic erosion in the path while traversing the Twin Peaks Trail. This area is hugely popular for mountain bikers, so pay attention to sharing the path with others. In between the 1.45-mile mark and the 1.72-mile mark, there will be several offshoots to your left and your right that you will need to bypass. The first offshoot you will come upon will be to your left. It is a shortcut to the other side of the Twin Peaks Trail. Continue heading south. In between there will be a picturesque inlet to your right.

The trail begins to head east at 1.87 miles, and views of Stillhouse Hollow Lake will open up to your right. From the 1.94-mile mark to the 2.3-mile mark, you will need to again bypass offshoots, this time to your right and left. Meanwhile the trail heads east along the shoreline and you will have up-close views of Stillhouse Hollow Lake. The trail begins to head away from the lake at 2.37 miles when the trail curves northwest. Take advantage of the shaded areas that occur in between the 2.61-mile mark and the 2.75-mile mark. With no shade on the Fire Line Trail and minimal shade on the Twin Peaks Trail, the shade during this segment of the trail provides some needed relief during the summer months.

When you reach the fork at 2.75 miles, there will be a bench. Feel free to take a break on the bench, and then bear right to continue on the Twin Peaks Trail. The left is an offshoot, again. The other end of the shortcut from the original 1.45-mile mark concludes at the 2.87-mile mark. At 2.94 miles, the Twin Peaks Trail ends and you will encounter a junction. Straight ahead is the connection to the Outback Trail; its markers are green. The path to the northwest is the Fence Line Trail; its markers are red. The path heading to the east and west is the Fire Line Trail. Bear left to return to

Twin Peaks Trail (combined with Dana Peak Hill Trail), Dana Peak Park

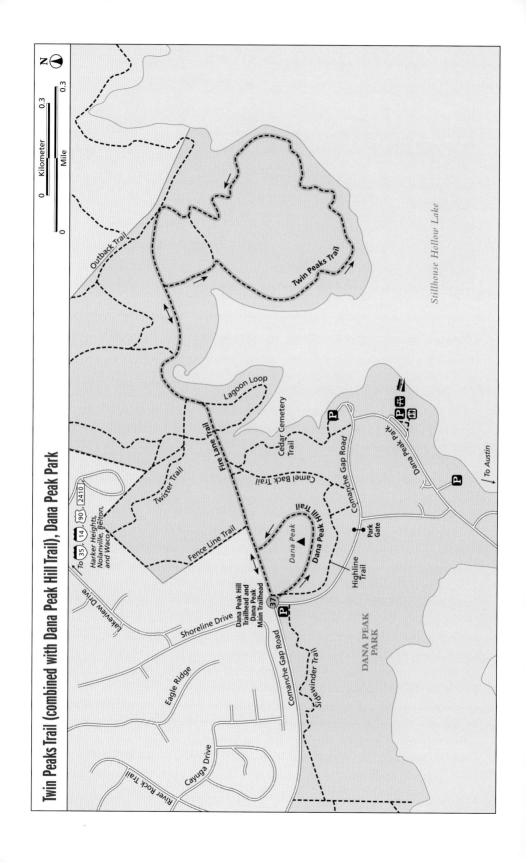

N

Kilometer
0 0.3

Mile
0 0.3

To 35, 14, 90, 2410
Harker Heights,
Nolanville, Belton,
and Waco

Outback Trail

Twin Peaks Trail

Stillhouse Hollow Lake

Lagoon Loop

Fire Lane Trail

Twister Trail

Cedar Cemetery Trail

Camel Back Trail

Fence Line Trail

Dana Peak Hill Trail

Dana Peak

Comanche Gap Road

Park Gate

Highline Trail

Dana Peak Park

P

To Austin

Lakeview Drive

Shoreline Drive

Dana Peak Hill Trailhead and Dana Peak Main Trailhead

P 37

Eagle Ridge

Cayuga Drive

River Rock Trail

Sidewinder Trail

Comanche Gap Road

DANA PEAK PARK

the Fire Line Trail and head toward the Twin Peaks Trail connection from the original 1.29-mile mark. Bypass the very last offshoot of the route to your right at 3.04 miles.

The mileage will read as 3.18 miles when you reach the Twin Peaks Trail connection from the original 1.29-mile mark. Continue straight on the Fire Line Trail all the way to the main trailhead for the Dana Peak Trail system, bypassing the Dana Peak Hill Trail connection from the original 0.45-mile mark. The route concludes at 4.16 miles.

Miles and Directions

0.0 Begin at the Dana Peak Hill Trailhead (south of the main trailhead for the Dana Peak Trail system).

0.02 Reach a fork. Continue straight. Make a rocky 100-foot ascent to the 0.14-mile mark.

0.14 Reach a vista of Stillhouse Hollow Lake.

0.35 Make a 90-foot descent from here to the 0.45-mile mark.

0.37 and 0.41 Bypass the offshoots to your left.

0.45 Reach the Fire Lane Trail. Bear right to head toward the Twin Peaks Trail. (Markers for the Fire Lane Trail are red.)

0.52 and 0.79 Bypass the connection to the Fence Line Trail to your left.

0.67 and 0.7 Bypass the connections to the Camel Back Trail and the Cedar Cemetery Trail to your right.

0.77 and 0.87 Bypass the connection to the Lagoon Loop to your right.

0.94 Bypass another connection to the Lagoon Loop to your left.

1.1 Bypass the connection to the Twister Trail to your left.

1.12 The trail splits and then merges.

1.29 Reach a fork. Bear right to begin on the Twin Peaks Trail. Watch for periodic erosion in the path throughout the Twin Peaks Trail.

1.45 to 1.72 Bypass several offshoots to your left and your right. The first offshoot to your left is a shortcut to the other side of the Twin Peaks Trail. Continue south.

1.87 Views of Stillhouse Hollow Lake open up to your right.

1.94 Bypass the offshoot to your right. Continue straight.

2.22 Bypass the offshoot to your left. The trail heads east along the shoreline.

2.3 Bypass several side trails to your right.

2.75 Reach a fork and a bench. Bear right to continue on the Twin Peaks Trail.

2.87 Bypass the other end of the shortcut from the original 1.45-mile mark.

2.94 Reach a junction. Bear left to return to the Fire Line Trail and head toward the Twin Peaks Trail connection from the original 1.29-mile mark.

3.04 Bypass the offshoot to your right.

3.18 Reach the Twin Peaks Trail connection from the original 1.29-mile mark. Continue straight to head toward the main trailhead for the Dana Peak Trail system.

4.01 Bypass the Dana Peak Hill Trail connection to your left. Continue straight toward the main trailhead and Dana Peak Trail System parking area.

4.16 Arrive back at the trailhead.

38 Springfield Trail (combined with Bur Oak Trail), Fort Parker State Park

With two lakes to enjoy, beautiful forests, a melodic spring, and an area rich with history, the route combining the Bur Oak Trail with the Springfield Trail is a must–do hike.

Lake or river: Fort Parker Lake and Lake Springfield
Photogenic factor: 5
Start: Springfield Trailhead
Elevation gain: 374 to 473 feet
Distance: 2.66 miles of a couple lollipops
Difficulty: Moderate
Hiking time: 1-2 hours
Seasons/schedule: Open year-round, 6 a.m. to 10 p.m.
Fees and permits: $5 per person 13 years and older (subject to change), free for Texas State Parks Pass holders
Trail contacts: Fort Parker State Park Headquarters, 194 Park Road 28, Mexia 76667; (254) 562-5751
Dog-friendly: Leashed dogs permitted

Trail surface: Dirt and gravel, at times can get rocky
Land status: Texas Parks and Wildlife Department
Nearest town: Mexia (north), Teague (east), Groesbeck (south), Waco (west)
Other trail users: Mountain bikers/cyclists, anglers; except on the Bur Oak Trail (hikers only)
Maps: USGS Groesbeck; Fort Parker State Park map (available online at www.tpwd.texas.gov/state-parks/parks-map and via the TX State Parks mobile app)
Special considerations: Yellow markers for the Springfield Trail and green markers for the Bur Oak Trail serve as trail guides.

Finding the trailhead: From the US 77 BUS N/La Salle Avenue and 3rd Street intersection south of Baylor University in Waco, head northeast on US 77 BUS N/La Salle Avenue for 1 mile. Exit for Martin Luther King Jr. Boulevard and S Loop Drive. After close to a mile, from the left lane, merge onto TX 484 Loop. TX 484 Loop changes into TX 6 S after 2.5 miles. Stay on TX 6 S for 6.6 miles. Turn left to get onto TX 164 E. Travel on TX 164 E for 25.6 miles. In the town of Groesbeck, turn left onto TX 14 N/Ellis Street. Continue on TX 14 N for 5.2 miles. Turn left onto Park Road 28 to enter Fort Parker State Park. After 1.4 miles, the floating bridge that starts off the trails will be to your left. There is parking available southwest of the floating bridge and near the Discovery Center. **GPS:** N31° 35.840' W96° 32.099'

The Hike

Nearby Fort Parker is famous for being attacked by the Comanche, Kiowa, and Kichais warriors in the spring of 1836. One of the five settlers that were kidnapped from the fort was the mother of Quanah Parker, Cynthia Ann Parker. (Her story is briefly shared in the hike from Copper Breaks State Park included in this guide.) Fort Parker State Park itself is more well known for the area that holds the remains of the

Fort Parker Lake

Birds visible from the bird blind

Lake Springfield

historic town of Springfield. This guide combines the Springfield Trail and the Bur Oak Trail to mingle nature with history. The Springfield Trail begins at the floating bridge, northeast of the parking area and Discovery Center. The Bur Oak Trail connects with the Springfield Trail after the bridge. Bear right to do the Bur Oak Nature Trail. The Springfield Trail continues southeast, and this guide will take that route after the Bur Oak Trail is completed. At 435 feet, a "Poison Ivy" interpretive wayside will be to your right. Several more interpretive waysides are placed throughout the route. These include interpretive waysides on the following topics: "Turks Caps," "American Basswood," "Water Oak," "Birds of Fort Parker State Park," "Hackberry," "Yaupon Holly," "Life of a Dead Tree," "Eastern Redbud," "American Beautyberry," "Welcome to Camp Mexia," "A Lasting Legacy," "Earning a Living," "Start of a New Day," "Fire in the Hole," "Time for Fun," "Building Bodies and Minds," Building a Park," "Segregation," "Reunion," and "Are You Ready to Join?"

When the mileage clocks at 0.11 miles, you will reach the loop portion of the first lollipop route. This guide takes the loop in a counterclockwise direction. Partial views of Fort Parker Lake will appear to your right shortly after. You will cross three wooden footbridges before you reach a bird blind to your right at 0.31 miles. Feel free to go to the bird blind to observe the view. Once you are done, continue the loop by heading east away from the lake.

Watch for some unearthed tree roots in the path at 0.36 miles. The trail heads northeast and then northwest before you reach the wooden footbridge at 0.45 miles. Pay attention to a possible fallen tree trunk in the area before you cross another wooden footbridge at 0.53 miles. The loop concludes at the 0.55-mile mark. Continue straight back toward the Springfield Trail connection. You will reconnect with the Springfield Trail at 0.63 miles. Bear right to continue on the Springfield Trail. Watch for unearthed tree roots in the path again at this point. The path surface gets a bit rocky and remains this way until you reach a wildflower area at 0.78 miles.

The trail eventually heads east when you get close to the Springfield Cemetery. The mileage reads as 0.94 miles when you reach the Springfield Cemetery to your right. Springfield Cemetery and the nearby springs are the only remnants of what was once a thriving town from the 1840s to the 1860s. The gravesites echo the names of those who lived there, including the diverse community that came about during the Reconstruction period after the Civil War. Look ahead for the yellow label at the 0.96-mile mark to begin the loop portion of the lollipop in a counterclockwise direction. To your left you will see another yellow label marker across the cemetery. The east side of the loop will be across Park Road 28 and a yellow marker is also at this point. That will be the return route of the loop. Continue southeast on the west side of the loop. When you come upon the group barracks and paved access road at 1.12 miles, watch for vehicles before crossing the access road. Bear right along the paved access road and head toward the park map exhibit. When you reach the park map exhibit, bear left toward the brown Springfield Trailhead sign at 1.23 miles. The path surface will change back to dirt and gravel at that point.

The trail heads east shortly after you go through another wildflower area. A clearing among the trees allows for partial views of Fort Parker Lake. Cross another wooden footbridge at 1.39 miles, and then the trail heads south briefly before heading east again toward Lake Springfield. The calm Lake Springfield is a perfect place to reflect and take a break. A bench by the lake makes it convenient to stop for a while and bask in the view. On the way around Lake Springfield, there will be a quick spur to the springs to your right. Once you head down the spur to check out the springs and come back, the trail begins to curve northeast. There will be access to Lake Springfield to your left at 1.56 miles. The trail then heads away from both Lake Springfield and Fort Parker Lake.

You will need to bypass the offshoot to your right before the trail heads west into another wildflower area at 1.8 miles. At the 1.87-mile mark, you will encounter Park Road 28 and a pedestrian crosswalk. Look straight ahead for the brown Springfield Trail sign and yellow marker. Watch for vehicles before crossing the crosswalk toward the sign and marker. The park headquarters will be at 1.91 miles, and then the path surface changes to a mowed grass surface for a brief period. You will reach the last wildflower area and wooden footbridge before you head northwest across a dirt access road at 2.08 miles. The trail continues to head west, and then at 2.25 miles, bear south toward the Springfield Cemetery. Reach the yellow marker from the original 0.94-mile mark. Watch for vehicles before crossing Park Road 28 to reconnect with the spur portion of the lollipop. The mileage will clock at 2.33 miles when you reach the spur portion of the lollipop from the original 0.96-mile mark. Head northwest back toward the trailhead bypassing the Bur Oak Nature Trail.

Miles and Directions

0.0 The Springfield Trail begins at the floating bridge.

0.03 Reach a fork. Bear right to do the Bur Oak Nature Trail.

0.11 Reach the loop portion of the lollipop route. This guide takes the loop in a counterclockwise direction. Partial views of the lake will be to your right shortly after.

0.14, 0.19, and 0.23 Cross a wooden footbridge.

0.31 Reach a bird blind to your right.

0.36 Watch for unearthed tree roots in the path.

0.45 Cross a wooden footbridge.

0.53 Cross a wooden footbridge.

0.55 Reach the spur portion of the lollipop from the original 570-foot mark. Continue straight back toward the Springfield Trail connection.

0.63 Reach the Springfield Trail connection from the original 140-foot mark. Bear right to start the Springfield Trail. Watch for unearthed tree roots in the path.

0.94 Reach the Springfield Cemetery to your right. Look ahead for the yellow label at the 0.96-mile mark to begin the loop portion of the lollipop in a counterclockwise direction. Continue southeast on the west side of the loop.

Springfield Trail (combined with Bur Oak Trail), Fort Parker State Park

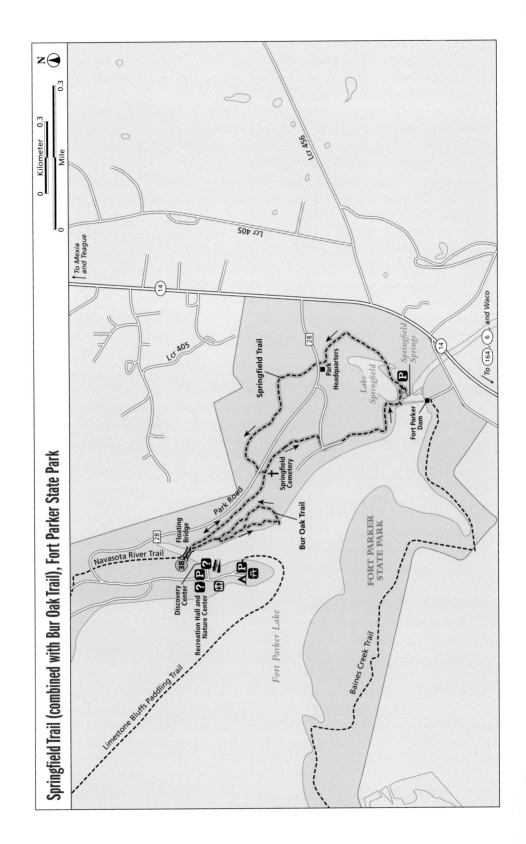

1.12 Reach the group barracks and paved access road. Bear right along the paved access road. Watch for vehicles before crossing and head toward the park map exhibit.

1.17 Reach the park map exhibit. Bear left toward the brown Springfield Trailhead sign at 1.23 miles. The path surface returns to dirt and gravel.

1.39 Cross a wooden footbridge.

1.45 A bench and the dam will be to your right. Lake Springfield will be to your left.

1.52 A spur to springs will be to your right.

1.53 Reach the springs. Enjoy the view and return.

1.54 Return to the trail. Bear right.

1.56 The trail heads away from the lakes.

1.75 Bypass the offshoot to your right.

1.87 Reach Park Road 28 and a pedestrian crosswalk. Watch for vehicles before crossing. Reconnect with the trail at the brown Springfield Trail sign and yellow marker.

1.91 Reach the park headquarters. The path surface changes to a mowed grass surface for a short period.

2.06 Cross a wooden footbridge.

2.08 Cross a dirt access road.

2.25 Bear south toward the Springfield Cemetery. Reach the yellow marker from the 0.94-mile mark. Watch for vehicles before crossing Park Road 28.

2.33 Reach the spur portion of the lollipop right from the original 0.96-mile mark. Bear right back to the trailhead bypassing the Bur Oak Nature Trail.

2.66 Arrive back at the trailhead.

39 Bluestem Bend Trail (entrance from Beautyberry Trail), Lake Somerville State Park (Birch Creek Unit)

In the spring, Lake Somerville State Park is a real treat. The assemblies of bluebonnets are in full fanfare around Lake Somerville on the Bluestem Bend Trail, and blooming wildflowers and prickly pear greet you along the Beautyberry Trail.

Lake or river: Lake Somerville
Photogenic factor: 5
Start: Beautyberry Trailhead
Elevation gain: 236 to 282 feet
Distance: 2.5-mile lollipop
Difficulty: Easy
Hiking time: About 1 hour
Seasons/schedule: Open year-round, 6 a.m. to 10 p.m.
Fees and permits: $5 per person 13 years and older (subject to change), free for Texas State Parks Pass holders
Trail contacts: Lake Somerville State Park Headquarters (Birch Creek Unit), 14222 Park Road 57, Somerville 77879; (979) 535-7763
Dog-friendly: Leashed dogs permitted

Trail surface: Dirt and gravel, with a mixture of rock and mowed grass
Land status: Texas Parks and Wildlife Department
Nearest town: Somerville and College Station (northeast), Caldwell (north), Brenham (southeast)
Other trail users: Mountain bikers/cyclists
Maps: USGS Somerville; Lake Somerville State Park (Birch Creek Unit) map (available online at www.tpwd.texas.gov/state-parks/parks-map and via the TX State Parks mobile app)
Special considerations: During the spring season with adequate rainfall, Texas bluebonnets bloom around Lake Somerville. Check with the park headquarters for current bluebonnet conditions.

Finding the trailhead: From the Texas Avenue and University Drive intersection near Texas A&M University in College Station, travel southwest on University Drive for 1.1 miles. University Drive changes into Raymond Stotzer Parkway. Raymond Stotzer Parkway merges into FM 60 W/Vincent Road after 6 miles. Travel on FM 60 W for 15.2 miles. Turn right onto TX 36 N. After 0.4 miles, turn left back onto FM 60. Continue for 7.1 miles. Turn left onto Park Road 57 and then stay on it for 4.2 miles. Once you reach the Birch Creek Unit of Lake Somerville State Park, go left into the park. After traveling for 1.4 miles (bypassing the road to the Yaupon Camping Area) you will reach a parking lot and the Cedar Elm Day-Use Area. The Beautyberry Trail starts north of the parking lot and can also be accessed close to the boat ramp. **GPS:** N30° 18.624' W96° 37.217'

The Hike

By combining the Beautyberry Trail with the Bluestem Bend Trail, you will have the opportunity to traverse through flourishing wildflower areas and also have views of Lake Somerville. One of the beautiful features of the Beautyberry Trail is its height-

Wildflowers along the Bluestem Bend Trail

of-land and the prickly pear that adorns the trail. The landscape of the Bluestem Bend Trail is gorgeous as well. Its topography is where the prairie meets the lake, with a mixture of bluebonnets. This guide begins the route with the Beautyberry Trail. The Beautyberry Trail starts north of the parking lot and the Cedar Elm Day-Use Area. Views of Lake Somerville will begin to your right. When you reach the connection to the Bucktail Run Trail to your left at 0.12 miles, bear right to continue on the Beautyberry Trail. Be cautious of any unearthed tree roots in the path and head across the footbridge at 0.23 miles.

You will come upon the first of several wildflower areas on the route at a quarter of a mile into the trail. The best time to see the wildflowers is in the spring when they are in full bloom. More wildflower areas appear at the 0.42- and 0.73-mile marks. The path surface changes to gravel and gets rocky in between those points. At three-quarters of a mile, you will encounter a connection to the Bluestem Bend Trail. This guide takes the Bluestem Bend Trail in a clockwise direction. Bear left to complete the Beautyberry Trail. Shortly after, you will reach Yaupon Camping Area Road. Look for vehicles before crossing the road toward the "Eagle Point" sign. When you reach the fork at 0.82 miles, the Beautyberry Trail ends. Bear right following the sign to start on the Bluestem Bend Trail. The left is the Eagle Point Trail. The path surface turns to mowed grass.

At 1 mile into the trail, views of the glistening Lake Somerville open up straight ahead. Continue straight along the shoreline at the fork shortly after. The right side

Bluestem Bend Trail (entrance from Beautyberry Trail), Lake Somerville State Park (Birch Creek Unit)

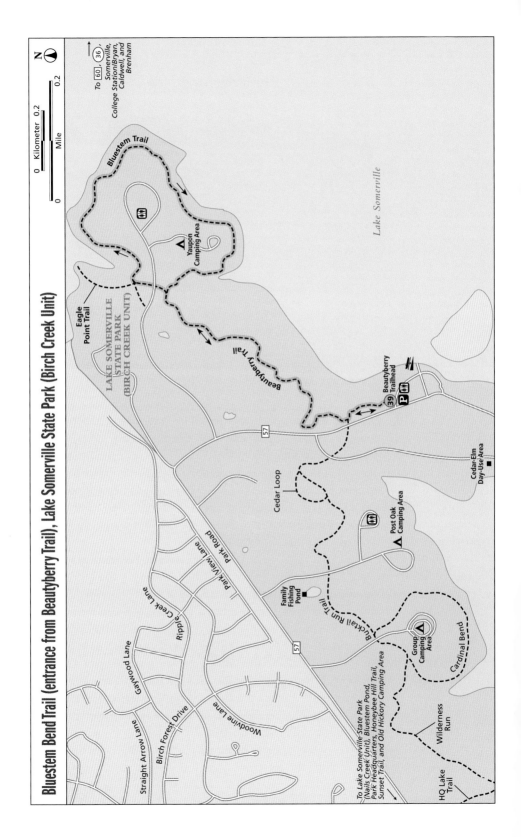

is an offshoot to the Yaupon Camping Area. An area covered in bluebonnets will welcome you at 1.15 miles, and then the trail surface turns sandy for a brief period before the trail heads southwest. At 1.27 miles, you will need to bypass the offshoot to the Yaupon Camping Area to the north and the offshoot to the lake to the south. Continue straight. You will repeat this at the 1.33-, 1.36-, 1.4-, and 1.48-mile marks, and then the trail curves northwest shortly after. The mileage will read 1.75 miles when you reach the Beautyberry Trail connection from the original 0.75-mile mark. Bear left and return the way you came.

Miles and Directions

0.0 The Beautyberry Trail starts north of the parking lot and the Cedar Elm Day-Use Area. Views of Lake Somerville will begin to your right.

0.12 Reach a fork. Bear right.

0.23 Be cautious of any unearthed tree roots in the path and cross the footbridge.

0.35 The path surface turns to gravel.

0.5 The path gets rocky for a brief period.

0.75 Reach a connection to the Bluestem Bend Trail. Bear left to complete the Beautyberry Trail.

0.78 Reach Yaupon Camping Area Road. Watch for vehicles before crossing to the "Eagle Point" sign.

0.82 Reach a fork. Bear right to start on the Bluestem Bend Trail. The path surface turns to mowed grass.

1.0 Views of Lake Somerville open up ahead.

1.03 Reach a fork. Continue straight along the shoreline.

1.17 The trail surface turns sandy for a brief period.

1.27, 1.33, 1.36, 1.4, and 1.48 Bypass the offshoots to the north and south. Continue straight.

1.75 Reach the Beautyberry Trail connection from the original 0.75-mile mark. Bear left to return to the trailhead.

2.5 Arrive back at the trailhead.

Bluebonnets blooming by Lake Somerville

40 Lake Loop, Bonham State Park

A trip to Bonham State Park is an enjoyable outing for those looking for a break from city life. The Lake Loop, which encircles the 65-acre Bonham State Park Lake, is full of surprises. Bois d'arc trees blend in with cedar and oak, Blackland Prairie pockets transpire within the woods, and if you are fortunate—you might encounter a speedy roadrunner.

Lake or river: Bonham State Park Lake
Photogenic factor: 4+
Start: Lake Loop Trailhead
Elevation gain: 577 to 630 feet
Distance: 1.98-mile lollipop, with an additional spur
Difficulty: Easy
Hiking time: 1-2 hours
Seasons/schedule: Open year-round, 6 a.m. to 10 p.m.
Fees and permits: $4 per person 13 years and older (subject to change), free for Texas State Parks Pass holders
Trail contacts: Bonham State Park Headquarters, 1363 State Park 24, Bonham 75418; (903) 583-5022
Dog-friendly: Leashed dogs permitted

Trail surface: Dirt
Land status: Texas Parks and Wildlife Department
Nearest town: Bonham (northwest), Dodd City (northeast)
Other trail users: Mountain bikers/cyclists, anglers
Maps: USGS Bonham; Bonham State Park map (available online at www.tpwd.texas.gov/state-parks/parks-map and via the TX State Parks mobile app)
Special considerations: Pay attention to unearthed tree roots that occur intermittently throughout the trail. Portions of this trail can get overgrown after a decent rainfall or during the spring and summer months.

Finding the trailhead: From the S TX 78 and TX 56 corridor in Bonham, travel on S TX 78 S for 1.4 miles. Turn left onto FM 271 S. Stay on FM 271 S for 1.9 miles, and then turn right onto Park Road 24 to head into Bonham State Park. The Lake Loop Trailhead will be to your right after 0.8 miles. **GPS:** N33° 32.732' W96° 08.531'

The Hike

The Lake Loop commences by the Park Road 24 sign, north of the Group Tent parking area. The trail heads west into a wooded area. Most of the trail will offer shade, with the exception of some segments that are in pocket prairie areas. At 160 feet, the trail heads south. Soon after, a "Wild Grape" interpretive wayside will be to your left. There will be several interpretive waysides along the trail. These include topics on the following: "Greenbriar," "Eastern Red Cedar," "American Elm," "Pocket Prairie," "Alabama Supplejack," "Hackberry," "Poison Ivy," "Bois d'Arc," and "Texas Red Oak." You will then cross a small wooden footbridge.

Lake Loop, Bonham State Park

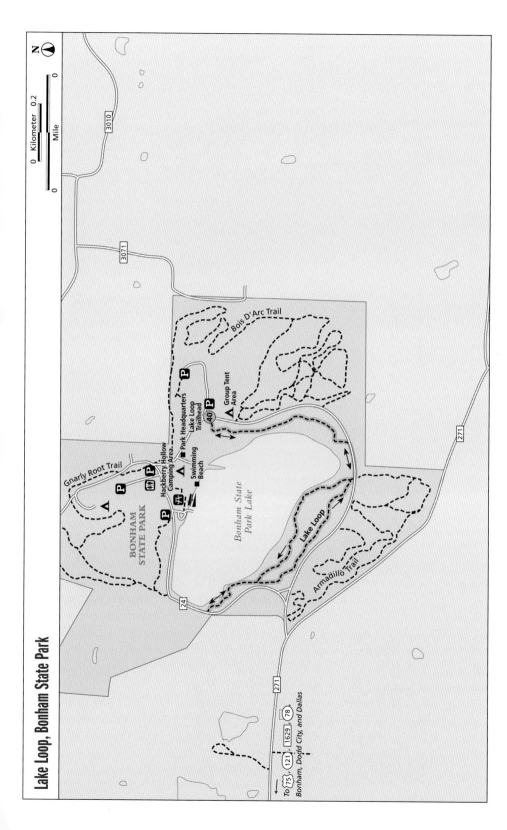

Vista of Bonham State Park Lake

Partial lake views will appear to your right at the 0.15-mile mark. During the winter months, the view is not as obstructed by the surrounding foliage. At 0.31 miles, you will cross another small wooden footbridge. Shortly after, you will go across a short boardwalk that leads you to Park Road 24. You will need to walk along the road to reconnect with the Lake Loop. Watch for vehicles before walking along the roadside. You will cross over a culvert before reconnecting with the Lake Loop at 0.47 miles. Bear right. To your left is a connection to the Armadillo Trail. Shy of half a mile into the trail, you will reach the loop portion of the lollipop route. Take the loop in a counterclockwise direction by bearing right.

Views of the lake begin to appear again to your right at 0.61 miles and you will reach a pocket prairie that blooms with wildflowers during the spring and summer. Take a moment to enjoy the view and the colors surrounding you. The prairie ends at 0.65 miles, and you will reenter a wooded area. The east side of the loop concludes at 0.84 miles, and you will reach an additional spur. Continue straight on the

additional spur. The other path to your southwest is the west side of the loop from the 0.49-mile mark. Partial lake views will be offered to you once again, shortly after.

The capstone of the trail is a vista of Bonham State Park Lake at 0.9 miles. Two benches and a picnic table are also available at this point. Take some time to have a snack, rest, or enjoy the scenery to your right. After you are done, you can turn around and return to the trailhead at this point. This guide does the spur all the way through to complete the Lake Loop and for extra mileage. If you choose to continue, head either straight or left. Both paths eventually merge at 0.94 miles. The spur eventually ends when the mileage clocks at 1 mile and you reach Park Road 24. Turn around and return to the fork at the original 0.84-mile mark.

You will encounter the loop portion of the lollipop route at 1.16 miles. This is the same spot where the loop concluded at the original 0.84-mile mark. Bear right to hike the west side of the loop. You can also choose to go back on the same side you came on. Bypass the offshoots to Park Road 24 to your right at the 1.21- and 1.32-mile marks. You will cross a small wooden footbridge in between these points.

Another pocket prairie will greet you at 1.38 miles, and then the loop portion of the trail ends at 1.49 miles. Return down the spur portion of the lollipop that you concluded at the original 0.49-mile mark. As before, watch for vehicles before going along Park Road 24. You will reconnect with the Lake Loop when the mileage reads 1.59 miles. Head across the short boardwalk back to the trailhead.

Miles and Directions

0.0   The trail starts by the Park Road 24 sign, north of the Group Tent parking area.

0.08 Cross a small wooden footbridge.

0.15 Partial lake views will be to your right.

0.31 Cross a small wooden footbridge.

0.38 Cross a small boardwalk.

0.39 Reach Park Road 24. Watch for vehicles before bearing right along the roadside.

0.4   Cross over a culvert.

0.47 Reconnect with the Lake Loop by bearing right.

0.49 Reach the loop portion of the lollipop route. Bear right to go in a counterclockwise direction.

0.61 Views of the lake appear to your right.

0.84 Reach a fork. Continue straight on the additional spur.

0.86 Partial lake views will be to your right.

0.9   Reach a vista, two benches, and one picnic table to your right. You can return to the trailhead at this point. This guide completes the lake loop route for extra mileage. Continue straight or left. Both paths eventually merge.

0.94 Bear right.

1.0   Reach Park Road 24. Return to the fork at the original 0.84-mile mark.

1.16 Reach the loop from the original 0.84-mile mark. Bear right to hike the west side of the loop. You can also choose to take the east side.

1.21 Reach a fork. Continue straight.

1.24 Cross a small wooden footbridge.

1.32 Continue straight.

1.49 Reach the spur portion of the lollipop from the original 0.49-mile mark. Return to Park Road 24 and watch for vehicles before going north alongside Park Road 42.

1.59 Reconnect with the Lake Loop and head across the boardwalk back to the trailhead.

1.98 Arrive back at the trailhead.

Roadrunner sighting on the trail

41 Beaver Slide Nature Path, Purtis Creek State Park

The popular Beaver Slide Nature Path is a beloved trail for good reason. It meanders through peaceful wooded areas and offers expansive views of the unruffled Purtis Creek State Park Lake and inlets. Fortunate hikers might see a beaver swimming through the water.

Lake or river: Purtis Creek State Park Lake
Photogenic factor: 5
Start: Beaver Slide Nature Path Trailhead
Elevation gain: 394 to 433 feet
Distance: 1.66-mile lollipop
Difficulty: Easy
Hiking time: 30 minutes–1 hour
Seasons/schedule: Open year-round, 6 a.m. to 10 p.m.
Fees and permits: $5 per person 13 years and older (subject to change), free for Texas State Parks Pass holders

Trail contacts: Purtis Creek State Park Headquarters, 14225 FM 316 N, Eustace 75124; (903) 425-2332
Dog-friendly: Leashed dogs permitted
Trail surface: Dirt
Land status: Texas Parks and Wildlife Department
Nearest town: Mabank (west), Eustace (south), Athens (southeast)
Other trail users: None
Maps: USGS Mabank; Purtis Creek State Park map (available online at www.tpwd.texas.gov/state-parks/parks-map and via the TX State Parks mobile app)

Finding the trailhead: From downtown Dallas, use I-45 S to get onto US 175 E. After traveling 54.3 miles on US 175 E, turn left onto CR 2938. Travel on CR 2938 for 3.9 miles. Go left onto FM 316. After 0.4 miles, turn left across the dam. Continue on FM 316 for 1.3 miles, and the trailhead will be to your left. It will be north of the parking area and east of the Purtis Creek Camping Area. **GPS:** N32° 21.817' W96° 00.176'

The Hike

The Beaver Slide Nature Path is more than just a leisurely hike through the woods and along the lake. Situated in a dreamy landscape and outfitted with scenic footbridges, the trail is worthwhile. The Beaver Slide Nature Path begins north of the parking area and east of the Purtis Creek Camping Area. It starts off by heading east through a mixed woodland. At 275 feet, the trail curves northwest. Bypass the offshoot to your right at the 380-foot mark by continuing straight.

When you head north down some stone steps at 0.14 miles, you will encounter the first of three footbridges. Bypass the offshoot to your left at 0.17 miles by continuing straight. You will cross the second footbridge, and head east at the 0.2-mile mark. An offshoot to an overlook of a cove to your right will appear shortly after.

Beaver Slide Nature Path

View of inlet from the footbridge

Continue straight. Once you reach the bird viewing blind to your right at 0.3 miles, you will need to bypass a few more offshoots to your right from this point to the 0.38-mile mark. The trail then heads north.

At 0.39 miles, you will reach the loop portion of the trail. Take the left side of the loop to take the loop in a clockwise direction. The third footbridge will be to your right on the return portion of the loop and a bench will be to your left. Another bench will be to your left soon after, and then you will cross over a seasonal stream-bed at 0.46 miles. The trail curves east at 0.6 miles, and then curves south at 0.7 miles. At the 0.7-mile mark, primitive campsites M through A will be dispersed from this point to the 1.2-mile mark. There will be partial views of the lake from this point to site B. Site D, if unoccupied, offers the best viewpoint out of all the campsites.

The trail curves northwest at 1.08 miles. When you cross the third footbridge, the loop segment of the lollipop route concludes. The best vantage point of the lake from the trail is at this point. Take a moment to relish the scene of the inlet and any wildlife. When you are ready, return the way you came.

Beaver Slide Nature Path, Purtis Creek State Park

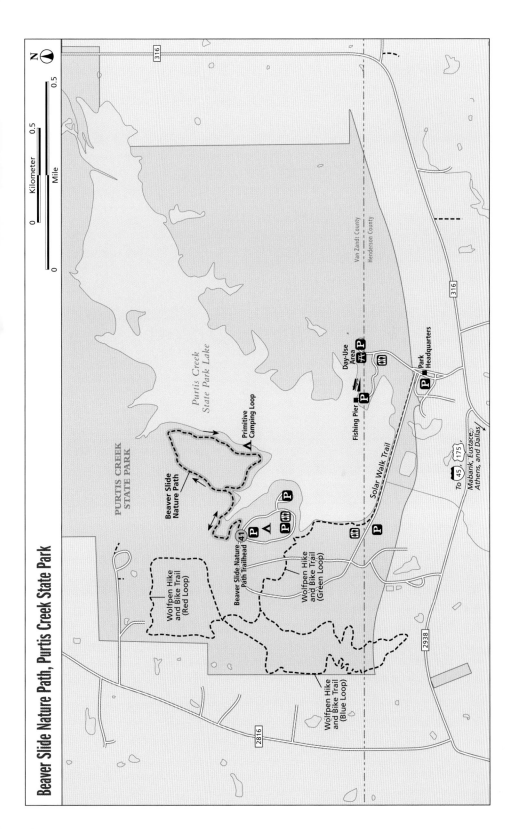

Sunset at Purtis Creek State Park Lake

Miles and Directions

0.0 The trail begins north of the parking area and east of the Purtis Creek Camping Area.

0.07 Bypass the offshoot to your right.

0.14 Go down some stone steps and cross a wooden footbridge.

0.17 Bypass the trail to your left.

0.2 Cross a footbridge.

0.24 Bypass the offshoot to an overlook to your right.

0.3 Reach a bird viewing blind to your right. Bypass a few offshoots to your right from this point to the 0.38-mile mark.

0.39 Reach the loop portion of the trail. Bear left to take the loop in a clockwise direction.

0.46 Cross a seasonal streambed.

0.7 Primitive campsites M through A will be from this point to the 1.2-mile mark.

1.27 Cross a footbridge and the loop segment of the lollipop route concludes. The best vantage point of the lake is at this point. Return the way you came.

1.66 Arrive back at the trailhead.

Honorable Mentions (Prairies and Lakes)

H Oxbow Lake Trail, Palmetto State Park

The swampy landscape around Oxbow Lake has its unique charm. Tropical dwarf palmetto trees thrive among lofty sycamores and cottonwoods. The petite and quiet lake, which originated from the powerful San Marcos River, now rests in topography unlike anywhere in the Lone Star State.

Lake or river: Oxbow Lake
Photogenic factor: 4
Start: Oxbow Lake Trailhead, south of restrooms
Elevation gain: 295 to 323 feet
Distance: 0.84-mile loop, portion in day-use area is undefined
Difficulty: Easy
Hiking time: 30 minutes
Seasons/schedule: Open year-round, 6 a.m. to 10 p.m.

Fees and permits: $3 per person 13 years and older (subject to change), free for Texas State Parks Pass holders
Trail contacts: Palmetto State Park Headquarters, 78 Park Road 11 South, Gonzales 78629; (830) 672-3266
Dog-friendly: Leashed dogs permitted
Trail surface: Dirt and gravel, asphalt in the day-use area
Land status: Texas Parks and Wildlife Department

View of Oxbow Lake from the trail

Nearest town: Gonzales (southeast), Luling (northwest)
Other trail users: Mountain bikers/cyclists, anglers

Maps: USGS Ottine; Palmetto State Park map (available online at www.tpwd.texas.gov/state-parks/parks-map and via the TX State Parks mobile app)

Finding the trailhead: From the TX 123 BUS N and I-10 corridor in Seguin, travel on I-10 E for 22.3 miles. Take exit 632 for US 183 S. After half a mile, keep right to merge onto US 183 S. Travel on US 183 S for 2.5 miles. Go left onto CR 261. Stay on CR 261 for 1.9 miles (it eventually changes to Park Road 11 N) past the park headquarters to your right. Turn left onto State Park Road and the day-use area. The Oxbow Lake Trailhead will be 0.4 miles down State Park Road, south of the restrooms and east of a small parking area. **GPS:** N29° 35.571' W97° 35.134'

Horseshoe Lake Trail, Attwater Prairie Chicken National Wildlife Refuge

The water lily–adorned Horseshoe Lake is one of the best highlights of the Attwater Prairie Chicken National Wildlife Refuge (besides catching a glimpse of the endangered Attwater prairie chicken). The beauty of the tranquil lake is fitting for artwork inspiration, and the lake makes a wonderful place for reflection.

The beauty of Horseshoe Lake showcased during daylight

Lake or river: Horseshoe Lake
Photogenic factor: 5
Start: Horseshoe Lake Trailhead
Elevation gain: 167 to 183 feet
Distance: 0.88-mile lollipop
Difficulty: Easy
Hiking time: 30 minutes
Seasons/schedule: Open year-round, sunrise to sunset; visitor center hours are 7:30 a.m. to 4 p.m. Mon through Fri
Fees and permits: None (subject to change)
Trail contacts: Attwater Prairie Chicken National Wildlife Refuge Headquarters, 1206 APC NWR Road, Eagle Lake 77434; (979) 234-3021
Dog-friendly: Leashed dogs permitted
Trail surface: Dirt and mowed grass
Land status: US Fish and Wildlife Service
Nearest town: Eagle Lake (southwest), Columbus (northwest), Sealy (northeast), Houston (east)
Other trail users: None
Maps: USGS Eagle Lake NE; Attwater Prairie Chicken National Wildlife Refuge map (available online at https://www.fws.gov/refuge/attwater-prairie-chicken)
Special considerations: To add more mileage, the Horseshoe Trail connects with the Sycamore Trail.

Finding the trailhead: From City Hall in downtown Houston, get onto I-45 N by heading northwest on Walker Street. After traveling on I-45 N for 5.5 miles, merge onto I-10 W. Stay on I-10 W for 43.5 miles. Exit off of I-10 W for TX 36 S. Curve around east to head south on TX 36 S. After 1.6 miles on TX 36 S, turn left onto FM 3013 W. Travel for 9.8 miles on FM 3013 W and then go right onto Attwater Prairie Chicken National Wildlife Refuge (APC NWR) Road. Stay on APC NWR Road for 1 mile. Turn right onto CR 140. CR 140 will change into CR 116 as you pass the refuge headquarters. The Horseshoe Lake Trailhead and parking area will be to your right after 1.5 miles. **GPS:** N29° 40.267' W96° 16.101'

J Towash Forest Trail, Lake Whitney State Park

The once-bustling town of Towash, named after the chief of the Hainai Tribe that originally settled there, remains at the bottom of southeast side of Lake Whitney due to a flood in 1908. The Towash Forest Trail, bearing the relic's name, traverses the west side of Lake Whitney State Park, taking hikers through a peaceful prairie and along the lakeshore.

Lake or River: Lake Whitney
Photogenic Factor: 4
Start: Towash Forest Trailhead
Elevation gain: 532 to 554 feet
Distance: 1.21-mile lollipop
Difficulty: Easy
Hiking time: 30 minutes–1 hour
Seasons/schedule: Open year-round, 6 a.m. to 10 p.m.
Fees and permits: $5 per person 13 years and older (subject to change), free for Texas State Parks Pass holders
Trail contacts: Lake Whitney State Park Headquarters, 433 FM 1244, Whitney 76692; (254) 694-3793
Dog-friendly: Leashed dogs permitted
Trail surface: Dirt and gravel
Land status: Texas Parks and Wildlife Department

Bluebonnets along the shoreline of Lake Whitney

Nearest town: Hillsboro (northeast), Waco (south), Dallas/Fort Worth (north)
Other trail users: Mountain bikers

Maps: USGS Whitney; Lake Whitney State Park Trails map (available online at www.tpwd.texas .gov/state-parks/parks-map and via the TX State Parks mobile app)

Finding the trailhead: From the US 77 BUS N/La Salle Avenue and 3rd Street intersection south of Baylor University in Waco, head northeast on US 77 BUS N/La Salle Avenue for 1.6 miles. Turn left to merge onto US-77 BUS N. At about 3.3 miles, make a left onto Industrial Boulevard. After 0.4 miles, turn right onto Gholson Road. Travel on Gholson Road for 15.3 miles, where it changes to FM 933, and continue on FM 933 for 15.4 miles. Turn left on FM1244, and then, after 2.5 miles, make a left onto State Park Road 47. After 0.8 miles, turn left at the fork. The trailhead will be to your left after 0.5 miles, right before the Sunset Ridge Camping Loop. **GPS:** N31° 55.013' W97° 21.295'

Pineywoods

Dusk in the forest (Honorable Mention Hike K)

42 Lakeview Loop (entrance from Brim Pond Trail), Lake Bob Sandlin State Park

Several different ecoregions converge in the Lake Bob Sandlin area, making the already lovely lake not just a sight to behold, but also a body of water that is abundant with a kaleidoscope of biodiversity. Hikers can find inspiration from the sunrise views of Lake Bob Sandlin and Brim Pond on the Lakeview Loop. A bonus—if hikers also like to fish, they can fish for bass, crappie, and catfish off the lighted fishing pier at the lake in the evening.

Lake or river: Lake Bob Sandlin and Brim Pond
Photogenic factor: 5
Start: Brim Pond Trailhead
Elevation gain: 236 to 389 feet
Distance: 1.19-mile lollipop
Difficulty: Easy
Hiking time: About 1 hour
Seasons/schedule: Open year-round, 6 a.m. to 10 p.m.
Fees and permits: $5 per person 13 years and older (subject to change), free for Texas State Parks Pass holders
Trail contacts: Lake Bob Sandlin State Park Headquarters, 341 State Park Road 2117, Pittsburg 75686; (903) 572-5531

Dog-friendly: Leashed dogs permitted
Trail surface: Dirt path occasionally laden with dried pine
Land status: Texas Parks and Wildlife Department
Nearest town: Mount Pleasant (northeast), Pittsburg (southeast), Mount Vernon (northwest), Winnsboro (southwest)
Other trail users: Mountain bikers/cyclists, anglers
Maps: USGS Monticello; Lake Bob Sandlin State Park map (available online at www.tpwd .texas.gov/state-parks/parks-map and via the TX State Parks mobile app)

Finding the trailhead: From Mount Pleasant, travel on FM 127/O'Tyson Avenue for 10.4 miles. Turn left onto FM 21 S. Travel south on FM 21 for 1 mile. Turn left onto Lake Bob Sandlin Road/Park Road 2117. Close to 0.4 miles and after passing the park headquarters, go left onto Lake Bob Sandlin Road toward the camping areas. There will be a parking area of about ten spaces and the Dogwood Trailhead to your left. The Brim Pond Trailhead will be to your right. **GPS:** N33° 03.262' W95° 05.792'

The Hike

On the Lakeview Loop, not only will you be afforded stunning views of Lake Bob Sandlin and Brim Pond, but you will also come upon a cornucopia of vegetation and trees in the area. The area where Lake Bob Sandlin lies is where the Pineywoods, Blackland Prairie, and Post Oak Savannah ecoregions intersect. This intermingling of sundry ecosystems creates the ideal environment for plentiful flora and fauna.

Sunrise at Lake Bob Sandlin

The Lakeview Loop can be accessed near the day-use area, but this guide begins at the Brim Pond Trailhead, to include an additional route through a beautiful forest and the opportunity to see the picturesque Brim Pond. From about 490 feet to the Lakeview Loop connection at the 0.3-mile mark, the Brim Pond Trail curves south and then north a couple of times. At 0.11 miles, you will make a 15-foot descent until you reach the footbridge at the 0.14-mile mark. In between, there will be a bench to your right. Bypass the side trail to your right at the 0.24-mile mark. Once you go down the log steps a little over a quarter of a mile into the trail and head east, Brim Pond will be to your right. Brim Pond is an ethereal beauty, especially on a quiet dawn, when the morning sunlight begins to stream in through the trees and luminate across the still pond. Be sure to bask in the stillness that is unmatched when you are in the city. When you reach one end of Brim Pond at 0.3 miles, you will encounter the Lakeview Loop connection and "Cast A Line" sign. Bear left to start on the loop in a clockwise direction.

Views of Lake Bob Sandlin will start to appear ahead of you at 0.4 miles and then the trail heads south. While remarkable all day, the lake scenery is especially mesmerizing around sunrise. Once you go across the footbridge at 0.46 miles, you will come upon the first of many interpretive waysides. It will be the "Standard Shumard Red Oak" sign to your right. The array of diverse flora and trees is remarkable, so if you have the chance, make sure to take a look at the signs that are along the trail. When you go across the footbridge half a mile into the trail, interpretive waysides will continue to be available until the 0.70-mile mark. They include topics on the following— "Coral Honeysuckle," "Devils Walkingstick," "Hackberry," "Mockernut Hickory," "Wild Grape," "Red Buckeye," "American Beautyberry," "Loblolly Pine," "Red Maple,"

Lakeview Loop (entrance from Brim Pond Trail), Lake Bob Sandlin State Park

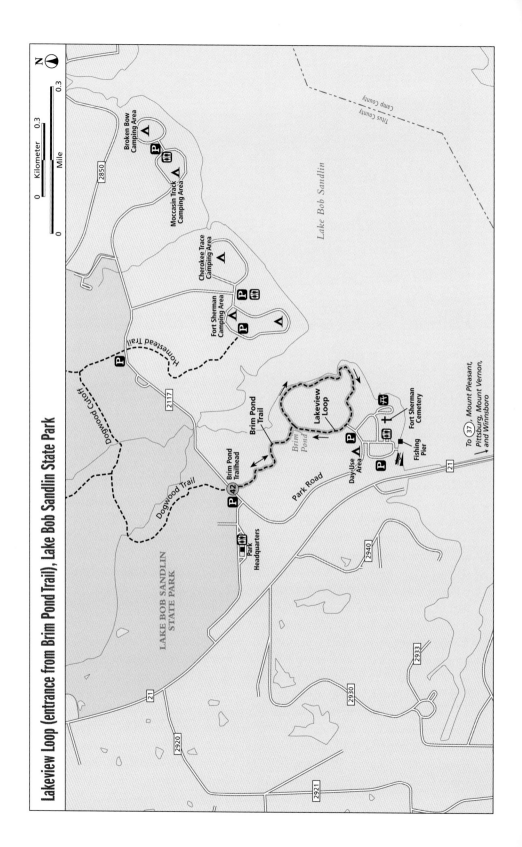

"Common Persimmon," and "Poison Ivy." In between the plethora of signs along the trail, there will also be a scenic viewing point and access to the lakeshore to your left at 0.58 miles. The trail then heads west shortly after. You will reach a grassy clearing at 0.72 miles.

The path becomes somewhat undefined in this grassy clearing. Look for the parking area and sign to the northwest (which would be the opposite direction of the day-use area, fishing pier, and Fort Sherman cemetery). Head northwest and reconnect to the Lakeview Loop at 0.78 miles. The trail then winds north. Additional interpretive waysides will appear from the 0.8-mile mark to the 0.83-mile mark. These signs will offer details on the "Hercules's Club," "Sassafras," "Winged Elm," "Sweet Gum," "Eastern Red Cedar," "White Oak," and "American Elm."

Quiet mornings at Brim Pond

You will come upon Brim Pond once again, as well as a bird viewing blind and a bench to your left at the 0.89-mile mark. The Brim Pond Trail connection from the original 0.3-mile mark will be at 0.91 miles onto the trail. Bear left back onto the Brim Pond Trail to return the way you came.

Miles and Directions

0.0 The trail begins at the Brim Pond Trailhead, southeast of the Dogwood Trailhead and parking area.

0.11 Make a 15-foot descent to the footbridge at the 0.14-mile mark.

0.24 Bypass the side trail to your right.

0.26 Go down the log steps. Brim Pond will be to your right.

0.3 Reach the Lakeview Loop connection. Bear left to start the loop in a clockwise direction.

0.4 Views of Lake Bob Sandlin will be ahead of you.

0.46 Cross the footbridge.

0.58 Reach a scenic viewing point and the lakeshore to your left.

0.72 Reach a grassy clearing. The path becomes somewhat undefined. Look for the parking area and sign to your northwest. You will reconnect to the Lakeview Loop at that point.

0.78 Reconnect with the Lakeview Loop.

0.89 Reach Brim Pond and a bird viewing blind to your left.

0.91 Reach the Brim Pond Trail connection from the 0.3-mile mark. Bear left to return the way you came.

1.19 Arrive back at the trailhead.

43 Lakeshore Trail, Tyler State Park

The lake in the heart of Tyler State Park is quite a spectacle to see, especially during the spring and autumn seasons when the 100-foot-tall trees showcase their colors. Dogwoods and redbuds bloom when winter has passed, and sweetgums start to blaze when the temperatures drop. In the summer, the cool waters of the spring-fed lake are a real treat for those looking for reprieve from the Texas summer heat.

Lake or river: Tyler State Park Lake and Beaver Pond
Photogenic factor: 5
Start: Lakeshore Trailhead at Brown's Point Picnic Area
Elevation gain: 394 to 459 feet
Distance: 2.14-mile lollipop, trail is undefined near the boat ramp and Lake Spring Picnic Area until the end of the swimming area
Difficulty: Easy
Hiking time: 1–2 hours
Seasons/schedule: Open year-round; headquarters hours are 8:30 a.m. to 4:30 p.m.
Fees and permits: $6 per person 13 years and older (subject to change), free for Texas State Parks Pass holders
Trail contacts: Tyler State Park Headquarters, 789 Park Road 16, Tyler 75706; (903) 597-5338
Dog-friendly: Leashed dogs permitted

Trail surface: Dirt
Land status: Texas Parks and Wildlife Department
Nearest town: Tyler (south)
Other trail users: None
Maps: USGS Tyler North; Tyler State Park map (available online at www.tpwd.texas.gov/state-parks/parks-map and via the TX State Parks mobile app)
Special considerations: Tyler State Park is popular for its spring flowering trees and fall colors. Be sure to make plans well in advance to visit the park during these prime times. Check ahead of time with park staff to confirm foliage conditions. There will be multiple offshoots to the camping areas and the Southside Day-Use Area from this trail. In order to protect the topography and fragile ecosystem from erosion, please do not go on these unofficial trails.

Finding the trailhead: From Tyler City Square in downtown Tyler, head north on Broadway Avenue for 1.3 miles. Turn right on W Martin Luther King Jr. Boulevard. After 0.3 miles, turn left on W Church Avenue. The road changes into FM 14/State Park Highway after 0.3 miles. Travel on FM 14 for 7.8 miles before turning left onto Park Road 16. Keep on heading west on Park Road 16 toward the Silver Canoe (the Tyler State Park store). The Lakeshore Trailhead will be southeast of the Brown's Point Picnic Area parking lot. **GPS:** N32° 28.730' W95° 17.663'

The Hike

Tyler State Park has no shortage of magnificent trees. The serene, 64-acre, no-wake lake within the park is surrounded by a mixed woodland. The forests are a mixture of dogwood, post oak, short leaf pine, mockernut hickory, redbud, American holly, loblolly pine, sweetgum, blackjack oak, eastern red cedar, and sassafras, just to name a few. The Lakeshore Trail lives up to its name—it takes hikers along the shores of Tyler State Park Lake. There are also a couple bonus opportunities after you hike. You can visit some of the Frank Lloyd Wright–inspired Prairie-style structures built by the Civilian Conservation Corps near the park headquarters. You can also have a nice picnic by the swimming area and enjoy the unspoiled waters of the lake.

The stone-bordered path that commences southeast of the Brown's Point Picnic Area parking lot is where you can start on the Lakeshore Trail. This guide takes the trail as a loop, in a clockwise direction. At 110 feet, the path merges with the trail coming north from the swimming area. Continue straight. When the stone borders end at 365 feet into the trail, there will be an overlook to your southwest. Continue southeast on the dirt path and across the long wooden footbridge. The footbridge ends at the 0.22-mile mark. You will eventually pass by remnants of fallen trees to your right. At 0.33 miles, you will reach the lily pad–studded Beaver Pond to your right. Enjoy the charming view, and perhaps do a little bird-watching. Then head west across a wooden bridge at 0.34 miles.

The trail eventually curves and heads northwest. The Sumac Bend Camping Area will be to your left at 0.37 miles. A little over half a mile into the trail, a bench will be available to your right. The Red Oak campsite will be to your right. The trail begins to head in a westerly direction right

Tyler State Park Lake

Dogwoods blossoming along the trail

after. From here to the 0.83-mile mark, there will be several unearthed tree roots in the path to watch out for. Pass through a fallen tree trunk and go over some log steps at 0.57 miles.

You will be afforded great views of Tyler State Park Lake to your right at 0.65 miles. At about three-quarters of a mile into the trail, you will reach some steps that lead to a bench to your right. The trail then winds north. At 0.81 miles, you will reach another bench to your right and the trail will curve west before eventually heading south. Another opportunity to view Tyler State Park Lake to your right will also occur at this point. Steps leading to the Southside Day-Use Area will be to your left and a fishing dock will be to your right at 0.89 miles. The trail begins to head south. Once you reach the fork shortly after, take either side, as they eventually merge. The left side at the time of publication is less overgrown. The trail then winds southwest. Cross a wooden footbridge a mile into the trail and come upon a small open clearing as you head north.

You will reach a dam at the 1.08-mile mark. The shade dissipates temporarily as you cross over the dam. Once you have crossed the dam, bear right between some large rocks to continue on the trail. Big Pine campsite #320 will be straight ahead of you to the north. After passing by Lakeview campsites #213 and #211 at 1.36 miles, go toward the stone-bordered path to the Lakeview Camping Area access road. Shortly after, green markers with yellow letters will indicate for you to bear right along the Lakeview Camping Area access road. Watch for passing vehicles and go around the campsites. At 1.55 miles, the trail reconnects near Lakeview campsites #218 and #201. Look for the stone-bordered path ahead of you that curves east around the amphitheater. After passing the amphitheater, go to the boat ramp and scenic overlook. Make sure to take a few minutes to enjoy the panoramic views of the stunning lake at the scenic overlook. Once you are ready, head toward Park Road 16 and the bridge. This portion of the trail becomes undefined until you reach the end of the swimming area. You also have the option to turn around and return the way you came. This guide continues through the Lake Spring Picnic Area to complete the route as a loop.

The mileage clocks at 1.66 miles when you reach Park Road 16 and the bridge. This bridge is used by vehicles. Watch for passing vehicles before heading east across the bridge. Stay close to the bridge walls just in case a vehicle needs to pass. Once you come upon the Lake Spring Picnic Area, look for the footbridge in between two picnic benches to your southeast. Go across the footbridge. Be careful as there will be several unearthed tree roots in the path. At 1.75 miles, you will reach the Northside Day-Use Area. Head toward the playground. Take either the ramp or stairs to the playground. Head south past the playground until you reach the most southern picnic bench and then look for the stone ledge at 1.84 miles. Take the farthest right side of the path that parallels the lakeshore. The left side of the path goes to other picnic areas.

Lakeshore Trail   Beaver Pond

When you reach the Boat House at the 1.86-mile mark, take the ramp toward the Silver Canoe (the Tyler State Park store). Bear right to curve around the Silver Canoe. Heading left will lead you to the Northside Day-Use Area parking lot. Go southeast along the concrete path parallel to the swimming area to reconnect with the trail at 2.02 miles. The trail becomes defined again. Continue straight on the dirt path. To the north will be stairs to the Northside Day-Use Area parking lot. Cross over the wooden plank at 2.05 miles. It is possible that a fallen tree trunk may be in the path shortly after. You will come upon the Brown's Point Picnic Area at the 2.07-mile mark. Continue straight and then bear left on the stone-bordered path from the beginning of the trail to return to the trailhead.

Miles and Directions

0.0 The trail begins southeast of the Brown's Point Picnic Area parking lot.

0.02 The path merges with the trail coming north from the swimming area. Continue straight.

0.07 An overlook will be to your southwest. Continue southeast across the long wooden footbridge.

0.33 Beaver Pond will be to your right.

0.34 Cross a wooden footbridge.

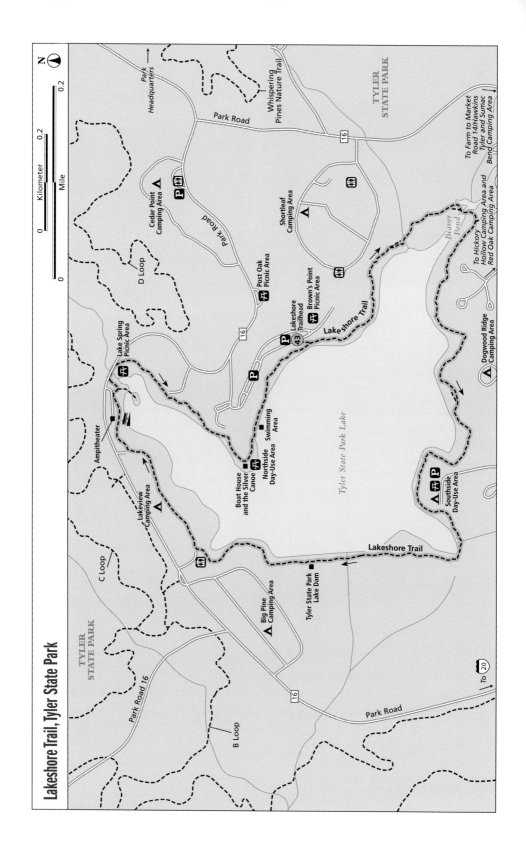

Lakeshore Trail, Tyler State Park

TYLER STATE PARK

N

Kilometer
0   0.2
Mile
0   0.2

Park Headquarters

Whispering Pines Nature Trail

Park Road

Cedar Point Camping Area

D Loop

Park Road

16

Shortleaf Camping Area

Post Oak Picnic Area

Brown's Point Picnic Area

Lake Spring Picnic Area

Lakeshore Trailhead

43

Lakeshore Trail

TYLER STATE PARK

Beaver Pond

To Hickory Hollow Camping Area and Red Oak Camping Area

To Farm to Market Road 14/Hawkins Tyler and Sumac Bend Camping Area

Dogwood Ridge Camping Area

16

Swimming Area

Tyler State Park Lake

Southside Day-Use Area

Ampitheater

Boat House and the Silver Canoe

Northside Day-Use Area

Lakeview Camping Area

C Loop

TYLER STATE PARK

Park Road 16

B Loop

Big Pine Camping Area

Tyler State Park Lake Dam

16

Park Road

To 20

Lakeshore Trail

0.51 A Red Oak campsite will be to your right. There will be several unearthed tree roots in the path to watch out for from this point to the 0.83-mile mark.

0.57 Pass through a fallen tree trunk and go over some log steps.

0.75 Reach some steps that lead to a bench to your right.

0.89 Reach steps leading to the Southside Day-Use Area to your left. A fishing dock will be to your right.

0.91 The path splits and then eventually merges.

1.0 Cross a wooden footbridge.

1.08 Cross over a dam. After crossing the dam, bear right between some large rocks.

1.36 Reach Lakeview campsites #213 and #211. Go toward the stone-bordered path to the Lakeview Camping Area access road.

1.38 Green markers with yellow letters will direct you to bear right along the Lakeview Camping Area access road. Watch for passing vehicles and go around the campsites.

1.55 The trail reconnects near Lakeview campsites #218 and #201. Look for the stone-bordered path that curves east around the amphitheater.

1.61 Reach a boat ramp and scenic overlook. This portion of the trail becomes undefined until you reach the end of the swimming area. You can turn around at this point and return the way you came. This guide continues to the Lake Spring Picnic Area to complete the loop route. Head toward Park Road 16 and the bridge.

1.66 Reach Park Road 16 and the bridge. Watch for passing vehicles before heading east across the bridge. Stay close to the bridge walls just in case a vehicle needs to pass.

1.69 Reach the Lake Spring Picnic Area. Look for the footbridge in between two picnic benches to your southeast.

1.71 Cross the footbridge.

1.75 Reach the Northside Day-Use Area. Head toward the playground.

1.77 Take either the ramp or stairs to the playground. Head south past the playground until you reach the most southern picnic bench.

1.84 Look for the stone ledge. Take the right side of the path that parallels the lakeshore.

1.86 Reach the Boat House. Take the ramp toward the Silver Canoe (Tyler State Park store).

1.88 Bear right to curve around the Silver Canoe.

1.95 Head southeast along the concrete path bordering the swimming area to reconnect with the trail.

2.02 The swimming area ends. Continue straight on the dirt path.

2.05 Cross over a wooden plank.

2.07 Reach the Brown's Point Picnic Area. Continue straight.

2.12 Bear left back to the trailhead.

2.14 Arrive back at the trailhead.

44 Prairie Branch Loop, Huntsville State Park

The nearly 200-acre Lake Raven is surrounded by endless congregations of oaks, sweetgums, and pine. The constant wet climate of the area makes the lake and its forests a conducive environment for coastal wetland wildlife, including the American alligator.

Lake or river: Lake Raven
Photogenic factor: 4+
Start: Prairie Branch Loop Trailhead
Elevation gain: 256 to 366 feet
Distance: 1.55-mile lollipop
Difficulty: Easy
Hiking time: 30 minutes–1 hour
Seasons/schedule: Open year-round, 6 a.m. to 10 p.m.
Fees and permits: $7 per person 13 years and older (subject to change), free for Texas State Parks Pass holders
Trail contacts: Huntsville State Park Headquarters, 565 Park Road 40 W, Huntsville 77340; (936) 295-5644
Dog-friendly: Leashed dogs permitted
Trail surface: Sandy in the beginning, dirt occasionally laden with dried pine for the remainder

Land status: Texas Parks and Wildlife Department
Nearest town: Huntsville (north), New Waverly and Conroe (south)
Other trail users: None
Maps: USGS Moore Grove; Huntsville State Park map (available online at www.tpwd.texas .gov/state-parks/parks-map and via the TX State Parks mobile app)
Special considerations: Purple squares with an egret symbol serve as guides on this trail. The west side of the loop along the shoreline can get highly eroded. Check with park headquarters for current trail conditions. Pay attention to unearthed tree roots that occur intermittently throughout the trail. Alligators live in the waters of Lake Raven. Exercise caution and maintain a distance of at least 30 feet if an alligator is sighted.

Finding the trailhead: From the TX 30 and I-45 corridor in Huntsville, turn right onto N Freeway Service Road/I-45 Frontage Road. Travel for 1.5 miles before merging onto I-45 S. Continue on I-45 S for 4.8 miles and then take exit 109. After 0.4 miles from the exit, turn left onto N Freeway Service Road. Travel on N Freeway Service Road for 0.3 miles. Turn right onto State Park Road 40. Continue on State Park Road 40 for 2.1 miles. Stay right at the fork toward the Prairie Branch Camping Area. After 0.1 miles, turn right toward the Prairie Branch Camping Area. The Prairie Branch Loop Trailhead will be 0.3 miles north of the last parking lot (past the restrooms and showers). **GPS:** N30° 37.283' W95° 32.120'

The Hike

The scenery of Lake Raven is mainly characterized by the forests reminiscent of trees from the East Texas Pine Belt region. For the most part, the Prairie Branch Loop trail is shrouded in a mixture of hardwoods, loblolly pines, and palmettos. Half of it

A still morning at Lake Raven

traverses along the shoreline of Lake Raven. Lake Raven has three sources—the Prairie Branch Creek, the Big Chinquapin Creek, and the Little Chinquapin Creek. You will notice that the Prairie Branch Loop and the soon-to-be mentioned Chinquapin Trail are named after these contributors. The Prairie Branch Loop begins north of the parking area in the Prairie Branch Camping Area. In 200 feet, you will reach a junction. Continue straight and take the route in the middle to take the Prairie Branch Loop in a counterclockwise direction. The right is a connection to the Dogwood Trail. The left is the return route of the Prairie Branch Loop.

At 0.13 miles, the path surface changes from sand to dirt and is intermittently laden with pine needles. A bench will be to your left just shy of a quarter of a mile into the trail. Another connection to the Dogwood Trail will occur to your right at this point as well. Continue straight. The trail converges with the Chinquapin Trail from the 0.72-mile mark to the 0.79-mile mark. Once you come upon the junction, take the far-left path that curves to the south to continue on the Prairie Branch Loop. Straight ahead is the Chinquapin Trail. To your right, a side trail heads toward Alligator Branch.

The sides of the trail become densely populated with ferns starting around 0.91 miles. In combination with the palmettos, a Jurassic-like aura can be felt on this portion of the trail. You will be greeted with views of Lake Raven to your right also at this point and until the 1.51-mile mark. Several wooden boardwalks are situated on this segment of the trail throughout the remainder of the route.

Prairie Branch Loop, Huntsville State Park

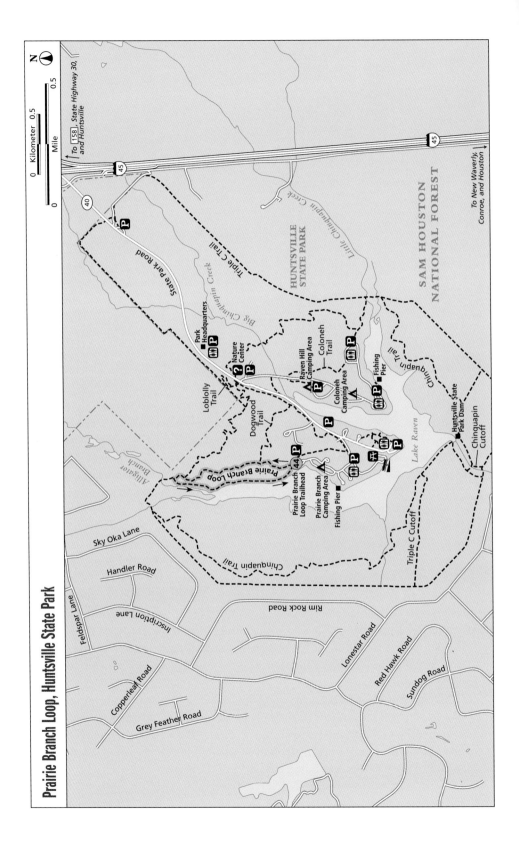

Prairie Branch Loop

Alligator sighting at Lake Raven

The trail begins to head southeast away from the lakeshore at 1.45 miles. You will reach the spur portion of the lollipop route from the original 200-foot mark when the mileage clocks at 1.51 miles. Bear right to return to the trailhead.

Miles and Directions

0.0 The Prairie Branch Loop begins north of the parking area.

0.04 Reach a junction. Continue straight and take the center route to take the Prairie Branch Loop in a counterclockwise direction.

0.24 Reach a fork. Continue straight.

0.72 The trail merges with the Chinquapin Trail up to the 0.79-mile mark.

0.79 Reach a junction. Take the far-left path that curves south to continue on the Prairie Branch Loop.

0.91 Views of Lake Raven will be to your right from this point to the 1.51-mile mark. Cross several wooden boardwalks starting from this point.

1.51 Reach the spur portion of the lollipop route from the original 0.04-mile mark. Bear right back to the trailhead.

1.55 Arrive back at the trailhead.

45 Volksmarch Trail (combined with Arrowhead Trail), Atlanta State Park

Spanning over 27,000 acres, Lake Wright Patman is home to many species, including herons, pelicans, eastern turkeys, butterflies, and armadillos. The peaceful, towering forests surrounding the lake were also home to the Caddoan people who dwelled among them.

Lake or river: Lake Wright Patman
Photogenic factor: 4
Start: Volksmarch Trailhead
Elevation gain: 187 to 266 feet
Distance: 1.92 miles out and back
Difficulty: Easy
Hiking time: About 1 hour
Seasons/schedule: Open year-round, 6 a.m. to 10 p.m.
Fees and permits: $3 per person 13 years and older (subject to change), free for Texas State Parks Pass holders
Trail contacts: Atlanta State Park Headquarters, 927 Park Road 42, Atlanta 75551; (903) 796-6476
Dog-friendly: Leashed dogs permitted

Trail surface: Dirt path
Land status: Texas Parks and Wildlife Department
Nearest town: Douglassville (southwest), Atlanta and Queen City (southeast)
Other trail users: Anglers
Maps: USGS Douglassville; Atlanta State Park map (available online at www.tpwd.texas.gov/state-parks/parks-map and via the TX State Parks mobile app)
Special considerations: Blue blazes on trees serve as guides for this trail. Portions of this trail consist of unearthed tree roots and seasonal creek beds. During rainy seasons and wet conditions, use extra caution—surfaces can be slippery and waterlogged.

Finding the trailhead: From Texarkana, travel south on TX 93 for 3.7 miles, where it changes to US 59 S. Stay on US 59 S for 15.6 miles. Turn right onto CR 3541 in the town of Lanark. After 1.1 miles, turn right onto CR 3542, and then left onto CR 3543. After 0.6 miles, turn right onto FM 96. Stay on FM 96 for 5 miles. Go right onto FM 1154. After 1.7 miles, turn left onto Park Road 42 you will enter Atlanta State Park. Continue on Park Road 42 for 0.7 miles before taking the right side of the fork. The Volksmarch Trailhead will be behind the restrooms after 0.1 miles. **GPS:** N33° 14.125' W94° 15.235'

The Hike

Lake Wright Patman is expansive and can be viewed from several trails within Atlanta State Park. The Volksmarch Trail is an easy stroll through an old-growth forest before it connects with the Arrowhead Trail and heads straight to the lakeshore. Various habitats can be enjoyed on this trail, including the aforementioned old-growth forest, new-growth forest, and prairie.

The Volksmarch Trailhead is located east of the Knight Bluff Camping Area restrooms. The trail heads primarily in an easterly direction until it connects with the Arrowhead Trail. About 90 feet into the trail, you will cross over a seasonal stream. The trail heads through a myriad of age-old shortleaf pines, oak, loblolly pines, and hickory. Make sure to stop and glance at the magnificent sight above, as the longstanding trees encircle you. You will make a slight descent of 5 feet in elevation from the 0.13-mile mark to the 0.14-mile mark, and then the trail heads north for a brief period. Cross over another seasonal stream at 0.16 miles, and then the trail heads back east. You will encounter a slight ascent of 5 feet in elevation from the 0.18-mile mark to the 0.19-mile mark. After half a mile into the trail, the trail winds in a southeast direction.

At 0.61 miles, you will make a longer descent of 20 feet in elevation until the 0.65-mile mark. The old-growth forest then

Old-growth forest

opens up to new growth. In 2016, a large amount of the forest was flooded with 10 feet of water for four months. Via prescribed burns, hardier new bottomland trees were established to promote a more deep-rooted forest that would better withstand future floods. In this area, the trail surface turns from dirt and unearthed tree roots to mowed grass. The connection to the Arrowhead Trail occurs at 0.72 miles. Bear left to take the Arrowhead Trail toward Lake Wright Patman. Most portions of this trail are characterized by prairie landscape. Be ready to be surrounded by beautiful buckeye butterflies and waltzing dragonflies. Red-headed woodpeckers also frequent the Arrowhead Trail.

Take the left side of the fork at 0.87 miles. This route leads to the lakeshore. The right side of the fork is a continuation of the Arrowhead Trail. You will come upon

Volksmarch Trail (combined with Arrowhead Trail), Atlanta State Park

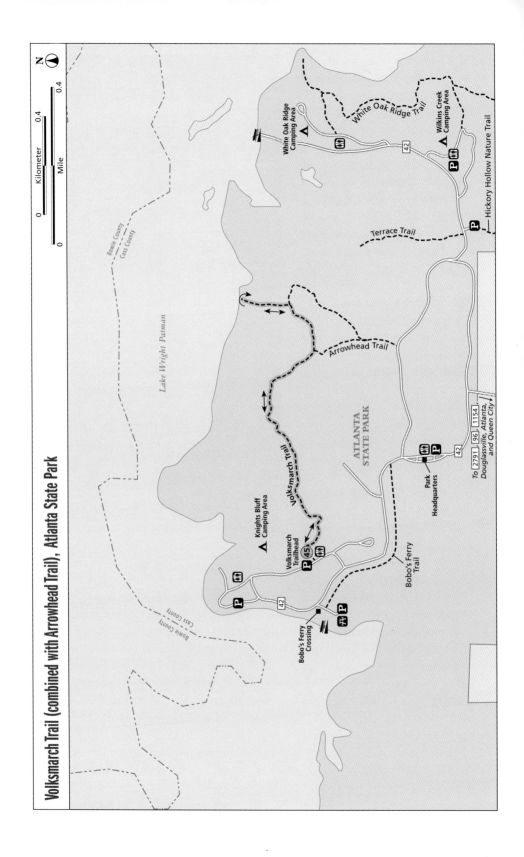

N

Kilometer
0   0.4

Mile
0   0.4

Bowie County
Cass County

Lake Wright Patman

White Oak Ridge Camping Area

White Oak Ridge Trail

Wilkins Creek Camping Area

42

Hickory Hollow Nature Trail

Terrace Trail

P

Arrowhead Trail

ATLANTA STATE PARK

Park Headquarters

P

42

To 2791, 96, 1154 Douglassville, Atlanta, and Queen City

Knights Bluff Camping Area

Volksmarch Trail

Volksmarch Trailhead

P 45

Bobo's Ferry Trail

P

42

P

Bobo's Ferry Crossing

P

Cass County
Bowie County

Lake Wright Patman

the lakeshore at the 0.96-mile mark. Enjoy the calm, panoramic view before you and then return the way you came.

Miles and Directions

0.0 The trail begins east of the restrooms in the Knights Bluff Camping Area.

0.02 Cross over a seasonal streambed.

0.13 Make a slight descent of 5 feet in elevation to the 0.14-mile mark.

0.16 Cross over a seasonal streambed.

0.18 Make a slight ascent of 5 feet in elevation to the 0.19-mile mark.

0.61 Make a 20-foot descent to the 0.65-mile mark. The path turns to mowed grass.

0.72 Reach the Arrowhead Trail connection. Bear left onto the Arrowhead Trail.

0.87 Reach a fork. Bear left to head toward the lakeshore.

0.96 Reach Wright Patman Lake. Return the way you came.

1.92 Arrive back at the trailhead.

46 Rustling Leaves Trail, Daingerfield State Park

Especially mesmerizing in the fall, Little Pine Lake is just as enchanting all year. It can attribute its year-round glory to the diverse forest that surrounds it. The Rustling Leaves Trail rings true to its name as it guides hikers along the reposeful banks of this spring-fed lake. The trees seem to echo in an appeasing symphony as the wind drifts through their branches.

Lake or river: Little Pine Lake
Photogenic factor: 5
Start: Rustling Leaves Trailhead
Elevation gain: 315 to 422 feet
Distance: 2.73-mile loop, trail is undefined in the day-use area portion
Difficulty: Easy to moderate due to uneven terrain
Hiking time: About 2 hours
Seasons/schedule: Open year-round, 6 a.m. to 10 p.m.
Fees and permits: $4 per person 13 years and older (subject to change), free for Texas State Parks Pass holders
Trail contacts: Daingerfield State Park Headquarters, 455 Park Road 17, Daingerfield 75638; (903) 645-2921

Dog-friendly: Leashed dogs permitted
Trail surface: Dirt
Land status: Texas Parks and Wildlife Department
Nearest town: Daingerfield (northwest), Hughes Springs (southeast)
Other trail users: None
Maps: USGS Daingerfield; Daingerfield State Park map (available online at www.tpwd.texas.gov/state-parks/parks-map and via the TX State Parks mobile app)
Special considerations: Daingerfield State Park is well-known for its fall foliage. Be sure to make plans well in advance to visit the park during this prime time, usually in mid to late Nov. Check ahead of time with park staff to confirm the status of fall colors in the area.

Finding the trailhead: From the US 259 and TX 11 intersection in Daingerfield, travel on TX 11 E for 2.3 miles. Turn right onto Park Road 17 and enter Daingerfield State Park. Head down Park Road 17 for about 1.1 miles and bypass the road to the Dogwood Camping Area. At the second fork with the concrete historic sign, turn right. (Heading straight will lead to the Little Pine General Store and Little Pine Interpretive Center.) Continue for 0.1 miles. The Rustling Leaves Trailhead will be to your left at the parking area, just past the road to the Cedar Ridge Campground and Mountain View Campground. **GPS:** N33° 00.633' W94° 41.983'

The Hike

The captivating Daingerfield State Park was established after the Civilian Conservation Corps (CCC) made a conscious effort in the 1930s to replant native trees in the area and to build a dam to create Little Pine Lake. The 507-acre park had once been deforested land due to the significant presence of sawmills and influx of

Autumn sunsets at Daingerfield State Park

ore mining. The types of trees that were replanted included a mixture of deciduous trees and evergreens. This undertaking is what allows Daingerfield State Park at this present day to be so beautiful during autumn. It is quite an experience to witness the mixture of hardwoods ablaze among the emerald-hued shortleaf and loblolly pines. Some of the trees that were planted by the CCC are now over 100 feet tall. Hikers will be able to get a glimpse of the twenty-plus types of trees that call Daingerfield State Park home when they traverse the Rustling Leaves Trail.

The Rustling Leaves Trailhead commences near the picnic area and to the left of the parking area. A connection to the Mountain View Trail will be to your north. This guide will take the trail in a clockwise direction, heading east. The route continues through an undefined route through the day-use area and past the swimming area to connect with the defined part of the trail at the 0.45-mile mark.

About 315 feet onto the trail, go across the small footbridge to avoid walking on Park Road 17. Continue through the grassy area to go along the shoreline and toward the day-use area. Clusters of lily pads provide an opportunity for a painting to your right. A bench is available to use for viewing this picturesque area. You will cross the last wooden footbridge when the mileage reads as 0.2 miles. The boat launch is also at this point. In the early morning or at dusk, you might be greeted by a raft of mallards or wood ducks, as they make ripples in the water and find shade underneath the various watercraft. The Little Pine Interpretive Center neighbors the boat dock. The trail curves west around the wooden dock of the Little Pine Interpretive Center. Paddle boats, canoes, kayaks, and paddleboards stationed at its wooden dock are available for rent. There is also a fishing pier in the day-use area, which you will pass by at a quarter of a mile into the trail.

Continue to head west toward the swimming area, which you will reach at 0.41 miles. The Little Pine General Store will be up the hill, to your north. The swimming area ends at the 0.44-mile mark and the trail becomes defined shortly after.

You will reach a wooden footbridge at 0.46 miles. There will be a series of side trails to cabins and the Big Pine Camping Area to your left afterward to the 0.73-mile mark, with the "Don't miss out" sign to your right and a couple more wooden footbridges to cross within the segment. Bear right at the fork at the 0.6-mile mark. After crossing over the footbridges from the 0.64 to the 0.80-mile mark, you will reach Dogwood Camp Road. You will see a sign and a small wooden footbridge to your right, where you will reconnect with the Rustling Leaves Trail. Watch for vehicles while heading toward that point on Dogwood Camp Road. The trail then picks up again at 0.84 miles and continues to head east.

Shy of a mile from the trailhead, the trail begins to head south. You will cross over a small footbridge shortly after. At the 1.05-mile mark, you will come upon the Dogwood Camping Area and restrooms. Follow the sign and continue straight. The trail begins to head southwest. A portion of the trail can get overgrown during the summer from the 1.17- to 1.21-mile mark. You will pass a bench to your right. The trail then heads west at the 1.29-mile mark, with another bench to its right shortly after.

Little Pine Lake

Bear right at the fork at the 1.54-mile mark to take the scenic lollipop route to the CCC Picnic Area. You will reach the loop portion of the route to the CCC Picnic Area at 1.68 miles. After surveying the panoramic view of Little Pine Lake, the swimming platform, and day-use area, turn around and return to the fork that was at the 1.54-mile mark. You will reconnect with the fork at 1.86 miles. Bear right to continue on the Rustling Leaves Trail.

At 1.93 miles, the trail curves, and heads northwest. You will encounter a few more wooden footbridges in between this point and when you reach the bench to your right at 2.1 miles. At the 2.31-mile mark, you will reach a natural-looking dam. This is the dam that was constructed back in the late 1930s by the Civilian Conservation Corps to create the 80-acre Little Pine Lake. The path across the dam ends at 2.45 miles into the trail. There will be a wooden bridge with a bench next to

Lilies floating near the shoreline

Rustling Leaves Trail, Daingerfield State Park

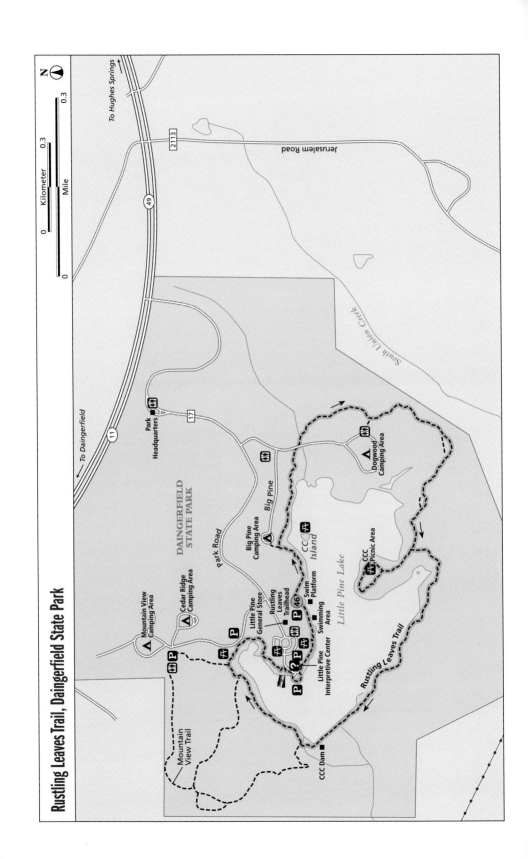

it soon after. Once you cross the bridge, bear right. To your left is a connection to the Mountain View Trail. Follow the sign at the 2.66-mile mark to continue straight on the Rustling Leaves Trail. Another connection to the Mountain View Trail will be to your left. Cross the small wooden footbridge at the 2.72-mile mark, with the trail closing the loop back at the trailhead at 2.73 miles.

Miles and Directions

0.0 Start at the Rustling Leaves Trailhead, near the picnic area. A connection to the Mountain View Trail will be to your north, and the parking area and Park Road 17 to your east. This guide will take the trail in a clockwise direction, heading east on an undefined route through the day-use area and past the swimming area to connect with the defined part of the trail at the 0.45-mile mark.

0.06 Go across a small footbridge. Continue through the grassy area along the shoreline.

0.2 Cross a wooden footbridge by the boat launch. Reach the Little Pine Interpretive Center. Go along the wooden dock.

0.25 Reach a fishing pier. Continue west toward the swimming area.

0.41 Reach the swimming area.

0.44 The swimming area ends. Connect with the defined portion of the trail shortly after.

0.46 Reach a wooden footbridge.

0.54 Bypass the side trail to the cabins to your left.

0.6 Reach a fork. Bear right.

0.64 Cross a wooden footbridge. Bypass several side trails to the Big Pine Camping Area to your left from here to the 0.73-mile mark.

0.67 You will cross three wooden footbridges from this point to the 0.80-mile mark.

0.82 Reach Dogwood Camp Road. Look to your right for a sign and a small wooden footbridge to reconnect with the trail. Watch for vehicles.

0.84 Reconnect with the trail.

0.98 Cross a small footbridge.

1.05 Reach the Dogwood Camping Area and restrooms. Continue straight.

1.17 The trail can get overgrown from this point to 1.21 miles.

1.54 Reach a fork. Bear right to take the scenic lollipop route toward the CCC Picnic Area.

1.7 Reach the scenic viewing point (CCC Picnic Area). Return to the fork that was at the 1.54-mile mark.

1.86 Reach the fork from the 1.54-mile mark. Bear right.

1.93 Encounter three more wooden footbridges from here to the 2.01-mile mark.

2.31 Cross a dam.

2.45 The dam ends. Cross a wooden bridge and then bear right.

2.66 Continue straight following the sign.

2.72 Cross a small footbridge.

2.73 Arrive back at the trailhead.

Honorable Mentions (Pineywoods)

K Lone Star Hiking Trailhead #6 to Lake Conroe, Sam Houston National Forest

The Lone Star Hiking Trail (LSHT) is the longest trail in Texas, and somewhat of a bucket list hike for backpacking enthusiasts. It cuts through the pine-dominated Sam Houston Forest and makes its way along the shoreline of 40-mile Lake Conroe to Stubblefield Campground. Hikers who are not able to do the LSHT as a whole can access Lake Conroe by starting from Trailhead #6.

Lake or river: Lake Conroe
Photogenic factor: 4+
Start: Lone Star Hiking Trailhead #6
Elevation gain: 167 to 269 feet
Distance: 1.58 miles out and back
Difficulty: Easy
Hiking time: 30 minutes–1 hour
Seasons/schedule: Open year-round; Sam Houston National Forest Ranger Office hours are 8 a.m. to 4:30 p.m. Tues, Thurs, and Fri
Fees and permits: None (subject to change)

Trail contacts: Sam Houston National Forest Ranger Office, 394 FM 1375 West, New Waverly 77358; (936) 344-6205
Dog-friendly: Leashed dogs permitted
Trail surface: Dirt
Land status: USDA Forest Service
Nearest town: Huntsville (north), New Waverly (east), Conroe (southeast)
Other trail users: Anglers
Maps: USGS San Jacinto; Lone Star Hiking Trail Club map for Stubblefield (available online at https://lonestartrail.org/maps.html)

Lake Conroe from the shoreline

Special considerations: Hunting is permitted in some areas of the Sam Houston National Forest. Try to avoid areas that are open to hunters during hunting season. This guide stops at the first point it reaches Lake Conroe. To add mileage, you can hike all the way to Stubblefield Campground and come back for an 8-mile round-trip hike.

Finding the trailhead: From the TX 105 and I-45 corridor in Conroe, travel north on I-45 for 15.2 miles. Get off exit 102 for FM 1375. In 0.3 miles, take the third exit at the traffic circle. After another 0.3 miles, take the second exit at the traffic circle. Continue west on FM 1375 for 8.3 miles. Turn right onto Forest Service Road 274. In 0.2 miles, the Lone Star Hiking Trailhead #6 will be south of the parking area. **GPS:** N30° 31.678' W95° 37.780'

⌐ Lakeshore Trail, Ratcliff Lake Recreation Area (Davy Crockett National Forest)

The 45-acre Ratcliff Lake is a hiker's and paddler's paradise. With a distinctive kind of serenity (thanks to it being a no-wake lake), Ratcliff Lake is photo-worthy every step along the way on the Lakeshore Trail. With a continuous canopy of pines and hardwoods, a designated vista, and several fishing piers, there is no shortage of places to view the lake from a different perspective.

Kayakers enjoying the still waters of Ratcliff Lake

Lake or river: Ratcliff Lake
Photogenic factor: 5
Start: Lakeshore Trailhead
Elevation gain: 299 to 329 feet
Distance: 0.96 miles out and back
Difficulty: Easy
Hiking time: 30 minutes–1 hour
Seasons/schedule: Open year-round; Davy Crockett National Forest Ranger Office hours are 8 a.m. to 4:30 p.m. Tues, Wed, and Fri
Fees and permits: $5 per vehicle (subject to change); pay at the self-pay station or via the Recreation.gov website or Recreation.gov mobile app
Trail contacts: Davy Crockett National Forest Ranger Office, 18551 TX 7 East, Kennard 75847; (936) 655-2299

Dog-friendly: Leashed dogs permitted
Trail surface: Dirt
Land status: USDA Forest Service
Nearest town: Crockett (west), Lufkin (east), Nacogdoches (northeast)
Other trail users: Anglers, paddlers
Maps: USGS Ratcliff; USDA Forest Service map for Ratcliff Lake (available online at https://www.fs.usda.gov/Internet/FSE _DOCUMENTS/fseprd524915.pdf)
Special considerations: Alligators live in the waters of Ratcliff Lake. Exercise caution and maintain a distance of at least 30 feet if an alligator is sighted.

Finding the trailhead: From the Angelina Street and Raguet Street intersection in downtown Lufkin, head northwest onto Raguet Street. The road changes to TX 103 W after 2.8 miles. Continue west on TX 103 for 11.7 miles, before it changes to TX 7 W. After 12.1 miles on TX 7 W, turn right onto Forest Service Road 520. In 0.4 miles, the Lakeshore Trailhead will be to your east, just south of the restrooms and designated swimming area. **GPS:** N31° 23.280' W95° 09.245'

M Island Trail, Martin Dies Jr. State Park (Walnut Ridge Unit)

The bayou–like tranquility of B. A. Steinhagen Lake is unmatched. It lies in the northern region of the Big Thicket, where several ecosystems unite. The topography of Martin Dies Jr. State Park is rich in biodiversity, including pine forests on the shore and bald cypresses standing in the lake waters. The Island Trail allows hikers to experience the natural splendor, as well as up–close views from a few coves and the observation bridge.

Lake or river: B. A. Steinhagen Lake
Photogenic factor: 4+
Start: Island Trailhead
Elevation gain: 59 to 84 feet
Distance: 0.95-mile lollipop, with an additional spur
Difficulty: Easy
Hiking time: 30 minutes
Seasons/schedule: Open year-round, 6 a.m. to 10 p.m.; headquarters located in the Hen House Ridge Unit

Fees and permits: $4 per person 13 years and older (subject to change), free for Texas State Parks Pass holders
Trail contacts: Martin Dies Jr. State Park Headquarters, 634 Park Road 48 South, Jasper 75951; (409) 384-5231
Dog-friendly: Leashed dogs permitted
Trail surface: Dirt occasionally laden with dried pine
Land status: Texas Parks and Wildlife Department

Nearest town: Jasper (northeast), Woodville (southwest)
Other trail users: Anglers
Maps: USGS Town Bluff; Martin Dies Jr. State Park map (available online at www.tpwd.texas .gov/state-parks/parks-map and via the TX State Parks mobile app)

Special considerations: Pay attention to unearthed tree roots that occur intermittently throughout the trail. Alligators live in the waters of B. A. Steinhagen Lake. Exercise caution and maintain a distance of at least 30 feet if an alligator is sighted.

Finding the trailhead: From the I-10 and College Street intersection in Beaumont, travel on I-10 E for 0.9 miles. Take a slight right to merge onto US 287 N/US 69 N/US 96 N. Stay on US 96 N for 16.1 miles, and then exit for US 96 BUS N. Travel on US 96 BUS N for 2.8 miles, and then it changes into FM 92 N/N 5th Street. Continue on FM 92 N/N 5th Street for 36.2 miles. Turn right onto US 190 E. After traveling east on US 190 for 3.4 miles, turn left into the Walnut Ridge Unit of Martin Dies Jr. State Park. (The Hen House Ridge Unit and park headquarters are just a little farther east off of US 190.) Travel on Park Road 48 for 1.1 miles. Make a slight right into the Walnut Slough Day-Use Area. The Island Trail will start at the small footbridge north of the parking area. **GPS:** N30° 52.204' W94° 10.556'

Bald cypress trees are a distinguishing characteristic of B. A. Steinhagen Lake

Gulf Coast

A roosting White Ibis (Hike 48)

47 Middle Lake Trail (entrance from Meadow Trail), William Goodrich Jones State Forest

A nice jaunt from the bustling city life of Houston, the lush William Goodrich Jones State Forest allows hikers to be one with nature. With only the chorus of birds as background music and a couple of unruffled ponds, both the Meadow Trail and Middle Lake Trail within the forest can be enjoyed as a metropolitan respite.

Lake or river: Twin Ponds
Photogenic factor: 4+
Start: Meadow Trailhead
Elevation gain: 167 to 192 feet
Distance: 1.52 miles out and back
Difficulty: Easy
Hiking time: 30 minutes–1 hour
Seasons/schedule: Open year-round, sunrise to sunset; Conroe District Office hours are 8 a.m. to 5 p.m. Mon through Fri
Fees and permits: None (subject to change)
Trail contacts: Conroe District Office, 1328 FM 1488, Conroe 77384; (936) 273-2261

Dog-friendly: Leashed dogs permitted
Trail surface: Dirt and gravel
Land status: Texas A&M Forest Service
Nearest town: Within Conroe city limits
Other trail users: Mountain bikers/cyclists, equestrians
Maps: USGS Tamina; William Goodrich Jones State Forest map (available online at https://tfsweb.tamu.edu/jones-state-forest/)
Special considerations: Green metal circles with hiker and arrow symbols on them placed on tree trunks serve as trail guides.

Finding the trailhead: From City Hall in downtown Houston, get onto I-45 N. Travel on I-45 N for 30.2 miles, and then take exit 79A. Travel on N Freeway Service Road for 3.8 miles. Take the right lane to do a turnabout and merge onto FM 1488 W. Travel west on FM 1488 for 2.1 miles. The parking lot and trailhead will be to your left. **GPS:** N30° 13.859' W95° 29.908'

The Hike

Named in honor of renowned Texan conservationist William Goodrich Jones, the William Goodrich Jones State Forest is a quiet paradise within the city limits of Conroe. The forest is dominated by pines, some over a hundred years old, and serves as a refuge for the federally listed endangered red-cockaded woodpecker.

To connect with the Middle Trail and reach the Twin Ponds, this guide will start at the Meadow Trailhead. A densely wooded trail, the Meadow Trail begins south of the parking lot. Forty feet into the trail, you will reach a fork. Bear right to go across the concrete pedestrian bridge. The left side is Gravel Pit Road. At 195 feet into the trail, you will need to go across a wooden pedestrian bridge. The trail heads southeast and then you will encounter a fork. Continue straight at the fork.

Twin Ponds

The right connects to the Jones Trail. There will be green metal circles at 0.1 miles directing you to bear right and head south. Straight ahead is again, Gravel Pit Road. Continue straight at the fork, a quarter of a mile into the trail. The right is another connection to the Jones Trail. The Meadow Trail eventually heads southeast, then at 0.2 miles, heads east. At 0.46 miles, the trail heads south and continues to do so until it reaches the Middle Lake Trail. The Middle Lake Picnic Area will be to your right at the 0.55-mile mark.

At 0.6 miles, you will reach the Middle Lake Trail connection. Bear right at the fork to continue onto the west segment of the Middle Lake Trail. The lovely

Twin Ponds will appear to your right soon after. A couple benches to rest on and enjoy the view from are positioned on opposite edges of the ponds. If you would like to see both ponds up close, bear right at 0.68 miles to take an optional spur in between the Twin Ponds. At 0.7 miles, bear right to go in between the two ponds. It will be a lovely stroll through this area; just be mindful of unearthed tree roots in the path. Another bench will be to your right at 0.72 miles. The spur ends at the wooden footbridge when the mileage clocks at 0.76. You could reconnect to the Middle Trail from this point, but the way to it is very overgrown. This guide avoids going through the unmaintained portion and heads back to the fork from the original 0.6-mile mark. At 0.92 miles, you will reach the Middle Lake Trail and

Middle Lake Trail (entrance from Meadow Trail), William Goodrich Jones State Forest

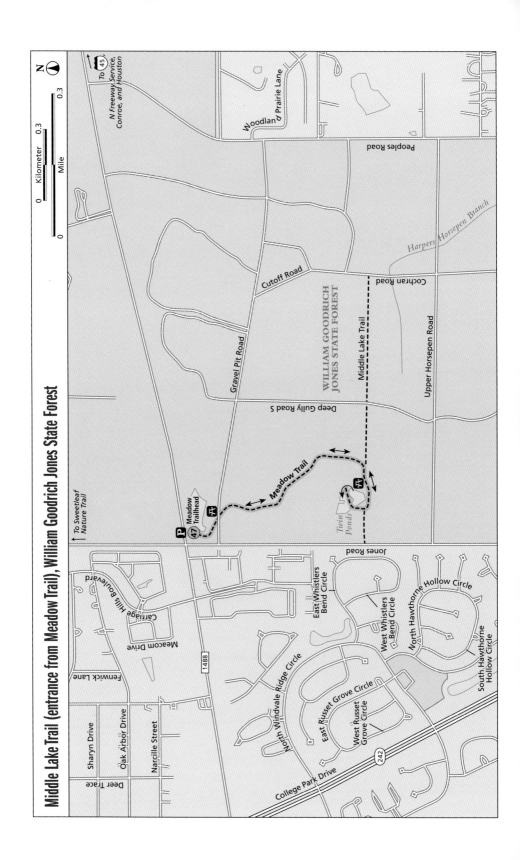

FATHER OF TEXAS FORESTRY

William Goodrich Jones was known for advocating conservationism, establishing parks, and implementing a designated Arbor Day. His appreciation for trees grew when he visited the Black Forest in Germany as a teenager and witnessed the forest management cycle performed by the local villagers. Nearly a decade later, he became the president of a bank in the city of Temple, Texas, and planted the first tree in the town in his front yard. He encouraged the residents to also plant trees, and soon the stark town became lush with greenery. Years later, William Goodrich Jones helped create the Texas Forestry Association and the Texas A&M Forest Service (originally the Department of Forestry). Remembered for his dedication to sustainable use of forests, the William Goodrich Jones State Forest is named after him. The forest was acquired by the Texas A&M Forest Service in 1926.

Meadow Trail connection from the original 0.6-mile mark. Bear left to return the way you came on the Meadow Trail.

Miles and Directions

0.0 The trail begins south of the parking lot.

0.01 Reach a fork. Bear right toward the concrete pedestrian bridge.

0.02 Cross the concrete pedestrian bridge.

0.04 Cross a wooden pedestrian bridge. Reach a fork shortly after. Continue straight.

0.1 Bear right.

0.25 Reach a fork. Continue straight.

0.55 The Middle Lake Picnic Area will be to your right.

0.6 Reach a fork. Bear right onto the Middle Lake Trail.

0.65 The Twin Ponds will be to your right.

0.68 Bear right to take an optional spur in between the Twin Ponds.

0.7 Bear right to go in between the two ponds. Be aware of unearthed tree roots in the path.

0.76 The spur ends at the wooden footbridge. You could reconnect to the Middle Trail from this point, but it is very overgrown. This guide avoids doing so and returns to the fork from the original 0.6-mile mark.

0.92 Reach the Middle Lake Trail and Meadow Trail connection from the original 0.6-mile mark. Bear left to return the way you came.

1.52 Arrive back at the trailhead.

Middle Lake Trail

48 Elm Lake Loop and 40 Acre Lake Trail, Brazos Bend State Park

The lakes in Brazos Bend State Park are a nature lover's dream. Teeming with wildlife, the lakes provide marshy wetland environments unmatched in other parts of Texas. Surrounded by stunning birds in flight, alligators hovering within the waters, or fun-loving ducks parading among the lily pads, hikers will constantly be delighted by all the activity. Both the Elm Lake Loop and 40 Acre Lake Trail best represent the diverse and enchanting ecosystems of Brazos Bend State Park.

Lake or river: Elm Lake, Pilant Lake, 40 Acre Lake, and New Horseshoe Lake
Photogenic factor: 5
Start: Elm Lake Loop Trailhead
Elevation gain: 26 to 59 feet
Distance: 4.39-mile figure 8, with 2 additional spurs
Difficulty: Easy
Hiking time: 2–3 hours
Seasons/schedule: Open year-round, 8 a.m. to 10 p.m.
Fees and permits: $7 per person 13 years and older (subject to change), free for Texas State Parks Pass holders
Trail contacts: Brazos Bend State Park Headquarters, 21901 FM 762, Needville 77461; (979) 553-5101
Dog-friendly: Leashed dogs permitted

Trail surface: Dirt and gravel
Land status: Texas Parks and Wildlife Department
Nearest town: Needville (west), Alvin (east), Houston (northeast), Angleton (south)
Other trail users: Mountain bikers/cyclists, anglers
Maps: USGS Thompsons; Brazos Bend State Park map (available online at www.tpwd.texas .gov/state-parks/parks-map and via the TX State Parks mobile app)
Special considerations: Brown wooden signs serve as trail guides. Alligators live in the waters of most of the lakes in Brazos Bend State Park. Exercise caution and maintain a distance of at least 30 feet if an alligator is sighted. Pets must be kept on a leash no longer than 6 feet.

Finding the trailhead: From City Hall in downtown Houston, get onto I-45 S. Travel on I-45 S for 1.4 miles, and then take exit 46B for TX 288 S and I-69/US 59 S. Travel on TX 288 S for 28 miles, and then take exit for FM 1462 to head toward the town of Rosharon. After 0.4 miles from the exit, turn right onto FM 1462. Travel on FM 1462 for 13 miles. Turn right onto FM 762. Stay on FM 762 for 1.4 miles. Turn right onto Park Road to enter Brazos Bend State Park. Continue on Park Road for 3.8 miles until you reach the parking lot for Elm Lake, bypassing roads to 40 Acre Lake and the Burr Oak and Red Buckeye Camping Areas. The Elm Lake Loop begins south of the parking lot. **GPS:** N29° 22.623' W95° 36.191'

The Hike

The Elm Lake Loop begins south of the Elm Lake parking lot. You can start on the Elm Lake Loop anywhere from the parking lot. This guide starts at the northeast

Elm Lake

Yellow-crowned Night Heron sighting along the
Spillway Trail

corner of Elm Lake and takes the loop in a clockwise direction. At 0.2 miles, the
trail heads west through the Spillway Trail to connect with the 40 Acre Lake Trail.
Several observation decks will be available to your right north at the 0.24-, 0.32-,
0.43-, 0.52-, 0.61-, 0.71-, and 0.81-mile marks. Sometimes in the mornings if you
go out on one of these decks, you might see an alligator. Continue straight at the
fork at 0.55 miles. The Pilant Slough Trail will be to your left. A "Bird Life at Brazos"
interpretive wayside will be to your right.

When you get to the fork at 0.85 miles, bear left onto the Spillway Trail. The right
is a continuation of the Elm Lake Loop. This guide will take this route on the way
back after completing the 40 Acre Lake Trail. The Spillway Trail connects the Elm
Lake Loop to the 40 Acre Lake Trail. It heads west immediately after you start on
it. A "Monarch of the Marsh" interpretive wayside will be to your right. Additional
interpretive waysides will be along the Spillway Trail. These include interpretive waysides with the following topics: "Long Legged Waders and Smaller Waders," "Family
Life of Alligators," and "Brazos River Floods." At 1.23 miles, you will cross over a
long wooden footbridge. Pilant Lake will parallel the footbridge to your right. Lots
of birds like to congregate near the bridge, so this would be a great place to see some
of them up close.

An impressive triple-level observation tower at the 1.44-mile mark indicates that
you have reached the 40 Acre Lake Trail. Bear left across the wooden footbridge to
take the 40 Acre Lake Trail in a clockwise direction. There will be several benches

afforded to you on this trail. They will be available at the 1.55- 1.64-, 1.73-, and 1.79-mile marks. Take advantage of these to take a break, especially if you choose to hike during the hot Texas summers. Prior to the fork at 1.84 miles, the trail heads west, and then south. Bear right at the fork to head toward the picnic area and to continue on the 40 Acre Trail. An offshoot to the Live Oak Trail will be to your left. You will cross over the first of two small wooden footbridges at the 1.88-mile mark. Bypass the connection to the Live Oaks Trail to your left shortly after. You will enter a densely forested area that will last until the second small footbridge at the 2.08-mile mark. Bypass the path to the picnic area to your right in between those points.

The dirt path changes to sidewalk when you reach the day-use area at 2.13 miles. Continue straight on the sidewalk. There will be an optional spur to the fishing pier at 2.15 miles. This guide includes the route to the fishing pier for the opportunity to see 40 Acre Lake up close. Bear right on the boardwalk toward the fishing pier. When the boardwalk ends and you reach the fishing pier, enjoy the panoramic view of the lily pad–adorned 40 Acre Lake. Turn around and return to the fork at the original 2.15-mile mark.

The mileage clocks at 2.33 miles when you reconnect with the 40 Acre Lake Trail. Bear right back onto the dirt and gravel path. For both of the forks at the 2.41- and 2.45-mile marks, bear right to continue on the 40 Acre Lake Trail. The left are offshoots back to the day-use area. When you reach the Hoot's Hollow Trail connection just shy of 2.5 miles into the trail, head straight toward the bench to continue on the 40 Acre Trail. The trail then heads east. The mileage will clock at 2.85 miles when you come back to the familiar triple-level observation tower that was at the beginning of the 40 Acre Lake Trail. Continue straight back onto the Spillway Trail to reconnect with the Elm Lake Loop. You will reach the Elm Lake Loop connection from the original 0.85-mile mark when the mileage clocks at 3.45 miles. Bear left to finish the remainder of the Elm Lake Loop.

Several more benches will be available to your left at the 3.56- and 3.79-mile marks. A connection to the Horseshoe Lake Loop will be to your left in between. The trail heads east and New Horseshoe Lake will appear to your left. There will be another bench to your right just before you reach the fork at 3.85 miles. Bear right to continue on the Elm Lake Loop. The left side goes to a picnic area. You will cross a small wooden footbridge at 3.98 miles, and then an observation deck for Elm Lake will be to your right at 4.19 miles. This guide takes the optional boardwalk spur to the observation deck. When you reach the observation deck, take a moment to enjoy the view of the halcyon Elm Lake. Signs identifying birds found in Brazos Bend State Park will be available at the observation deck. Once you are ready, turn around and reconnect with the Elm Lake Loop at 4.25 miles. Bear right to complete the loop. From here, you can either have lunch at one of the picnic tables, return to your car, or return to the trailhead.

If you have additional time to spend within Brazos Bend State Park, make sure to purchase tickets ahead of time (online only) to visit the George Observatory. It is

Anhinga sighting at the fishing pier at 40 Acre Lake

Many bird species call Brazos Bend State Park home

40 Acre Lake

Elm Lake Loop and 40 Acre Lake Trail, Brazos Bend State Park

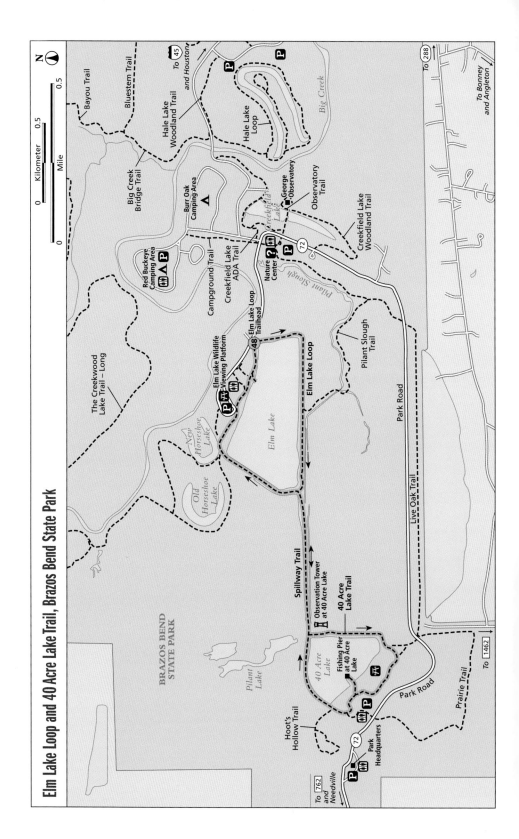

managed by the Houston Museum of Natural Science. Open each Saturday night, weather permitting, the George Observatory offers stargazing opportunities. Also, visit the award-winning Nature Center free of charge where you can touch a hatchling alligator and view one of the park's native snakes up close. The Nature Center is open 11 a.m. to 3 p.m. Monday through Friday and 9 a.m. to 5 p.m. on weekends.

Miles and Directions

0.0 Start at the northeast corner of Elm Lake and take the Elm Lake Loop in a clockwise direction.

0.24 An observation deck will be to your right. Several more will become available at the 0.32-, 0.43-, 0.52-, 0.61-, 0.71-, and 0.81-mile marks.

0.55 Reach a fork. Continue straight.

0.85 Bear left onto the Spillway Trail.

1.23 Cross a wooden footbridge and Pilant Lake will be to your right.

1.44 Reach a triple-level observation tower and the 40 Acre Lake Trail. Bear left across the wooden footbridge to take the trail in a clockwise direction.

1.84 Reach a fork. Bear right toward the picnic area.

1.88 Cross a small wooden footbridge. Bypass the connection to the Live Oaks Trail to your left shortly after.

2.02 Bypass the path to the picnic area to your right.

2.08 Cross a small wooden footbridge.

2.13 Continue straight on the sidewalk.

2.15 Bear right on the boardwalk toward the fishing pier.

2.24 Reach the fishing pier and the boardwalk ends. Enjoy a panoramic view of 40 Acre Lake. Return to the fork at the original 2.15-mile mark.

2.33 Reconnect with the 40 Acre Lake Trail. Bear right.

2.41 and 2.45 Reach a fork. Bear right.

2.49 Reach a fork. Head straight.

2.85 Reach the triple-level observation tower from the original 1.44-mile mark. Go straight back onto the Spillway Trail.

3.45 Bear left onto the Elm Lake Loop.

3.56 and 3.79 A connection to the Horseshoe Lake Loop will be to your left. New Horseshoe Lake is visible to your left.

3.85 Reach a fork. Bear right.

3.98 Cross a small wooden footbridge.

4.19 An observation deck will be to your right. Head down the boardwalk to the observation deck.

4.22 Reach the observation deck and the boardwalk ends. Take a moment to enjoy the view of Elm Lake. Return to the Elm Lake Loop.

4.25 Reconnect with the Elm Lake Loop. Bear right.

4.39 Arrive back at the trailhead.

49 Peach Creek North and South Loops, Lake Houston Wilderness Park

The painterly Lake Dabney and refreshing Peach Creek are just some of the jewels that can be enjoyed while hiking on the Peach Creek North and South Loops. Those looking for some peace and time away from the concrete jungle will be able to have that experience while on the trails in Lake Houston Wilderness Park.

Lake or river: Lake Dabney and Peach Creek
Photogenic factor: 5
Start: Peach Creek North Loop Trailhead
Elevation gain: 33 to 92 feet
Distance: 3.34 miles of a couple lollipops
Difficulty: Easy
Hiking time: 1–2 hours
Seasons/schedule: Open year-round, 7 a.m. to 6 p.m. Sun, Mon, Wed, Thurs (closed Tues) and 7 a.m. to 8 p.m. Fri and Sat
Fees and permits: $3 per person ages 13 to 65 (subject to change), free for children under 12, seniors, and military personnel (with ID)
Trail contacts: Lake Houston Wilderness Park Office, 25840 FM 1485, New Caney 77357; (832) 395-7690
Dog-friendly: Leashed dogs permitted

Trail surface: Dirt and gravel
Land status: City of Houston Parks and Recreation Department
Nearest town: Within New Caney city limits
Other trail users: Mountain bikers/cyclists, anglers, paddlers, horseback riders on specific trails (please call ahead of time as rain closes this option)
Maps: USGS Splendora; Lake Houston Wilderness Park map (available online at https://www.houstontx.gov/parks/lake houstonpark.html)
Special considerations: Venomous snakes can be encountered on this trail. Pay attention to unearthed tree roots that occur intermittently throughout the trail. There will be several vehicle roads to cross during this route. Please watch for passing vehicles before crossing.

Finding the trailhead: From City Hall in downtown Houston, get onto I-45 N. Travel north on I-45 for 0.6 miles, and then merge onto I-10 E. Stay on I-10 E for 1.4 miles, and then take exit 770C for I-69/US 59 N. Travel on I-69/US 59 N for 27.4 miles, and then take exit 159A. After 0.8 miles on Eastex Freeway Road, turn right onto FM 1485 S. Within 0.2 miles, turn right onto TX 494 Loop S. Travel on TX 494 Loop S for 0.3 miles. Turn left onto FM 1485 E. Continue on FM 1485 E for 2.2 miles. Go left to stay on FM 1485 E. In half a mile, the entrance and fee station for Lake Houston Wilderness Park will be on your right. Turn right on Wilderness Road. After 0.1 miles, the parking area for the Peach Creek North Loop Trail will be to your right. The trailhead will be southwest of the parking area. **GPS:** N30° 08.776' W95° 10.148'

The Hike

Lake Houston Wilderness Park was purchased for only $10 from the state of Texas in 2006. Prior to being owned by the state, it was owned by Champion Paper Company. Some of the trails within the park are remnants of old logging roads used by the

Daybreak at Lake Dabney

company. Although Lake Houston cannot be accessed by the Peach Creek trail system, hikers will still be able to enjoy Lake Dabney and Peach Creek. Several benches are dispersed throughout the route, allowing for optimal breaks to enjoy Peach Creek or rest during the summer heat.

The Peach Creek North Loop begins southwest of the parking area. The trail heads south before heading east at 0.15 miles, and then back south at 0.17 miles. When you come upon the fork shortly after, bear right to continue on the Peach Creek North Loop. The left is the Dogwood Trail. At the next fork at 0.34 miles, bear right to take the loop portion of the lollipop in a counterclockwise direction. The left will be the return route after you complete the Peach Creek South Loop. There will be a 5-foot descent from here to the 0.35-mile mark. From the 0.37-mile mark to the 1.43-mile mark, the trail heads primarily south.

Peach Creek starts to become visible and parallel to your right at 0.45 miles and continues to do so all the way to the 1.23-mile mark. Continue straight toward the Peach Creek South Loop when you encounter the fork at 0.72 miles. This is the spur segment of the lollipop route for the Peach Creek South Loop. The left is the other end of the loop route for the Peach Creek North Loop. Three-quarters of a mile into the trail, you will cross over the first of four wooden footbridges on this route. At 0.79 miles, you will reach the loop portion of the lollipop route for the Peach Creek South Loop. Bear right to take the Peach Creek South Loop in a counterclockwise direction. The left is the other side of the loop route for the Peach Creek South Loop.

After you cross over a culvert, public restrooms and a parking lot will be to your left at the 0.91-mile mark. You will soon reach Peach Creek Lane/Nature Center Road. Watch for vehicles before crossing the road to reconnect with the dirt and gravel path to the south of you. At 0.95 miles, there will be a dirt path to your left that goes to the Peach Creek Group Camping Area. Continue straight on the dirt and gravel path to continue on the Peach Creek South Loop. There will also be several offshoots to Peach Creek to your right from this point to the 1.23-mile mark. At 1.03, you will cross over the second wooden footbridge. Bypass the offshoot to your left that leads to the Peach Creek Group Camping Area.

The path splits at 1.1 miles and then converges. You will cross over the third wooden footbridge shortly after. From the 1.2-mile mark you will make a short 5-foot ascent to the 1.21-mile mark. The trail switches between heading east and heading south all the way until you bypass the Ameri-Trail connection to your right. Continue heading east and then bypass the Yaupon Trail, also to your right. The trail heads north at 1.72 miles. At the fork at 1.91 miles, continue straight. The right connects to Highland Loop Road.

When you reach Stable Road at 2.04 miles, again, watch for vehicles before crossing the road to reconnect with the dirt and gravel path to the north. A series of interpretive waysides will appear from the 2.06-mile mark to the intersection with the Forest Trail at the 2.14-mile mark. These interpretive waysides include the

Peach Creek North and South Loops

following titles: "Agriculture," "Invasive Species," "Night Pollinator," "Yellow-Bellied Sapsucker Tree," and "Native Plants." Continue straight on the Peach Creek South Loop at the intersection with the Forest Trail and the following intersection at 2.18 miles. As usual, when you reach Nature Center Road at 2.23 miles, watch for vehicles before crossing the road. Look for the four wooden posts to the north and reconnect with the dirt and gravel path.

The trail heads west at 2.32 miles, and then you will reach Lake Dabney shortly after. Any shade dissipates when the trail curves around south of Lake Dabney until the 2.54-mile mark. While you meander along the shoreline, there will be a fishing pier to your right. The pier is a fantastic vista point for Lake Dabney, especially in the mornings. Enjoyable looking A-frame structures congregate on the northwestern shore of the lake, while larger, lakeside cabins line up around the east side. (Lake Houston Wilderness Park is currently the only park owned by the city of Houston that offers overnight lodging. All structures are reservable online at: https://www .houstontx.gov/parks/lakehoustonpark.html.) Take some time to go out on the pier to take photos of Lake Dabney or eat a snack at one of the picnic benches. Once you are done with your break, continue on the trail around Lake Dabney. The trail begins to head west away from Lake Dabney at 2.47 miles. You will reach Red Oak Road shortly after. Watch for vehicles before crossing the road. Look for the one wooden post to the west and reconnect with the dirt and gravel path.

When the mileage clocks at 2.59 miles, you will come upon the fork from the original 0.79 mark (the spur segment of the Peach Creek South Loop lollipop). Bear right to return to the Peach Creek North Loop. When the mileage reads as 2.66 miles, you will reach the fork from the original 0.72-mile mark. At this point you can continue heading back the way you came from the Peach Creek North Loop Trailhead. This guide, for variety, takes the other side of the loop for the Peach Creek North Loop by bearing right. At 2.76 miles, you will cross the fourth and final wooden footbridge. Three miles into the route, you will encounter the fork from the original 0.34-mile mark (the spur segment of the Peach Creek North Loop lollipop). Bear right to return to the trailhead.

Miles and Directions

0.0 The Peach Creek North Loop begins southwest of the parking area.

0.19 Reach a fork. Bear right.

0.34 Reach a fork. Bear right to take the loop portion of the lollipop in a counterclockwise direction. Make a 5-foot descent from here to the 0.35-mile mark.

0.45 Peach Creek parallels to your right from this point to the 1.23-mile mark.

0.72 Reach a fork. Continue straight.

0.75 Cross a wooden footbridge.

0.79 Reach a fork. Bear right to take the Peach Creek South Loop in a counterclockwise direction.

0.86 Cross over a culvert.

Peach Creek North and South Loops, Lake Houston Wilderness Park

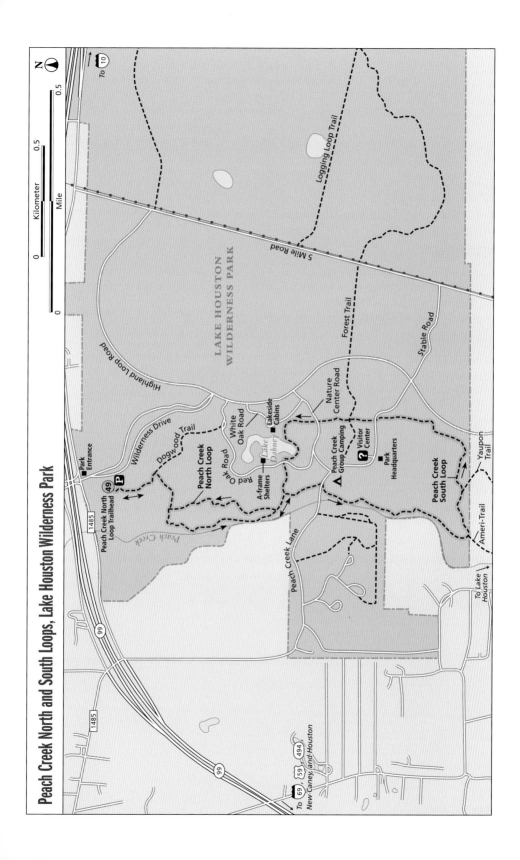

0.91 Public restrooms and a parking lot will be to your left. Reach Peach Creek Lane/Nature Center Road. Watch for vehicles before crossing the road to reconnect with the dirt and gravel path to the south.

0.95 Reach a fork. Continue straight on the dirt and gravel path to continue on the trail. Bypass several offshoots to Peach Creek to your right from this point to the 1.23-mile mark.

1.03 Cross a wooden footbridge. Bypass an offshoot to your left that leads to the Peach Creek Group Camping Area.

1.11 The path splits and then merges shortly after.

1.15 Cross a wooden footbridge.

1.2 Make a 5-foot ascent from here to the 1.21-mile mark.

1.43 Reach a fork. Bear left.

1.57 Reach a fork. Continue straight.

1.91 Reach a fork. Continue straight.

2.04 Reach Stable Road. Watch for vehicles before crossing the road to reconnect with the dirt and gravel path to the north.

2.14 Reach an intersection with the Forest Trail. Continue straight.

2.18 Reach another intersection. Continue straight.

2.23 Reach Nature Center Road. Watch for vehicles before crossing the road to reconnect with the dirt and gravel path with four wooden posts to the north.

2.36 Reach Lake Dabney.

2.41 A fishing pier will be to your right.

2.49 Reach Red Oak Road. Watch for vehicles before crossing the road to reconnect with the dirt and gravel path with one wooden post to the west.

2.59 Reach the fork from the original 0.79-mile mark. Bear right to return to the Peach Creek North Loop.

2.66 Reach the fork from the original 0.72-mile mark. At this point you can continue heading back the way you came from the Peach Creek North Loop Trailhead. This guide, for variety, takes the other side of the loop for the Peach Creek North Loop by bearing right.

2.76 Cross a wooden footbridge.

3.0 Reach the fork from the original 0.34-mile mark. Bear right to return to the trailhead.

3.34 Arrive back at the trailhead.

50 Shoveler Pond Trail, Anahuac National Wildlife Refuge

The 220-acre, freshwater Shoveler Pond is a picturesque and peaceful haven for many waterfowl, reptiles, and amphibians. With coastal wetland habitats continuing to be threatened by urban development, Shoveler Pond and the Anahuac National Wildlife Refuge protect and shelter many species. This allows people the opportunity to experience the treasured wildlife up close.

Lake or river: Shoveler Pond
Photogenic factor: 5
Start: Butterfly Garden and Willows Trailhead
Elevation gain: 6 to 15 feet
Distance: 4.32-mile lollipop, with an additional spur
Difficulty: Easy
Hiking time: 2-3 hours
Seasons/schedule: Open year-round, 1 hour before sunrise until 1 hour after sunset; visitor center hours are 9 a.m. to 4 p.m. Fri through Sun
Fees and permits: None (subject to change)
Trail contacts: Anahuac National Wildlife Refuge Visitors Center, 4017 FM 563, Anahuac 77514; (409) 267-3337
Dog-friendly: Leashed dogs permitted
Trail surface: Dirt and boardwalk (ADA accessible) on the Butterfly Garden and Willows Trail, asphalt on the Shoveler Pond Trail

Land status: US Fish and Wildlife Service
Nearest town: Stowell and Beaumont (northeast), Anahuac and Baytown (northwest)
Other trail users: Mountain bikers/cyclists
Maps: USGS Frozen Point; Anahuac National Wildlife Refuge map (available online at https://www.fws.gov/refuge/anahuac/library)
Special considerations: There is no shade on this trail. Start your hike early and bring adequate amounts of water. There are two versions of the Willows Trail. This guide takes the ADA-accessible version. The Shoveler Pond Trail is also an auto tour loop. Please be alert for vehicles as you hike on the trail and stay on the side to allow vehicles to pass. The Visitor Center is located about 16 miles northwest of the main entrance to the Anahuac National Wildlife Refuge.

Finding the trailhead: From City Hall in downtown Houston, get onto I-45 N. Travel on I-45 N for 0.6 miles, and then merge onto I-10 E. Stay on I-10 E for 43.2 miles, and then take exit 812 for TX 61. After 0.9 miles, turn right onto TX 61 S. In 3.8 miles, it will change to FM 562 S. Continue on FM 562 S for 8.2 miles. Turn left onto Whites Ranch Road/FM 1985. After traveling on Whites Ranch Road for 4.3 miles, turn right into the main entrance of the Anahuac National Wildlife Refuge. The butterfly garden and parking lot will be to your right in 3.2 miles. **GPS:** N29° 36.829' W94° 32.053'

The Hike

The main purpose of the Anahuac National Wildlife Refuge is to preserve the coastal wetland ecosystem. As more of the Gulf Coast gets developed, salt water begins to

The boardwalk at Shoveler Pond

invade freshwater habitats, and wildlife is driven out. One species that has been a prime example of this fate is the mottled duck. Mottled ducks have made the Ana-huac National Wildlife Refuge one of their primary habitats and find shelter in the waters of Shoveler Pond all year round. Hikers who visit Shoveler Pond will have the chance to see the mottled duck, as well as other waterfowl, and reptiles, such as the American alligator and turtles.

This guide starts at the butterfly garden where there is adequate parking available and adds some additional sightseeing along the way. Head west and there will be a small pond to your left. In 215 feet, the path splits and then merges. Take the left side that leads to the bridge over the pond. You will reach the boardwalk at 635 feet into the trail. At 0.22 and 0.25 miles into the trail, a bench and observation deck will be to your right. You will come upon a parking area and the Shoveler Pond Trail at 0.3 miles. The trail surface will now be paved asphalt. Another observation deck with a bench and two water features for birding will be to your right. Continue heading west. Keep in mind that the Shoveler Pond Trail is also an auto tour route. Pay atten-tion to vehicles and stay on the side of the path to allow vehicles to pass. You will pass another parking lot and a connection to the primitive version of the Willows Trail to your right at 0.35 miles.

At 0.69 miles, you will reach the loop portion of the lollipop route and halcyon Shoveler Pond comes into view. Bear right to take the loop in a counterclockwise direction and to move at the same flow with any vehicles. A "Wildlife You May See"

View from the trail

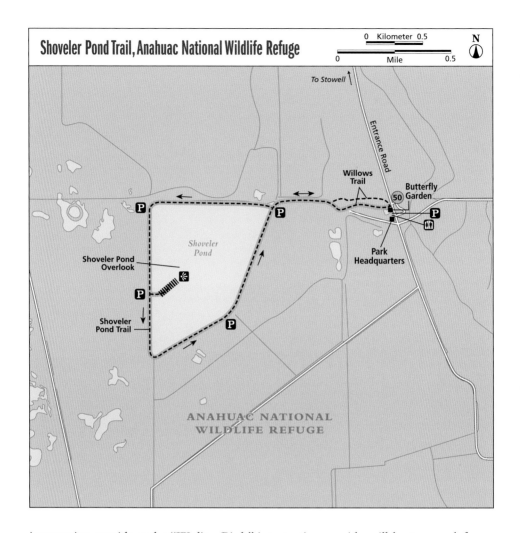

0   Kilometer 0.5

0   Mile   0.5

N

To Stowell

Entrance Road

Willows
Trail

Butterfly
50 Garden

P

P

P

Shoveler
Pond

Shoveler Pond
Overlook

Park
Headquarters

P

Shoveler
Pond Trail

P

ANAHUAC NATIONAL
WILDLIFE REFUGE

interpretive wayside and a "Wading Birds" interpretive wayside will be to your left at the 0.82-mile mark and 1.07-mile mark, respectively. The trail then heads west at 1.37 miles. At 1.46 miles, a "Living in the Water" interpretive wayside will be to your left. When you reach the boardwalk at 1.86 miles, take advantage of this scenic spur. During the summer or a drought this portion of the pond may be dry, however do not let those conditions deter you from seeing the beauty and wildlife thriving around the boardwalk. An "Alligators Thrive" interpretive wayside will be to your left as you head east down the boardwalk. The boardwalk ends at the 2.01-mile mark. When there is water, the cane to the north of the boardwalk is a rookery for plenty of wading birds. After surveying the scenery and hopefully catching some glimpses of mottled ducks, red-eared sliders, and American alligators, turn around and return to the original 1.86-mile mark. The mileage will clock at 2.16 miles when you reach the original 1.86-mile mark. Bear left to continue the loop.

A "Waterfowl" interpretive wayside will be to your left at 2.17 miles, and the trail heads south at 2.48 miles. The final interpretive wayside, titled "Wetlands Are Valuable," will appear to your left at 2.75 miles. The trail then heads southeast after 3 miles. At 3.60 miles, the loop concludes. Return the way you came, heading south back to the butterfly garden and Willow Trail.

Miles and Directions

0.0 Start the trail at the butterfly garden.

0.04 The path splits and then merges. Take the left side that goes to the bridge over the pond.

0.12 Reach a boardwalk.

0.22 and 0.25 An observation deck with a bench will be to your right.

0.3 Reach a parking area and the Shoveler Pond Trail. The trail surface will now be paved asphalt. Another observation deck with a bench and two water features will be to your right. Shoveler Pond Trail is also an auto tour route. Pay attention to vehicles and stay on the side of the path to allow vehicles to pass.

Alligators at Shoveler Pond

0.35 Pass another parking lot to your right.

0.69 Reach the loop portion of the lollipop route and Shoveler Pond comes into view. Bear right to take the loop in a counterclockwise direction and to go with the correct flow of traffic.

1.86 Reach a boardwalk. Head east down the boardwalk.

2.01 Reach the end of the boardwalk. Turn around and return to the original 1.86-mile mark.

2.16 Reconnect with the original 1.86-mile mark. Bear left.

3.6 The loop ends. Return the way you came.

4.32 Arrive back at the trailhead.

Honorable Mentions (Gulf Coast)

N Catfish Point Trail, Lake Corpus Christi State Park

About half an hour away from the outskirts of Corpus Christi, the 21,000-acre Lake Corpus Christi is one of the largest man-made bodies of water in the state of Texas. With a marshy shoreline holding at bay a valuable brushy landscape, Lake Corpus Christi is a hospitable habitat for waterfowl and aquatic life. The Catfish Point Trail traverses along the banks of the lake providing hikers a "Gulf Coast" feel and at times, sights of American white pelicans and roadrunners.

Lake Corpus Christi at sunset

Lake or river: Lake Corpus Christi
Photogenic factor: 4
Start: Catfish Point Trailhead
Elevation gain: 49 to 121 feet
Distance: 0.93-mile lollipop
Difficulty: Easy
Hiking time: 30 minutes
Seasons/schedule: Open year-round, 7 a.m. to 10 p.m.
Fees and permits: $5 per person 13 years and older (subject to change), free for Texas State Parks Pass holders
Trail contacts: Lake Corpus Christi State Park Headquarters, 23194 Park Road 25, Mathis 78368; (361) 547-2635
Dog-friendly: Leashed dogs permitted
Trail surface: Dirt
Land status: Texas Parks and Wildlife Department
Nearest town: Mathis (northeast), Corpus Christi (southeast)
Other trail users: Anglers
Maps: USGS Sandia; Lake Corpus Christi State Park map (available online at www.tpwd.texas.gov/state-parks/parks-map and via the TX State Parks mobile app)
Special considerations: There is minimal shade on this trail. Start your hike early and bring adequate amounts of water. To add more mileage, the Catfish Point Trail connects with the Longhorn Trail.

Finding the trailhead: From the I-37 and US 181 corridor in Corpus Christi, travel on I-37 N for 34.2 miles. Take exit 34 and after 0.2 miles, head onto I-37 Frontage Road. After 0.2 miles on I-37 Frontage Road, turn left onto TX 459 Spur. Travel on TX 459 Spur for 0.6 miles. Go left onto TX 359 W. Stay on TX 359 W for 4.6 miles. Turn right onto Park Road 25. After 1.4 miles on Park Road 25, turn left to stay on Park Road 25 and enter Lake Corpus Christi State Park. Continue on Park Road 25 for a mile. The Catfish Point Trailhead will be to your left, across the road from the Catfish Cove Camping Area. **GPS:** N28° 03.517' W97° 52.596'

◯ Clay Family Eastern Glades Trail, Memorial Park

The Clay Family Eastern Glades made its debut within Houston's Memorial Park in the summer of 2020, and it continues to amaze visitors. It encompasses the stunning, 5.5-acre Hines Lake, a verdant promenade, a wetlands section, and lakeside boardwalks. Situated in an area where a former World War I military training camp once stood, the Clay Family Eastern Glades is rich in its history and its charming scenery.

Lake or river: Hines Lake
Photogenic factor: 5
Start: Trail can be accessed from multiple points of the Seymour Lieberman Exer-Trail
Elevation gain: 36 to 61 feet
Distance: 1 to 2-mile lollipop, depending on route taken
Difficulty: Easy
Hiking time: 30 minutes–1 hour
Seasons/schedule: Open year-round, 5 a.m. to 11 p.m.
Fees and permits: None (subject to change), small fee to park in certain sections of Memorial Park
Trail contacts: Memorial Park Conservancy Office, 7575 North Picnic Lane, Houston 77007; (713) 863-8403
Dog-friendly: Leashed dogs permitted
Trail surface: Dirt and gravel

The boardwalk around Hines Lake

Land status: City of Houston Parks and Recreation Department, managed by the Memorial Park Conservancy

Nearest town: Within Houston city limits

Other trail users: Mountain bikers/cyclists

Maps: USGS Houston Heights; Memorial Park map (available online at https://www.memorialparkconservancy.org/visit/map-directions/)

Finding the trailhead: From City Hall in downtown Houston, travel on Bagby Street for 0.3 miles to reach Memorial Parkway. Turn left on Memorial Parkway and stay on it for 3.9 miles. Turn right onto E Memorial Loop Drive. After 0.4 miles on E Memorial Loop Drive, the trail can be accessed to your left. Paid parking ($1 for 3 hours, subject to change) is available in multiple areas within Memorial Park. Refer to https://www.memorialparkconservancy.org/visit/map-directions/parking/ for a parking map. **GPS:** N29° 46.168' W95° 25.821'

Hike Index

THE TEN ESSENTIALS OF HIKING

American Hiking Society

American Hiking Society recommends you pack the "Ten Essentials" every time you head out for a hike. Whether you plan to be gone for a couple of hours or several months, make sure to pack these items. Become familiar with these items and know how to use them.

1. Appropriate Footwear
Happy feet make for pleasant hiking. Think about traction, support, and protection when selecting well-fitting shoes or boots.

2. Navigation
While phones and GPS units are handy, they aren't always reliable in the backcountry; consider carrying a paper map and compass as backups and know how to use them.

3. Water (and a way to purify it)
As a guideline, plan for half a liter of water per hour in moderate temperatures/terrain. Carry enough water for your trip and know where and how to treat water while you're out on the trail.

4. Food
Pack calorie-dense foods to help fuel your hike, and carry an extra portion in case you are out longer than expected.

5. Rain Gear & Dry-Fast Layers
The weatherman is not always right. Dress in layers to adjust to changing weather and activity levels. Wear moisture-wicking clothes and carry a warm hat.

6. Safety Items (light, fire, and a whistle)
Have means to start an emergency fire, signal for help, and see the trail and your map in the dark.

7. First Aid Kit

Supplies to treat illness or injury are only as helpful as your knowledge of how to use them. Take a class to gain the skills needed to administer first aid and CPR.

8. Knife or Multi-Tool

With countless uses, a multi-tool can help with gear repair and first aid.

9. Sun Protection

Sunscreen, sunglasses, and sun-protective clothing should be used in every season regardless of temperature or cloud cover.

10. Shelter

Protection from the elements in the event you are injured or stranded is necessary. A lightweight, inexpensive space blanket is a great option.

Find other helpful resources at AmericanHiking.org/hiking-resources